Working with Faculty in the New Electronic Library

Papers and Session Materials Presented at the Nineteenth
National LOEX Library Instruction Conference
held at Eastern Michigan University
10 to 11 May 1991, and related
resource materials gathered
by the LOEX Clearinghouse

edited by
Linda Shirato, Director
LOEX Clearinghouse
University Library
Eastern Michigan University

Published for Learning Resources and Technologies
Eastern Michigan University
by
Pierian Press
Ann Arbor, Michigan
1992

ISBN 0-87650-294-X
Copyright © 1992, The Pierian Press
All Rights Reserved

The Pierian Press
Box 1808
Ann Arbor, Michigan 48106

LIBRARY ORIENTATION SERIES

(Most volumes in the series are still in print; those that are out of print are so designated.)

Table of Contents

Articles

Instructive Sessions

Poster Sessions

LOEX Conference—Panel Summary   165

Rachel Gardner (Monmouth College)
Abigail Loomis (University of Wisconsin-Madison)
Marsha Miller (Indiana State University at Terre Haute)
Shirley Black (University of Detroit)
Sharon Mader (DePaul University)
Evan Farber (Earlham College)

Bibliography   170

Roster of Participants   184

Preface

In 1975, LOEX presented a conference on "Faculty Involvement in Library Instruction." Since that time, the library world has changed dramatically with the introduction of online searching, online catalogs, CD-ROM indexes and databases, and a host of other electronic resources. How has this changed our relationship with the faculty? In many ways it has brought about unprecedented opportunity. Faculty themselves need to learn to use the new resources, and can hardly ignore that their students need to learn them too.

At the same time, the more things have changed the more they have remained the same. Librarians still need to develop relationships with faculty, take the initiative, reach out to them, and to develop programs that meet their needs and those of their students. This is unlikely to change no matter what technological wonders await us in the future.

LOEX was lucky to have as its keynote speaker one of the most experienced and knowledgeable of experts on the subject of working with faculty: Evan Farber of Earlham College. Evan spoke of the changes that he has seen as he has worked in library instruction and reminded us of the work that remains to be done. He emphasized the primary place of teaching and learning in the academic institution, and helped us focus on the primary importance of our relationships with faculty in that process. Faculty as both teachers and learners are our primary bridge between student and library.

Our second speaker, Anne Lipow, described why we should try to teach faculty and how she and colleagues did it so ably at the University of California-Berkeley. Ms. Lipow emphasized the importance of making faculty a primary concern because they themselves are an important constituency, and because they provide the most effective access to their students. She explained the whys and hows of the successful faculty seminars produced under her leadership.

Illustrating how faculty and librarians might work together to produce library instruction (though in this case the colleague was a graduate student in instruction-al technology), Nathan Smith, Jr., Mary Piette, and Betty Dance of Utah State University presented their "Project FORE" program as a prototype of what might be accomplished. With HyperCard, they produced a computer assisted instruction program for basic freshman library skills. In their presentation, they explain the general guidelines for such a project. Emphasis was placed on following sound educational principles as well as on exploiting the possibilities of HyperCard. Project FORE aims to provide a new type of learning experience for the student, not just provide a workbook in computer form. Those interested in developing such a program can learn from this presentation and develop a feel for the amount of thought and work required.

The final main presentation was concerned with how librarians and administrators might work together. Fred Roecker, user education librarian at Ohio State University, and Thomas Minnick, an assistant dean in Ohio State's University College presented a two-part introduction to the impressive "Gateway to Information" program. Fred Roecker explained the history of Gateway, how it had been implemented, and its successful use to date. Tom Minnick spoke about the cooperative effort between the library and administrators in Ohio State's freshman program to make the Gateway a part of every freshman's introduction to college study. This is a example of an outstanding collaborative effort between librarians and faculty on a truly large scale.

In addition to the four excellent main presentations, the LOEX Conference was enriched by the contributions of nine instructive sessions and three poster sessions, each exhibiting practical ways in which cooperation with faculty can lead to good instruction.

I am indebted to Carolyn Kirkendall, former LOEX Director and now Instructional materials Librarian at Eastern Michigan University, for reporting on the panel discussion which ended the 19th LOEX Conference.

Linda Shirato
Director

TEACHERS AS LEARNERS—
THE APPLICATION OF BI

Evan Ira Farber

Before I get to the body of my talk, I should point out that it's based on two major premises. Both are working, not just theoretical, premises and both are fundamental to my approach to BI in the undergraduate library. (Keep in mind that throughout this work I'm talking about undergraduate education. Some of what I say may apply to graduate education, or to BI in schools or public libraries, but if it is relevant for those situations, it's purely accidental—my experience, my expertise lies in undergraduate education.)

The first premise is my belief (it's more than a belief—it's a basic working principle for administering my library) that BI should be the focus, the common denominator of the library's programs and policies, of almost everything that goes on in the library. And when I talk about BI, unless noted otherwise, I'm talking about course-related or course-integrated instruction, not separate courses. In one of my first pieces on BI, in John Lubans' book, *Educating the Library User*, which was published in 1974 (one of the first books on BI), I almost apologized for taking that approach: "Given the realities of the situation...one must come to the conclusion (regretfully, perhaps) that only by working through the courses, and that means through individual faculty members, can the objectives of library instruction presently be achieved....Working with faculty, then, becomes a given." I felt, in other words, that course-related instruction was based on political necessity, not on educational desirability. I've changed my view: now I think that course-related

Farber is Director, Lilly Library, Earlham College.

instruction has more advantages than the separate course, but I'd be glad to argue that.

My second premise is the paramount importance of the teaching/learning process. This premise really has two parts. The first is something I say in almost every talk I give; and that is, of course, that the library is not an end in itself—(it is not "the heart of the college")—but exists to support, to promote, to *enhance* what is the heart of the college—the teaching/learning process—those interactions between faculty and students that go on in classrooms, in laboratories, in tutorials, over cups of coffee, wherever—interactions that contribute to students' intellectual and critical skills, disciplinary and interdisciplinary knowledge, cultural and cross cultural awareness—all those outcomes we hope for in an undergraduate education. It's by how well the library supports and enhances those interactions that it should be evaluated, not by its size or budget. Those quantitative measures are important only insofar as they contribute to the library's role in the teaching/learning process. (And, of course, one of the most effective ways of contributing to that process is BI.) That's one part of my second premise.

The other part is a long-time interest in, experience with, and reading about classroom teaching, and particularly the improvement of classroom teaching. Part of my commitment to BI comes from my interest in undergraduate education: effective teaching is surely the most important component of that education and BI can make a real contribution to that. I also believe that most teachers are interested in improving, in becoming good teachers. Kenneth Eble is one of the most prolific and respected writers on college and university teaching (we have 18 books written or edited by him). In his 1983 book, *The Aims of College Teaching*, he talks about this interest in improving. The particular chapter focusing on that is titled "Teachers as Learners," and that's what I'm going to talk about, but primarily with relation to BI. If BI can make teaching more effective (as I believe and think you believe), faculty—who are interested in being better teachers—should be open to working with us. But too many are still not, and we need to look at them as learners.

Let me expand a bit on my first premise, BI as the focus of a library's program. I think I didn't realize how true this had become in my own case until about five years ago, when I was asked to give a talk at a conference on the integration of library services; my assignment of course was to approach that topic from the perspective of BI. As I thought about that I began to see that from almost every aspect of administration and service, our BI program was in mind—sometimes in the background, but much more often on the table—when we made decisions or had to choose among

options: personnel selection, budgetary decisions, book selection, even aspects of furnishings and building. "BI, though it began because of some other perceived needs, and then seen as an important end in and of itself, soon became the focus, the common denominator of most of our efforts. There are very few decisions made about programs or practices that don't take it into account." It's tempting for me to go into this even more, but that's not part of our agenda today. But I think you need to understand how basic it is in my approach to library administration.

Let me get to our present agenda, the teaching faculty and building relationships with them. In 1978 I gave a paper on library-faculty communication techniques. The thrust of that paper was not so different from this one—that is, if BI is so good, and can make such an important contribution to student learning and to teaching effectiveness, why is there so much resistance to it by teaching faculty? And how can that resistance be overcome? Well, since I wrote that paper 13 years have gone by. During these years I have looked at many other situations, talked to lots of librarians and teaching faculty around the country, done a lot of reading on the subject, and have 13 years more experience of working with and observing faculty, not just in a BI context, but in 10 of those years as a member of the college's personnel committee. In that committee I looked over scores of faculty members' self-evaluations, gaining insights into their abilities, shortcomings, attitudes, concerns, frustrations, and aspirations.

What's changed since then? Well, for one thing, the BI movement has grown steadily, perhaps dramatically. In 1978 the BI librarians had just established their own section in ACRL, and it's now the largest activity section of that organization, with over 4,000 members. Whereas LOEX provided one of the few conferences on BI and was one of the few places that gathered materials, now there are many conferences and a number of centers. Now there's a periodical, *Research Strategies*, devoted to BI, and articles on BI appear in just about every other library periodical with some frequency (though there still aren't enough in the disciplinary journals). The number of advertised library positions that stress or include BI as a responsibility has grown enormously. To my way of thinking, however, one of the most significant events came in 1987 when one of the most important recent books on undergraduate education, *College: The Undergraduate Experience*, by Ernest Boyer was published. It is especially important for us because it's the first major publication on undergraduate education that not only mentioned but promoted BI. "The college library must be viewed as a vital part of the undergraduate experience....The library staff should be considered as important to teaching as are classroom teachers....We further recommend that every undergraduate student be introduced carefully to the full range of resources for learning on campus. Students should be given bibliographic instruction and be encouraged to spend at least as much time in the library—using its wide range of resources—as they spend in classes."[1]

That's very significant, not just because, as I noted, it's the first major work to mention BI, but also because the study was sponsored by the prestigious Carnegie Foundation for the Advancement of Teaching. Even more significantly, perhaps, certainly from a practical viewpoint, two regional accrediting associations, Middle States and Southern, now include BI as part of their criteria for libraries.

That may not seem like a lot in 13 years, but remember—the wheels of change in education move very slowly.

But there's still resistance. Why? Well, again let me go back to 1978. I thought then there were two major explanations for the resistance. The first was simply that BI was an innovation, and faculty almost always respond to innovation cautiously, but if they do at all they do according to the risks and rewards involved with accepting that innovation. In other words, if an institution rewards innovation, its faculty will respond more readily. But 13 years ago most institutions did not reward good teaching—they rewarded publication, and BI is not only no help in getting published, it takes time away from it. Has this changed? Not entirely. But it is changing. There's much more attention now to improving classroom teaching. One has only to look at the spate of books on the subject (one publisher, Jossey-Bass, devotes practically its entire list to it), or the number of conferences and workshops on teaching, or the increase in the number of institutions where teaching is evaluated by students and help for improving teaching has been institutionalized. So the arena we work in should be friendlier.

The other major factor I addressed was that of personality. "Many teachers have fragile egos, and because someone wants to work with their students—someone who can point out materials and methods with which they may be unfamiliar—it is easy for them to infer that others think them inadequate....Further, most teaching faculty have never met librarians serving in a teaching capacity, and cannot think of librarians as peers with whom one can share the responsibility of teaching."

Was I too severe? I think not, though I might change the "fragile egos" phrase. (Although I do know a number of faculty with very fragile egos.) In her recent book, *Improving College Teaching*, Maryellen Weimer says it this way:

"Many faculty members respond to attempts to encourage them to better teaching with open resistance....What is it about instructional improvement that brings out this overtly negative faculty reaction? Quite simply, faculty feel threatened when attention is directed toward their teaching."[2] That's not quite the same as fragile egos. But I have come to realize how possessive faculty feel about their classes. They are in charge—it's their territory. As Professor Weimer says: "Teachers occupy positions of power in the classroom. They are supposed to know, to be the learned experts, to manage the classroom....If they do not or have not and find that out, from their position of power, they have far to fall."

A few years ago I was visiting one of the California universities. At dinner my host introduced me to one of her faculty, a guy in the drama department. When she introduced us, she commented on how much she enjoyed giving BI to his classes and what a pleasure he was to work with. "That's interesting," I said. "I love to work with our drama people, too. Why do you suppose they're so easy to work with?" He thought a moment, then gave what I think was a very useful insight: "It's probably because theater people are used to working with others." Of course! Directors don't run the whole show; they have to work with scenic designers, lighting technicians, a stage crew, and others. So they're used to sharing the platform. As I said, that was a useful insight, and it made me even more aware of the problem of the classroom as personal territory.

That problem is still with us. Many faculty members are still unwilling to share their classrooms, to give up some control over their classes. Does the changing constituency of the professoriat affect this? That is, now with a younger, more liberal group of faculty. Are they less defensive, less possessive, more willing to share? I think so, but I can't say for sure. How about the increase in the number of women faculty members? Are women easier to work with? I think so, and here I feel more certain. I wonder if anyone has done any comparative studies.

Another obstacle to working with faculty is their lack of time, and really, the better the teacher, the less time he or she has. Early on, I didn't even consider this—after all, I knew that BI would improve almost any course, so certainly every conscientious instructor would be glad to give me time. Well, an experience some years later caused me to now give it some weight. I was teaching one section of a humanities course—a course that all first-year students had to take. Mine was one of 15 or so sections, but I was not only teaching my section but giving BI to all the other sections. Now, I was very careful to get in touch with each of the other instructors and meet with their students, but I completely neglected to give my own section any BI. When I reflected on this later I realized that I had been so busy with the everyday business of the course—reading the assignments, making notes for lectures, thinking about tests, meeting with individual students, choosing and ordering texts for the following term—I was so busy with that that I forgot about the BI. The lesson for me? Teaching—good teaching—requires lots of time, and we just can't expect BI to be the major concern of a good teacher. It's up to us to take the initiative, to get in touch with individual faculty members. Sure, occasionally a faculty member I've worked with over the years will call me first, but I'm always pleasantly surprised when that happens.

Another part of that reluctance to work with us is due to faculty members' inability to see us as colleagues, persons with whom they're willing to share the responsibility for teaching their classes. There are several reasons for this, some of them quite obvious, but all, I think, possible to respond to.

First, we need to gain their respect for what we're supposed to do—that is, what we're traditionally supposed to do: in my own case, be a good administrator, keep up the book collection....For many of you, it probably would be being a good reference librarian. (That's one reason I say, if you're looking for another position, try to get one where the person you replace was a dud, a failure—then you automatically look good—at least, you have a honeymoon period.) But of course, doing our traditional job well is just the beginning.

I have another device for making inroads with new faculty. (This device is much easier in smaller institutions, but it's worth mentioning.) Find out the names of faculty who have been hired for the coming year. Write them, tell them how glad you are that they're coming, and ask if there's anything you can do for them before their arrival—check their bibliographies, see about ordering items, and the like. You have no idea how pleased these people are to get such a note. If they respond, fine, but even if they don't, you've established contact. Most of the time, however, the need is to establish a working relationship with faculty members already there. Now, this is an important thing to do, not only from the BI perspective, but from the wider administrative perspective. That is, a good working relationship with faculty members not only permits better service to students, but it helps gain support for the library—moral as well as financial support—from the faculty, and through the faculty, from the administration.

The most effective way of establishing a working relationship is by indicating a shared interest in the faculty member's courses. Most faculty love to talk about their teaching. That's natural, isn't it? Yet they're often reluctant to talk to faculty colleagues—there is, after all, a certain sense of competition among faculty, within departments, even between departments. If you doubt this, let me quote from an item in *The Teaching Professor*: "Colleagues don't talk much to each other about teaching....[a researcher] surveyed 1680 faculty at 14 institutions and found that 42 percent of them said that *never* during their entire career had anyone talked with them in detail about their teaching....Only 25 percent said that discussions on [teaching] had taken place more than once....To talk openly about teaching...implies one has a problem...."[3]

Preparing for BI provides an ideal opportunity to talk about one's teaching with an interested but non-threatening figure, the BI librarian. How to encourage this? Well, the letter to new faculty. For faculty already there, by sending him or her material that might be useful for the course: notices of new books, articles they might not see (not from journals they would be expected to see), then by setting up a time to talk about the course. We're seen, then, as someone who's interested in what the course is trying to do and how it does it, and maybe even having suggestions for improving it. Then, by talking with the instructor, we can find out more about the faculty member's interests, and later, after the course is over, talk about how it went. Did the BI take? Should it have been done differently? How can it be improved next time? Thus, you've built a working relationship that will be enhanced by using the same devices over the years.

I've really just touched on a few ways of working with faculty. I could go on and on—and I often do. But each of us has to work out his/her approaches, depending on a variety of factors—the institutional context, administrative support, the nature and size of the faculty, our individual personalities, interests and talents, and so forth.

There are times when you may get discouraged, when the resistance to your best efforts, to all that you believe is right, seems impenetrable. Think of the parallel with classroom teachers and their students, especially those I see in junior high school. How do they manage to keep going, with so much working against them: the problems, the anti-intellectualism of pre-adolescents, uncooperative parents, unsympathetic administrators. They do keep going, and I think what does keep them going are the successes, those kids for whom education has become a means of growth, of intellectual and psychological and social development. In other words, those for whom education has made a real difference in their lives, for whom the mission of education has had some validity.

Well, we believe in the validity of BI, that it can make a difference in higher education, in the effectiveness of the teaching/learning process. We have an advantage over those junior high school teachers. Their learners are going to leave and they'll have to start all over again with a new group. Our learners, the teaching faculty, will stay—most of them, anyway, for a while—and we can continue working on them—or better, working with them...perfecting that working relationship. Then we can use *them* as change agents, helping to carry our message to their colleagues.

Sure, we'll continue to have failures, but let's look rather at our successes, at the students we've helped, who because of us have done better work, saved time, gotten better grades, and feel better about using libraries. Let's look at those professors, who, having learned from us, are more effective teachers and en-joying teaching more. Let's learn from our failures, to be sure, and continually improve our methods, but let's keep in mind and feel good about our successes—if our objectives are worthy, as you and I believe they are.

NOTES

1.   Ernest L. Boyer, *College: The Undergraduate Experience* (New York: Harper and Row, 1988), 164-165.

2.   Maryellen Weimer, *Improving College Teaching* (San Francisco: Jossey-Bass, 1990), 16-17.

3.   *The Teaching Professor* (July 1987).

OUTREACH TO FACULTY:

WHY AND HOW

Anne G. Lipow[1]

There are four key reasons why efforts to work with faculty in new ways are, in my opinion, important. In fact, it may be just a trifle melodramatic to say that such efforts are not just important, but critical to the viability of librarianship in an academic institution.

The four reasons are outlined on the top page of your handout:

- First, there are new bibliographic concepts to be learned, and faculty must learn them if they are to be successful library users and information seekers.

- The second reason has to do with faculty as a particular group of information seekers.

- A third reason to work with faculty is that they are an important entree to students.

- And the fourth reason comes down to survival: working directly with faculty in new ways plays a crucial part in our changing role as professionals in the changing information industry.

I'd like to first talk about these four reasons, not in depth, but with a broad brush of supportive evidence to make the case from a variety of approaches, any one of which we could talk about further as you like in the discussion period that follows. And then, because ours is a practical occupation, I'd like to talk quite specifically about what I call on your outline "some nitty

Lipow is a library consultant and principal of Anne G. Lipow and Associates, Berkeley, California.

gritty": particular forms of outreach, how to make them happen, how they might look, what benefits result from them, especially as they relate to the four reasons. The attachments in your handout are examples of some of the applications I'll be talking about. And then, I'd want to invite open discussion about what I've said that you'd like to comment on, argue with, know more about.

Turning to Reasons 1-4

There are new BASIC information-seeking skills to be learned, and there's no one else to teach them but us. In the days of the standardized 3x5 card catalogs and printed reference works, the basic search skills were known by everyone from the time you first used a library in grade school; we librarians were brought into the picture when the patron's first line of attack in the library failed, and except for that category of patron who always immediately asks for help—having missed our message that they should be trying on their own first—that first line of attack usually included some shelf browsing, the card catalog, and perhaps one (two at the most) printed reference source. Most people, of course, got something and stopped there, though there were probably better things we could have led them to had they asked. The only **basic** skill a library user needed to know to get that far was the alphabet. The bibliographic concepts that you needed you learned from visual cues: you could *see* how the database you were searching was organized; you could see where it began and where it ended, you could tell how big it was; you knew to look in the beginning of the reference work for a description of the content, and in the back of the book for an index that you could browse through easily for the term you needed.

Those skills and concepts don't work with online catalogs and other electronic information resources. Today, knowing the order of the alphabet is not so important (keying the letters gets you to your alphabetical place), and you have none of the visual cues you've been used to that tells you something about the organization, the size, or the content of the database you are searching. You don't even have the visual cues you're used to, which tell you that the database even exists to be searched! Also, once you learn one catalog, you mustn't make assumptions about the next catalog or database you search. The fact is that to be a successful user of electronic resources today, you need to be the type of person who absorbs new information by noticing and reading words. That may not be the way most of us—not even faculty—learn this type of information.

Of course, everyone—faculty and all other information seekers—need help with these new concepts. But I believe we should be devoting special attention to teaching these concepts to faculty—as much if not more attention than we give to their students.

Which brings me half-way to the second reason it is important to work with faculty: *faculty as information seekers*. The faculty as an information-seeking constituency (which includes but is not limited to the *library-using* faculty) are in some ways the biggest information consumers on campus. Unlike other constituencies, they have a long-term and continuing need for information for their own benefit and for the benefit of their students. I'll say something about reaching the non-library using faculty when I talk about our changing role. But for the moment, let's assume that faculty use the library to prepare for class or in the course of a research project: check the current journal literature in their field, plow through some older materials if they work in the humanities, familiarize themselves with a new subject that their curiosity or research or student has led them to, compose their assignments to students, sometimes even to obtain a fact.

So I ask you (or you have to ask yourself): what are you doing to teach this big or significant constituency those concepts? NOT their students. Faculty. Not about specific electronic titles and databases; not in how to search your local online catalog; but concepts that they can use to ask themselves the right questions when they approach any electronic database for the first time. Not the bibliographic concepts of comprehensive versus selective, recent versus retrospective, basic introductory information versus research-level information. But new concepts: such as menu-driven versus command-driven; searching versus displaying; Boolean logic; keyword versus controlled vocabulary; the concepts of record, field, and index; impact on retrieval of word order in the search statement or of the MARC record structure; the changing definition of catalogs and how that affects searching; how to evaluate the databases and how to evaluate what was retrieved; the issues of publication format, full-text databases, truncation, authority control; and on and on.

In other words, the objective world of information has a different look to it. And we need to tell the faculty about it. Where else will they get it? If they pick it up on the streets, so to speak, or by the seat of their pants, or from a (God forbid) computer expert, you know they'll get it wrong.

Leaving the objective information world, I want to move squarely over to the information seeker side of the equation and examine what's similar about faculty to other information seekers on the one hand, and what's special about them on the other—and how that might influence whether and how you work with faculty.

To think about faculty as information seekers we need to understand something about the **nature** of information seekers. According to J.C.R. Licklider, who wrote in 1965 about the libraries of the future,[2] there are some universal truths about them. To recast Licklider's "criteria...that pertain to the needs and desires of users": If I asked you (this audience or any other audience), in the perfect world, what would you like the nature of your interaction with information to be? You would say you would want your information instantly; you would want it to be accurate; you'd like it summarized when you want it summarized, detailed when you want it detailed; you'd like to be able to absorb it at your reading speed (or listening speed, if the instrument talks rather than displays); you'd like it to be highly portable, lightweight to carry; you'd like to be able to read it, or view it in any position: sitting, lying in bed, waiting at the bus stop, lounging at the beach; you'd like to be able to transmit it easily to someone else so that you could both talk about the same thing; and you'd like the information-seeking-and-dispensing device to facilitate discovery of and access to deeper levels of information or related information.

That's what information seekers want; that's what people have always wanted.

Isaac Asimov's *Book of Facts* tells about the Persian scholar Abdul Kassem Ismael, who in the tenth century had a library of 117,000 volumes.[3] "On his many travels as a warrior and statesman, he never parted with his beloved books. They were carried about by 400 camels—trained to walk...in alphabetical order. The camel-driver librarians could put their hands instantly on any book their master asked for."

Not a bad information system (this may be the first instance of online voice-activated access to a complete library); I'm not sure I care for the model, but certainly we'd enjoy full employment.

A better system might be the one L. Frank Baum foresaw in his 1920 book *Glinda of Oz*: "[Dorothy] ran over to a big table on which was lying open Glinda's Great Book of Records. This Book is one of the greatest treasures in Oz and the Sorceress prizes it more highly than any of her magical possessions...I do not suppose there is any magical thing in any fairyland to compare with the RECORD BOOK, on the pages of which are constantly being printed a record of every event that happens in any part of the world, at exactly the moment it happens. And the records are always truthful, although sometimes they do not give as many details as one could wish...the records have to be brief or even Glinda's Great Book could not hold them all."[4]

(You see, even in magicland they compromise with quick and dirty records. And you can *bet* that will guarantee the future of librarians.)

Getting back to the real world, studies of faculty's information-seeking preferences show that they, like the rest of us, want their information quick and easy. With today's technologies, that utopia becomes possible. Professor Nancy Van House, library school professor at UC Berkeley, says that faculty want control over and responsibility for the process of their information seeking; and when stuck, they want advice from an expert; they want evaluated service ("what do you recommend?"); they want personalized service; they want efficient service; and they want immediate service so as not to break the flow of the process, so as not to interrupt the progress of their work. Their ideal, she says, is to call someone on the telephone, get the "answer," hang up, and continue the process: convenience with control.[5] The first source they go to is their home or office library—their personal information files, the journal collection on their shelves. It's there and it is familiar. Friends and colleagues come next (They'll call their colleague and ask, "Does the chapter in the book you told me about contain what I need?"). Convenience and control is important. In fact, there is evidence that faculty, like others, consider convenience with control paramount over quality.

You can understand then why mediated search services never caught on in a popular way, and why mediated search services take a precipitous decline as CD-ROM services are introduced in the library. Going through a mediator, the information seeker is giving up too much control. Particularly in the case of faculty and researchers, mediated services mean not only delay in getting information, but also giving up some control over and responsibility for the information. As Van House puts it, how can they be sure their intermediary is truly acting on their behalf—as they would act—as distrustful of the sources as they would be? (With CD-ROM, information is immediate AND the client maintains control. But the down side of their using CD-ROM and other such databases is that chances are high that they are not getting as good a service as they THINK they're getting because of their inability to exploit the system and their ignorance of its potential.)

So faculty prefer to do it themselves as far as they can conveniently go. The trouble is, these days they may not be able to go very far. The finding tools we're offering to our patrons are getting bigger and bigger, covering more and more. It's easy to observe that the larger the finding tool and the greater the information universe it covers, the more difficult it is for the user to search. The irony of that is that though more information than ever is conveniently available to the information seeker, they have less access. Or, to put it in another way, on the one hand we have increasingly sophisticated tools providing greater availability of collections; on the other hand, users are able to do less sophisticated searching on their own.

Now if faculty are no different from other information seekers in wanting their information fast and convenient, what's special about them? Why pay special attention to them? What's special is that they stay put and we know where they are! We know their telephone numbers—both work and home—their electronic mail addresses, their academic interests, their committee memberships. That's a huge advantage for us over any other group we serve. We can't claim that about our student or community users. In that sense, we have the opportunity to serve a segment of our users in a way that is standard operating procedure in special libraries.

With today's new information retrieval tools and the ease of remote access to them, we can create an environment that approaches an information seeker's utopia; we can offer a smorgasbord of highly personalized, convenient, and speedy services depending on the faculty member's particular need of the moment. So, because faculty are big information consumers, and because we know who they are and where they are, *and* because we are the only ones in a position to keep up with the fast-changing tools that offer faculty the speed, convenience, and control they want, there can be no excuse for our not working in partnership with faculty.

The third reason for working with faculty needs only to be stated: *Faculty can be a help or a hindrance in our efforts to reach students*. They see the students more often, much more often, than we do. They initiate their students' library assignments. To the extent that faculty are misinformed or uninformed about the library, their students will be misinformed or uninformed; and conversely, the better the faculty's understanding of the library, its resources and services for themselves, the more likely their students will have that better understanding. Working directly with faculty, in my opinion, is a giant step better than getting untutored faculty to allow us into their classes to lecture to their students. I was moved by Tom Eadie's exaggerated but provocative argument (which boils down to—BI is ineffective and hard to justify in the face of declining budgets and staffing) that appeared in *Library Journal* several months ago.[6] My qualification to Eadie's position goes: unless your lecture is tied in time to the *execution* of the class assignment, and followed up in substance, your lecture may well be a waste of everyone's time, largely because you are answering questions that aren't yet being asked; and, though we can proclaim loudly that they *should* be asked, they may never get asked.

On to the fourth reason: *as the information industry is changing, so must the way we work change*. Our mission doesn't change—linking information seekers with the information they need—but the way we accomplish our mission must change. And the faculty should be the primary focus in our efforts to change because the payoff is the greatest—for them, for their students, and therefore for us. One of the things that needs to change is the locus of our worksite—we should be where the faculty is. And hand in hand with that change is a change from waiting for them to come to us—because that won't happen—to our using every ploy in the book to initiate contact with them and following up: that's what I mean by OUT-REACH: initiating and following up. I'm not the first to say that we need to change what we do; it has been said differently and better by the important thinkers in our occupation: people like Hugh Atkinson, Pat Battin, Richard Rowe, Richard De Gennaro.[7] And I won't be the last you'll hear it from. So I won't belabor the point. I will assume that you agree that something has to change, and that the agenda now is to consider not whether but what should change and how to make it happen.

Let's talk about candidates for change that would make a difference. One of them is the attitude of the faculty about what librarians do for a living. We must work to change their belief that what we do is keep order on the shelves, reluctantly check out the books, purchase titles from lists, and perhaps help a few of their students who somehow got through high school not knowing the ABCs of using the catalog and finding materials—elementary tactics, which they the faculty expect everyone to know. The more advanced faculty are willing to sacrifice a bit of precious class time and they invite us into the classroom to cover these basics.

This misguided sense they have of us doesn't come out of the blue. We do a lot to reinforce it. Faculty think we can't be of help to them in their work because if they need help at all they believe it must to be from a subject specialist who is expert in research methods; and a reference librarian who can answer quickie questions off the top of the head doesn't fit that bill. Why do they believe that? Because when reference librarians are not in the faculty's class imparting basic search strategy, they are seen behind the reference desk giving short answers to undergraduates' questions. (A tangent to this picture of how we look to faculty, which I will only raise because it's really the subject of another conference, is a discussion of the consequences when they do seek help of their asking their question unaware that they are at a circulation desk, or of the likelihood that they will get a paraprofessional at the reference desk.) So faculty believe that "reference service" can't work for their problems. Therefore, if the faculty attitude about librarians is to change, then another thing that needs to change is the LOOK of our work. How we're seen doing business. Not just behind a desk giving out quick answers, but in places where they see us using our special knowledge to provide in-depth consultant services.

Another change we need to make is in how seriously we see our role as teachers. Our most common type of teaching situation is the one-shot lecture/demonstration, for which there are special skills to be learned and techniques to apply. Those skills and techniques should be taught in library schools as well as to practicing librarians in continuing education courses and in-service training programs. We need to understand how people learn, what's special about adult learners, why people fail, why they forget, and what makes learning stick.

We need also to change the message that we send to our users that says "You can successfully use the library independently, and IF by some chance you run into a snag, you can seek out a reference desk and ask for help." We should be sending out the opposite message: that these days you're doing right if you START at the reference desk. I think our libraries should be redesigned so you have to trip over a librarian when you walk in the door. And we should change our terminology: our reference desks should be renamed "advice desk" or "information consulting services." No one but us knows what "reference" means. Think, too, about changing wherever possible the word "library" (which to readers translates to a building) to "librarian" (which translates to a professional, an expert). For example, in printed matter directed to faculty, rather than inviting readers to visit the library, invite them to get to know their librarian.

A final change: For those of us in public service, our expertise is in the *process* of getting around the information universe. And we use our expertise in the course of providing general reference guidance: assisting clients with the process itself or directly retrieving the information wanted; and in specialized consultations, in which we bring to bear on the patron's research-level problem our knowledge of the structure of the literature in given fields, interdisciplinary sources, recently appearing reference works, trends in reference tools, and the latest technologies. That's how I see what we're about. Today, with the rapid expansion of the bibliographic universe, we need to become good at negotiating with the users the contradiction between their requirement of convenience and speed on the one hand and on the other, the reality that they must tolerate much trial-and-error searching and sometimes a delay in retrieving the chosen material if they are to achieve quality results.

When we make these kinds of changes, wonderful things happen: faculty view us differently; they make better use of our expertise; non-library using faculty become library users; their students begin to see us differently; we see ourselves differently.

Now, let us turn to some concrete examples of ways to work with faculty to accomplish changes in look, message, attitude, and use of our expertise and services.

In your handout are some outreach programs that have been offered at the University of California Berkeley, some for several years, with excellent results. Let me review those, and tell you about some others that are not in your handout:

Seminars for faculty (attachments 1a-1d, 2, 3a-3b)[8]

Series of several sessions; average length of session: 2 hours; offered annually since 1976. The plan is to offer them more often throughout the year. Topics cover searching electronic files; using communications software and bibliographic file management software; and resources in particular subjects of current interest. Some 200 attend, mostly faculty, some graduate students, some noncampus community members. Tips about publicity: importance of logo in establishing recognition; clear description of content of sessions and intended audience. Individual sessions are repeated for groups at request of department. A fee of $10 was charged for the most recent series; it defrayed the cost of handouts and minimized no-shows. The results of charging: (a) participants enrolled only in one or two sessions and attended them, as opposed to previous patterns of enrolling in several sessions but failing to attend most or all; and (b) the level of attention and participation was noticeably higher than in sessions that were free.

Newsletters (attachments 4, 5)

Primary objectives: to maintain regular contact; keep faculty informed of changes, such as new tools and services, how the library is managing reduced budget or staffing; solicit opinions, cooperation; prevent or reduce surprises and rumors; publicize the library's side of the story. Make them attractive, keep them short, lively, and to the point.

Mailings that make responding easy (attachment 6)

Form (sent to new and visiting faculty member with "welcome" cover letter) enabling them to request information about "library research resources and services, special seminars, ongoing classes." Primary purposes: increase awareness of library services; provide convenient way to respond.

Other programs not represented in handout:

- Library Research Consultancy Program.

Funded by Council on Library Resources, the core concept is that of the library research consultant, a librarian who serves as a "primary care" consultant to a faculty member or graduate student in the humanities and who is responsible for providing appropriate guidance through the research process, as well as providing resources. Goal—promoting a partnership between librarian and researcher.

Indirect routes to faculty:

- Classes for campus administrative and secretarial staff in library resources and services;

- Document delivery service (personalized, convenient, fast);

- Invitations to academic departments, one by one, to chat with library administrators. Goal—to establish rapport, clear up misunderstandings, learn what faculty want, close gap between faculty's unrealistic expectations and reality;

- "Distinguished Librarian Award"—faculty (and librarians) nominate a librarian for outstanding service, achievement, and other accomplishments. The award provides the opportunity for faculty to recognize their librarian liaisons; and publicizing the winners of the award in both librarian and faculty circles and celebrating the highest expressions of our expertise and services, raises everyone's (including librarians') consciousness about what librarians do.

These, then, are some outreach initiatives that serve to redefine us in the eyes of our constituencies.

To close, I believe, as I said at the beginning of this talk, that if we don't adopt some clear strategies for new forms of outreach to faculty, librarianship is in trouble: some of the indicators of that are the closing of library schools and the downgrading of professional positions to nonprofessional ranks at lower salaries. I worry that some other occupation will fill the vacuum. It would be a mistake to take our future for granted. I like to think about the future the way Saint Augustine thought about it—as quoted by Daniel Bell in his introduction to the deliberations of the American Academy of Arts and Sciences Commission on the Year 2000:[9] "Time, said St. Augustine, is a three-fold present: the *present* as we experience it, the *past* as a present memory, and the *future* as a present expectation." By that criterion," Bell says, "the world of the year 2000 has already arrived, for in the decisions we make now, in the way we design our environment, and thus sketch the lines of constraints, the future is committed. The future is not an overarching leap into the distance; it begins in the present."

We can guarantee our future as a viable important profession by committing ourselves to new directions now. It's not a foregone conclusion that we will meet the challenge. Change isn't easy. As inevitable as change is, we're built to resist it. We like a predictable environment, with no surprises, and change undermines prediction and guarantees surprises. On the other hand, wholesale transformation isn't required here either. Step-by-step changes will begin to draw those new lines of constraint that move us is new directions and commit our future.

NOTES

1.   Until April 1991, the author was director for Library Instructional Services at the University of California, Berkeley, where she launched, directed, and participated in several of the outreach programs discussed in this paper.

2.   J.C.R. Licklider, *Libraries of the Future* (Cambridge, MA: MIT Press, 1965), 35f.

3.   Isaac Asimov, *Isaac Asimov's Book of Facts* (New York: Grosset & Dunlap, 1979), 215.

4.   L. Frank Baum, *Glinda of Oz* (New York: Ballantine, 1981, ©1920), 3.

5.   Paraphrased from remarks that Dr. Nancy Van House (School of Library and Information Studies, University of California, Berkeley) delivered in an unpublished lecture presented at a Reference Service Forum, University of California, Berkeley, Library, 14 March 1991.

6.   Tom Eadie, "Immodest Proposals: User Instruction for Students Does Not Work," *Library Journal* (15 October 1990): 42-45.

7.   See, for example, Hugh C. Atkinson, "Strategies for Change," *Library Journal* (January 1984): 58-59 and (15 March 1984): 556-557; Patricia Battin, "The Electronic Library—a Vision for the Future," *EDUCOM Bulletin* (Summer 1984): 12-17; Richard Rowe, "You, the CIO," *American Libraries* (April 1987): 297; Richard De Gennaro, "Shifting Gears: Information Technology and the Academic

Library," *Library Journal* (15 June 1984): 1204-1209; and Richard De Gennaro, "Integrated Online Library Systems: Perspectives, Perceptions, & Practicalities," *Library Journal* (1 February 1985): 37-44.

8.   For a description of the early development of this program, see Anne Lipow, "Teaching the Faculty to Use the Library: A Successful Program of In-depth Seminars for University of California, Berkeley, Faculty," in *New Horizons for Academic Libraries* (New York: Saur Publishing, 1979), 262-267.

9.   Daniel Bell, ed., "Toward the Year 2000: Work in Progress," *Daedalus* (Summer 1967): 639.

OUTREACH TO FACULTY: WHY AND HOW

presented by

Anne G. Lipow
Library Consultant

19th National LOEX Library Instruction Conference
"Working with Faculty in the New Electronic Age"
Ypsilanti, May 10 and 11, 1991

• **New information-seeking concepts and skills**

• **Faculty as information seekers**

• **Faculty as library liaisons to students**

• **The changing role of the librarian**

• **Some nitty gritty**

Anne G. Lipow and Associates
2135 Oregon Street
Berkeley, California 94705

Voice: (415) 841-2933
Fax: (415) 841-2926
Internet: allpow@library.berkeley.edu

Outline

TO THE UC BERKELEY FACULTY AND RESEARCHERS:

- ■ If you want to make more productive use of the UCB libraries . . .
- ■ If you want to keep current with changing Library resources that make use of new technologies . . .
- ■ If you want to help students improve their skill in using the Library . . .

THEN YOU WANT TO ENROLL IN . . .

LIBRARY UPDATE/1990

Faculty Seminars on Research Resources in the Libraries and Beyond

THERE'S A SESSION HERE FOR YOU

This year's annual program offers a smorgasbord of sessions on the "catalogs plus": take your pick among sessions that make you an expert searcher, or that cover search techniques in less depth but include how to download bibliographic records to your microcomputer, or that cover only downloading, or that provide software and instruction in managing your personal bibliographic files (Sessions A,B,C, and D).

Also offered are 3 sessions on specialized instructional and research resources (Sessions E, F, and G).

ENROLLMENT

Mail your reservation form (last page) early. Seating is limited and heavy demand is anticipated in some of the sessions. Enrollment is free of charge to UCB faculty, research appointments, and graduate students; for all others, the charge is $30 per session to help defray costs of preparing handouts. No refunds after two weeks before scheduled session. In addition to providing handouts that support each session, many sessions will have additional materials available for sale.

THE SCHEDULE   See inside for description of sessions.

	Monday	Tuesday	Wednesday	Thursday	Friday
OCTOBER 1990	22	(A1) 23 HOW TO USE THE ONLINE CATALOGS and other Electronic Library Resources Focus: Humanities/Soc. Sci. 9–11am	(A2) 24 HOW TO USE THE ONLINE CATALOGS and other Electronic Library Resources Focus: Humanities/Soc. Sci. 3–5pm	(C1) 25 TWO IN ONE: THE CATALOGS AND REMOTE ACCESS 9–11am	26
	29	(C2) 30 TWO IN ONE: THE CATALOGS AND REMOTE ACCESS 3–5pm	(B1) 31 REMOTE ACCESS TO CATALOGS 3–5pm	(B2) 1 REMOTE ACCESS TO CATALOGS 9–11 am	2 **NOVEMBER 1990**
		(D1) MANAGING PERSONAL FILES 6 9–11pm (A3) HOW TO USE THE CATALOGS, etc. Focus: Science & Technology 3–5pm	(A4) HOW TO USE THE 7 CATALOGS, etc. Focus: Science & Technology 9–11am (D2) MANAGING PERSONAL FILES 3–5pm	8	
	12	(E) 13 ACCESS TO STATISTICAL INFORMATION 9–11 am	(F) 14 MEDIA RESOURCES AT UCB 9–10:30 pm	(G) 15 NEW AND UNDERUSED RESOURCES IN THE HUMANITIES 9–11 am	16

NOTE: By special arrangement, any of the sessions may be repeated for departmental groups, faculty meetings, and classes.
For more information, call Anne Lipow, 642-3773.

A. HOW TO USE THE ONLINE CATALOGS AND OTHER ELECTRONIC LIBRARY RESOURCES

Social Sciences and Humanities focus:

A1. Tuesday, October 23, 9:00–11:00am
A2. Wednesday, October 24, 3:00–5:00pm

Sciences and Technology focus:

A3. Tuesday, November 6, 3:00–5:00pm
A4. Wednesday, November 7, 9:00–11:00am

Instructors:
Jan Carter
Bill Whitson
Sonya Kaufman

Ann Jensen
Ralph Moon

You can ask much, much more of the Library's online catalogs than the location of a title you want to see. But much of what they can do for you and how to make them do it is not immediately obvious. Unless you know HOW the online catalogs work, you can fail at very simple searches, retrieve misleading results, or miss possibilities altogether.

For example, online catalogs can unscramble vague citations; cull through thousands of citations to come up with just what you need; tell you whether a book is out and when it is due back; keep track of your search strategies and redo past ones; reduce large listings to more manageable ones by retrieving only material within a certain date range or in a particular language or NOT on a particular subject. And you can retrieve more than book and periodical titles: switching to "CURRENT CONTENTS" on MELVYL, you can search journal indexes for citations, and you can browse the tables of contents of the latest issues of major scholarly journals. And using MEDLINE on MELVYL, you can search for biomedical articles. If you have a printer attachment or access via a remote terminal, you can compile your personalized bibliography as you search, in preparation for printing or downloading (See Session B below). In addition, you should know about the Library's many databases on compact disc) that enable convenient, efficient searching for journal articles. These CD products also provide access to textual and statistical files, directories, government information and more.

This seminar will cover the powerful features of both GLADIS and MELVYL that can save you hours of looking and recording; how to avoid the common and not-so-common mistakes people make. CD-ROM database searching will also be demonstrated. Confirmed enrollees will receive a hands-on exercise in using GLADIS and MELVYL, to complete before the session. *Optional:* Publications that cover different aspects of the catalogs will be available for sale at the session. (For in-depth training in MEDLINE on MELVYL, check with the Public Health Library, 2-2511, for sessions offered.)

Intended for new and visiting faculty and researchers, and those who have been using the catalogs with discouraging results or without benefit of formal guidance.

B. HOW TO ACCESS THE ONLINE CATALOGS FROM YOUR HOME OR OFFICE

B1. Wednesday, October 31, 3:00–5:00pm
B2. Thursday, November 1, 9:00–11:00am

Instructors: *Vivienne Roumani*
Jan Carter

From your personal computer, you can search Berkeley's GLADIS catalog or the statewide MELVYL catalog to find out about books, journals, articles, and nonprint materials; create tailored bibliographies; and then download them to your personal files. Before you come to the library you can search GLADIS to find out if the material you want is in or you can save a trip to the library altogether by sending an electronic mail request to BAKER to deliver the material to your office. Without setting foot in the library, you can check the tables of contents of journals and stay abreast of new catalog developments.

Participants will be shown how to use their personal computer, a modem, and communications software to access the catalogs; how to adjust software settings, download to personal files, and transmit requests to BAKER for delivery of the material – using PROCOMM, an IBM compatible communications software package. *Optional:* At the session, PC owners may purchase for $10 a PROCOMM disk programmed for automatic dialup to GLADIS and MELVYL Macintosh owners of Red Ryder or Microphone may purchase a disk containing GLADIS and MELVYL command files which they can transfer to their communications software.

*Note: This session does **not** cover how to search the online catalogs. See Sessions A & C.*

C. TWO IN ONE: THE CATALOGS AND REMOTE ACCESS TO THEM

Social Sciences and Humanities focus:

C1. Thursday, October 25, 9:00–11:00am

Sciences and Technology focus:

C2. Tuesday, October 30, 3:00–5:00pm

Instructors:

Anne Lipow

Ralph Moon

This session combines the contents of sessions A and B (see descriptions above) – though coverage of the catalogs is in less depth than in A. *Optional:* Publications that cover different aspects of the catalogs will be available for sale at the session. Also PC owners may purchase for $10 a PROCOMM disk programmed for automatic dialup to GLADIS and MELVYL. Macintosh owners of Red Ryder or Microphone may purchase a disk ($10) containing GLADIS and MELVYL command files which they can transfer to their communications software.

D. WHERE DID I PUT THAT PAPER? MANAGING YOUR PERSONAL INFORMATION FILES

D1. Tuesday, November 6, 9:00-11:00am
D2. Wednesday, November 7, 3:00-5:00pm

Instructor: *Vivienne Roumani*

Personal information files are intended to be an efficient and economical means of saving information that you expect to consult again. But without organization, these important files can quickly degenerate into unruly and unusable collections, never to be found when needed. Now you can toss out those yards of 5X8 cards organized in a way you hope you'll remember, envelopes that contain scraps of paper with your notes on new research ideas you want to get back to, or folders labeled "Miscellaneous" with citations to articles you've read and annotated with your impressions that you'll need to recall later.

In this seminar, participants will collectively organize and manage files by creating a bibliographic database from scratch easily and efficiently using PRO-CITE, a personal information management

program and an IBM-compatible microcomputer. We will experiment with citations representing material in various media; produce tailored bibliographies in several styles (Chicago, MLA, Science, etc.); create a record for a conversation or other non-bibliographic information; detect duplicate citations; edit and sort files; and retrieve our citations using multiple search approaches. This session is intended for anyone who is interested in managing personal information efficiently and economically. Participants may purchase PRO-CITE at the seminar for $100 (a 75% discount). (Note: UCB Library is working with the producers of PRO-CITE to add a catalogs link that will enable you to download records from GLADIS and MELVYL to automatically-formatted records in PRO-CITE.)

E. ADVANCES IN ACCESS TO GOVERNMENT STATISTICAL INFORMATION

E. Tuesday, November 13, 9:00-11:00am

Instructors: *Chuck Eckman*   *Wendy Diamond*
Phil Hoehn   *Fred Gey*

This program will highlight new products on compact disc (CD-ROM) relating to government-produced statistics found in the Business/Social Sciences Library, Government Documents Library, Map Library, and UC DATA (formerly State Data Program). Speakers will describe available and expected databases, demonstrate selected ones, and discuss the services that assist you in the use of these products.

The following CD-ROMs will be demonstrated:

County & City Data Book 1988 (basic U.S. county and city demographic information); **Business Indicators** (contains current and historical data from the U.S. Bureau of Economic Analysis, including the complete National Income and Products Accounts,

Survey of Current Business Tables, and more); **Statistical Masterfile** (index, with abstracts, to a wide assortment of federal, state, and international statistical publications); **Supermap** (enables user to generate maps and tables based on 1980 U.S. Census data down to the block level, and various public and private demographic data by county, 1960-1985); **U.S. Exports and Imports of Merchandise** (detailed data regarding U.S. foreign trade); **1987 Economic Censuses** (results of all seven 1987 economic censuses aggregated above the census tract level).

The session will be useful for faculty and students doing current or historical research in any social science field, or who are researching public policy issues.

F. MEDIA RESOURCES AT UCB

F. Wednesday, November 14, 9:00-10:30am

Instructor: *Gary Handman*

You can bring fresh perspectives to your classroom using new types of media support. The resources available today for classroom teaching enable the instructor to demonstrate concepts, visually juxtapose unlikely ideas, or bring alive a historical or cultural event. With a minimum of training you can use computer-based sound and video systems, and other forms of instructional technology to open new windows on the world, to explore new intellectual roads.

The electronic media hardware and software available for classroom use at Berkeley are rich and varied, but they are frequently

far flung and underpublicized. This seminar will explore the major media collections on the Berkeley campus, and will cover the online and printed catalogs and guides to these collections. New and evolving forms of computer-interactive media will be demonstrated— for example, a visual encyclopedia of Italian art and culture, and a historical and biographical teaching resource on Martin Luther King, Jr. The session is aimed at faculty, teaching assistants, and staff who use non- print materials in connection with instruction or training.

G. NEW AND UNDERUSED RESOURCES IN THE HUMANITIES

Instructor: *Michaelyn Burnette*

G. Thursday, November 15, 9:00-11:00am

Looking for primary source material by and about George Gissing? Searching for works on dance published in 18th century Britain? Desperate for *The Mystery of Edwin Drood* in machine readable text? Need articles on Aristotle or Jacques Derrida? Answer these and related questions by learning about RLIN and its subfiles: Archives, Manuscripts, and Special Collections; the Eighteenth

Century Short Title Catalogue; and Machine Readable Data file. Also, discover the value of *Current Contents on MELVYL* and the *Modern Language Association International Bibliography* on compact disc. Basic searching techniques will be demonstrated. Most useful for researchers in literature, philosophy, linguistics, rhetoric, film, or drama.

ENROLLMENT FORM for *LIBRARY UPDATE/1990*

DEADLINES:

UC research staff, and graduate students whose enrollment form is received by October 8 have priority.
After October 8, enrollment is open to others as space is available.

SEND THIS ENROLLMENT FORM TO: Andrea Spurgeon, 245 Main Library, or fax 643-7891.
Make a copy for your records.

FEE SCHEDULE Check your category.

U ☐	UCB faculty, graduate student, research appointment	no charge for all sessions
S ☐	Scholar Services Card holders (#29)	no charge for all sessions
O ☐	All others	$30 for each session

INDICATE THE SESSIONS YOU WISH TO ATTEND:

___	A–1	Online Catalogs/Electronic Information (Soc. Sci. / Humanities)	Tuesday, October 23	9–11am
___	A–2	Online Catalogs/Electronic Information (Soc. Sci. / Humanities)	Wednesday, October 24	3–5pm
___	A–3	Online Catalogs/Electronic Information (Science/Technology)	Tuesday, November 6	3–5pm
___	A–4	Online Catalogs/Electronic Information (Science/Technology)	Wednesday, November 7	9–11am
___	B–1	Remote Access to Catalogs	Wednesday, October 31	3–5pm
___	B–2	Remote Access to Catalogs	Thursday, November 1	9–11am
___	C–1	Catalogs and Remote Access (Soc. Sci. / Humanities)	Thursday, October 25	9–11am
___	C–2	Catalogs and Remote Access (Science/Technology)	Tuesday, October 30	3–5pm
___	D–1	Managing Personal Files	Tuesday, November 6	9–11am
___	D–2	Managing Personal Files	Wednesday, November 7	3–5pm
___	E	Access to Government Statistical Information	Tuesday, November 13	9–11am
___	F	Media Resources at UCB	Wednesday, November 14	9–10:30am
___	G	New and Underused Resources in the Humanities	Thursday, November 15	9–11am

For sessions A, B, C, and D, please provide the following information (for purposes of preparing sufficient quantities).
I tentatively plan to purchase the items marked below:

☐	Guides to GLADIS and MELVYL catalogs	$6.00	(Sessions A and C)
☐	Current Contents Guide	$10.00	(Sessions A and C)
☐	PROCOMM communications software, with autodial to catalogs *Purchaser must also register with software producer for additional $25.*	$10.00	(Sessions B and C)
☐	Disk with catalog command files for MacIntosh users	$10.00	(Sessions B and C)
☐	PRO–CITE bibliographic management software	$100.00	(Session D)

NAME _____ UCB TITLE/CATEGORY_____

ADDRESS* _____ PHONE _____

If you checked category O in FEE SCHEDULE above, CALCULATE YOUR FEE here: $30 X _____ no. of sessions = $ _____
Enclose check payable to **UC Regents**.
Refunds for cancellations only until two weeks preceding the date of session(s) covered by your payment.

* If off campus, include self-addressed stamped envelope to receive enrollment confirmation.

TO THE UC BERKELEY FACULTY AND RESEARCHERS:

- ■ If you want to make more productive use of the UCB libraries . . .
- ■ If you want to keep current with changing Library resources enabled by technological developments . . .
- ■ If you want to help students improve their skill in using the Library . . .

THEN YOU WANT TO ENROLL IN . . .

LIBRARY UPDATE/1988

Faculty Seminars on Research Resources in the Libraries and Beyond

Library Update/1988 marks the UC Berkeley Library's 15th annual program. Over 1800 faculty and researchers, including graduate students, have attended in the past. Their comments indicate that they now make more enlightened use of the Library than before.

The seminars, described on the next pages, range from one-and-a-half to three hours in length.
They consist of lectures, demonstrations, and discussions led by librarians and other specialists.

THERE'S A SESSION HERE FOR YOU

This year's program includes 7 seminars in new and changing tools for information access (sessions B, C, D, E, G, I, and J) and 3 seminars in how to find materials on interdisciplinary topics dispersed throughout the Library system and beyond (sessions A, F, and H).

ENROLLMENT: Enrollment deadline: two weeks before your scheduled session.

Mail your reservation form (last page) early. Seating is limited and heavy demand is anticipated in some of the sessions. If a session is filled, you will be placed on a waiting list and notified as space becomes available through cancellations.

THE SCHEDULE   See inside for description of sessions.

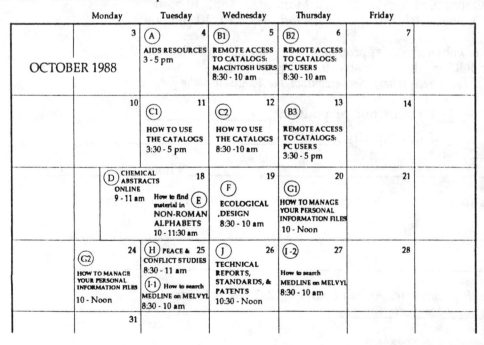

	Monday	Tuesday	Wednesday	Thursday	Friday
OCTOBER 1988	3	(A) 4 AIDS RESOURCES 3 - 5 pm	(B1) 5 REMOTE ACCESS TO CATALOGS: MACINTOSH USERS 8:30 - 10 am	(B2) 6 REMOTE ACCESS TO CATALOGS: PC USERS 8:30 - 10 am	7
	10	(C1) 11 HOW TO USE THE CATALOGS 3:30 - 5 pm	(C2) 12 HOW TO USE THE CATALOGS 8:30 -10 am	(B3) 13 REMOTE ACCESS TO CATALOGS: PC USERS 3:30 - 5 pm	14
		(D) CHEMICAL ABSTRACTS ONLINE 18 9 - 11 am (E) How to find material in NON-ROMAN ALPHABETS 10 - 11:30 am	(F) 19 ECOLOGICAL .DESIGN 8:30 - 10 am	(G1) 20 HOW TO MANAGE YOUR PERSONAL INFORMATION FILES 10 - Noon	21
	(G2) 24 HOW TO MANAGE YOUR PERSONAL INFORMATION FILES 10 - Noon	(H) PEACE & 25 CONFLICT STUDIES 8:30 - 11 am (I-1) How to search MEDLINE on MELVYL 8:30 - 10 am	(J) 26 TECHNICAL REPORTS, STANDARDS, & PATENTS 10:30 - Noon	(I-2) 27 How to search MEDLINE on MELVYL 8:30 - 10 am	28
	31				

NOTE: By special arrangement, any of the sessions may be repeated for departmental groups, faculty meetings, and classes.
For more information, call Anne Lipow, 642-3773.

LIBRARY CLASSES FOR FACULTY AND OTHER RESEARCHERS
See other side for description of classes
✶✶✶✶✶✶✶✶✶✶✶✶✶✶✶✶✶✶✶✶✶✶✶✶✶✶✶✶✶✶✶✶✶✶✶

February and March sessions
ENROLLMENT FORM ✶✶✶✶✶✶✶✶✶✶✶✶✶✶✶✶✶✶✶✶✶✶✶✶✶✶✶✶✶✶✶✶✶✶✶

ENROLL EARLY. CLASSES WILL BE LIMITED TO 15.
Your enrollment will be confirmed.

Fees.   UCB faculty and researchers......$10 per session
         All others...................................... $30 per session

>>*Note.--Due to limited resources, a modest fee for UCB-affiliated enrollees, as well as a surcharge for non-UCB enrollees, is necessary to contribute toward the costs of materials and minimize no-shows. No refunds after two weeks before scheduled session. The Library is interested in knowing if the fee presents a prohibitive hardship to any UCB researcher who wishes to attend.*

Please complete #1-4 below.

1. *Please enroll me in the following class(es):*

    ____A1 Current Contents...................Fri. Feb. 22, 10:10-noon
    ____A2 Current Contents...................Fri. Mar. 8, 9:10-11am
    ____B1 Procite...............................Mon. Feb. 25, 3:10-5pm
    ____B2 Procite...............................Fri. Mar. 1, 10:10-noon
    ____C1 Remote/Downloading..........Mon. Mar. 11, 3:10-5pm
    ____C2 Remote/Downloading..........Wed. Mar. 13, 9:10-11am
    ____D1 Online Catalogs.....................Mon. Mar. 18, 3:10-5pm
    ____D2 Online Catalogs.....................Wed. Mar. 20, 10:10-noon

2. *Enclosed is my payment (appropriate fee x number of classes):* $_____
   (Enclose IOC or check payable to UC Regents.)
   ____*I am a UCB researcher; please contact me to discuss the fee.*

3. Check one: ___Campus title or position:_____

              ___Other (specify):_____

4. Name:_____ Phone_____

   Address (*use campus address or enclosed stamped self-addressed envelope*):

   _____

   _____

   MAIL with payment to: Andrea Spurgeon, 245 Main Library.
   Make a copy for your records.

Description of Classes

A. FINDING ARTICLE CITATIONS VIA MELVYL's CURRENT CONTENTS

Search "CURRENT CONTENTS"--one of the 6 databases that comprise the MELVYL System--to find recent citations in journal literature, or browse the tables of contents of the recent issues of 6700 major scholarly journals worldwide in all disciplines. This session covers the strengths and shortcomings of CC and special search techniques for getting the most out of the database. Participants will receive an excellent user's guide.

B. USING PROCITE TO MANAGE YOUR BIBLIOGRAPHIC FILES

PRO-CITE software is one of the more powerful user-friendly systems for organizing and managing bibliographic citations, and is widely used in the academic community. It enables you to create, sort, index, and search very large files. The UC system has a site-license agreement with PRO-CITE producer PBS, Inc., enabling purchase of PBS software products at 75% discount. This session will demonstrate how to use PRO-CITE to (a) organize and manage files by creating from scratch a bibliographic database representing material in various media; (b) produce tailored bibliographies in several styles (Chicago, MLA, Science, etc.); and (c) edit, detect duplicate files, and retrieve citations using multiple search approaches.

C. USING PROCOMM FOR REMOTE ACCESS TO CATALOGS AND DOWNLOADING

With a personal computer, a modem, and communications software, you can do a lot of library work from your home or office: search the Library's 2 online catalogs, create tailored bibliographies, and then download them to your personal files; check the tables of contents of journals; find out if the material you want is in; send an electronic mail request to BAKER to deliver material to your office. This session demonstrates how to use an IBM-compatible personal computer and PROCOMM communications software to access the catalogs; adjust software settings, download to personal files, and transmit requests to BAKER for delivery of material. Optional: At the session, PC owners may purchase for $10 a PROCOMM disk programmed for automatic dialup to GLADIS or MELVYL. MacIntosh owners of Red Ryder or Microphone may purchase a disk containing GLADIS and MELVYL command files which they can transfer to their communications software.

Note.--This session does not cover how to search the online catalogs (see D below).

D. HOW TO MAKE THE MOST OF THE ONLINE CATALOGS

You can ask much, much more of the Library's two online catalogs than the location of a title you want to see. But much of what they can do for you and how to make them do it is not immediately obvious. (For example, you can unscramble vague citations; limit results to a date range or a particular language or NOT on a particular subject; keep track of your search strategies and redo past ones, ...) Also, unless you know HOW the online catalogs work, you can fail at very simple searches, retrieve misleading results, or miss possibilities altogether. This session covers the powerful features of both GLADIS and MELVYL that can save you hours of looking. Participants will receive an assignment in using the catalogs to complete before they come to class to ensure a baseline level of catalog searching experience.

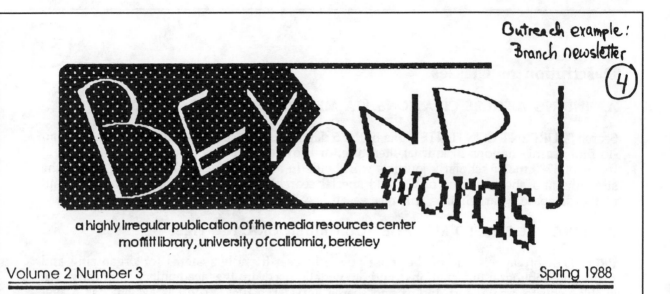

a highly irregular publication of the media resources center
moffitt library, university of california, berkeley

Volume 2 Number 3   Spring 1988

MRC Acquires The Video Encyclopedia of the 20th Century

One day in 1877, William K. Dickson, an assistant in Thomas Edison's Menlo Park, New Jersey lab, discovered an odd phenomenon: run a series of sequential photographic images printed on a roll of celluloid film stock past a strong light source at a certain speed and you get a startling, shadowy form of magic. As the separate illuminated images replace each other on the screen, the retina tricks the brain into persistence of vision—a neural illusion which makes the phantoms on the screen seem to move and live real as life.

> One of the most important visual resouces developed in the last decade. The single most significant acquisition made by the Center since its opening.

Since the day of Mr. Dickson's discovery, the cameras have rolled almost ceaselessly. Each decade has seen it own parade of real and fictional heroes and villains strut and fret across a backdrop of cultural catastrophes and triumphs. And at each turn, the unblinking lense has been near at hand to capture the essence and the moment—nearly a century's worth of cultural illuminations, visual images, icons, and archetypes enbalmed on millions of feet of film. Until recently, much of the film and video treasure trove has remained buried in far flung private collections and industry archives. While some of the classic newsreels of the 1930's and 1940's are slowly making their way into the home video market, obtaining access to the great store of this century's primary documentary film footage has remained a largely haphazard frustrating endeavor for teachers and students. Enter the **Video Encyclopedia of the 20th Century.**

Produced by CEL Communications of New York, the Video Encyclopedia is, we feel, one of the most important visual resources developed in the last decade. The set comprises over 80 hours of unedited silent and sound documentary film footage covering the major events, personalities, fads and fashions of the last century. A roughly chronological compendium of over 3,000 segments on 39 optical disks, the encyclopedia covers everything and everybody from Clarence Darrow at the Scopes Trial, to FDR's "Nothing to Fear" speech, to Martin Luther King Jr.'s march on Montgomery; from the San Francisco earthquake,

— ANNE G. LIPOW —

what's new in business information

⑤

Outreach example:
Branch library newsletter

Social Science/Business Library
30 Stephens Hall
University of California-Berkeley

```
*****************************************************************
Number 2: August, 1985
*****************************************************************
```

A Reminder About the Catalogs
Please remember that the Library's card catalog (Catalog 1)
ceased to be updated in 1980. Materials more current than 1980
will be found in the microfiche catalog (Catalog 2). Sets of
Catalog 2 are located on the counter in the lobby of the Library.
If you have not used the microfiche catalog, feel free to ask
for an explanation at the Reference Desk.

We have Rearranged the Book Stacks
Between the Spring semester and the Summer session, Library
staff spent eight days moving the circulating book collection.
The books you were used to having paged from behind the Circulation Desk are no longer there; they have been integrated
into the open book stack areas. Please note that there are
now two open stack areas in the Social Science/Business Library.
The call numbers A-HG are located on the mezzanine level, HJ-Z
will be found on the first floor in a room off the lobby.

The Northern Regional Library Facility
Due to the space limitations of the Stephens Hall facility,
many backruns of serials have been sent to the Northern Regional
Library Facility in Richmond. Requests for specific items to
be retrieved are taken between the hours of 9:00 a.m. to 3:00
p.m. Monday-Friday. Turnaround time is usually two days. Individuals may also go to the NRLF to use materials, where a reading
room and photocopier are available. Ask at the Reference Desk
for directions.

Baker: the Library Delivery Service
Business School faculty who have not used the General Library's
Baker Service may find it a great time saver. The Baker staff
delivers books, photocopies of periodicals, and other library
materials to your campus address for a small fee. Call 642-2537
for further details.

HOW TO GET TO KNOW THE LIBRARY BETTER

Use this order form to request information about library research resources and services, special seminars for faculty, and ongoing classes.

Mail to: Andrea Spurgeon, 245 Main Library, University of California at Berkeley, 94720

Please send the information checked below to:

NAME: _____   TITLE: _____

CAMPUS ADDRESS: _____   PHONE: _____

_____

INFORMATION LEAFLETS

Quantity **GENERAL INTRODUCTION TO THE LIBRARY**

☐ LOL 9   Map of the Libraries

☐ LOL 13   Hours (Current Semester)

☐ LOL 16   Library Facts

☐ LOL 29   An Introduction to the Library
             for UCB students, faculty, and staff

☐ CIRC 12   Answers to Frequently Asked Questions
             about the Main Stack

SERVICES

☐ LOL 11   Interlibrary Borrowing Service

☐ LOL 25   Stanford/Berkeley Cooperative Program

☐ LOL 35   BAKER Document Delivery Service

☐ LOL 57   Library Services for Users with Physical
             and Learning Disabilities

CATALOGS AND ELECTRONIC DATABASE GUIDES

☐ LOL 10   Library Catalogs

☐ LOL 18   Computerized Information Services

☐ LOL 27   "Current Contents" on MELVYL

☐ LOL 39   Databases on Compact Disc

☐ LOL 62   Dialup Access to Library Catalogs

CLASSROOM SUPPORT SERVICES

☐ LOL 56   Instructional Support Services

☐ MOFF 5   Moffitt Undergraduate Library

CLASSES

**SEMINARS IN RESEARCH RESOURCES FOR
FACULTY AND GRADUATE STUDENTS**

I would like to be notified of the Library's
October/November schedule of seminars
on the following topics:

___ New and Underused Research Resources in
     the Humanities

___ How to Use the Online Catalog to find
     Books and Articles

___ How to Access the Catalogs from Home or
     Office, and Download to Your Personal
     Information Files

___ Media Resources at UCB

___ New Access to Government Documents

___ ONGOING CLASSES IN HOW TO USE
     THE ONLINE CATALOGS

DLIS 9-90

EFFECTIVE COMPUTER-BASED/HYPERMEDIA INSTRUCTION FOR LIBRARIES:

THE DESIGN, EVALUATION,

IMPLEMENTATION AND CHALLENGE!

Nathan M. Smith, Jr., Mary I. Piette, and Betty Dance

Advances in technology, particularly computer hardware and software, have opened educational possibilities undreamed of a decade ago. James Mecklenberger spoke of "The New Revolution" happening in education:

> Revolutions occur first in the mind. The idea that modern information and communications technologies can play a major role in learning, teaching, and schooling is revolutionary. From its implementation, new educational practices rise and electronic schools appear. Moreover, when educators and students use technology *effectively*, they break through stereotypes and exceed normal expectations of what "school" can be. Unique powers of modern information and communications technologies allow us to create educational systems that produce remarkable results...."[1] (author's italics)

Many remarkable results have been achieved, yet a chronic complaint has been that much of the commercial software is poorly designed or simply inadequate. Today, it doesn't take a computer scientist to create educational programming on computers. The newest generation of authoring tools is available and their elegant, yet powerful design makes it easier for anyone to create programs. The introduction of HyperCard, an authoring tool bundled with Apple Macintosh computers, is a case in point. In the short span of a few years many HyperCard programs have been created

Piette and *Dance* are librarians with the Merrill Library, Utah State University, Logan, Utah. *Smith* was an instructional designer with the Instructional Technology Department.

and mostly created by nonprogrammers with special needs. Are these programs sophisticated? Definitely, yes. Well-designed? Often not.

This article's purpose is to provide an outline for creating valid, well-designed instruction, particularly computer-based instruction. We include some reflection on our experiences in designing, evaluating, and implementing Project FORE. As we refer to computer-based or computer assisted instruction (CAI), we include hypermedia instruction. CAI has been part of our instructional world for some time. Hypermedia, while computer-based, is distinct. While having the same advantages as CAI, hypermedia adds the power to use graphics, video, slides, sound, hypertext, and animation. While many of the principles and procedures described here are valid for any type of instruction, they become vital considerations when planning in the hypermedia environment. Our experiences in designing and implementing Project FORE led us to endorse these principles. We feel that our program has been successful since we have tried to consider these principles in our design. Certainly, this is a subject that volumes could be written about, and much has been written! A "references and recommended readings" section has been included for in-depth study of this subject.

Where Do You Begin? A Process to Follow...

Creating effective instruction can be time-consuming and costly. One proven methodology of developing instruction in education, business, and the armed services is the Systems Approach Model for Designing Instruction (see figure 1). It is called a systems approach because each component is vitally interrelated with all others to bring about learning. No one component can be skipped without seriously compromising instruction. A short description of each component follows.

1. Conduct needs assessment and identify instructional goals.

When do you decide instruction is needed? Obviously, a problem exists that creates a learning need. In other words, there is a discrepancy between "what is" and "what should be." A needs assessment is the first step to solving such a problem. To do a needs assessment, the problem and the needs of those affected by it must be clearly identified. How did it come to your attention? What are the indicators that there is a problem? Sometimes, the obstacle to "what should be" is an environmental problem, an absence of needed or proper tools, a lack of motivation, or a personnel problem. Problems of these kinds usually cannot be solved through instruction. Creating a system

of instruction should be undertaken only when there is a true lack of skills or information.

If a problem can be solved through instruction, identify the sources that will be affected by the solution to the problem. Now, the needs should be clearly stated. The needs statement should then be translated into instructional goals. Each instructional goal should have the following traits:

- It should clearly state student outcomes.[2]

- It must describe what the student will accomplish.

- It should relate to an identified need or problem from the needs assessment.

- It can be achieved through instruction rather than some other solution.

2. Conduct instructional analysis of each instructional goal.

Instructional analysis is a procedure through which the required subskills for each instructional goal are identified. Each instructional goal has required subskills that must be mastered before that goal can be learned.

Instructional tasks can fall into one or more of several domains of learning. The type of instructional analysis performed on a goal depends on its domain. These domains are psychomotor skills, intellectual skills, verbal information skills, and attitudes.[3]

3. Identify student entry behaviors and characteristics.

All of us have had the experience of being in a class where the material presented was either far beyond our understanding or was much too easy. Effective instruction meets the needs of the learner. Therefore, it is essential to identify the entry behaviors and general characteristics of the population you plan to teach. Entry behaviors are defined as the essential sets of subskills a student must have mastered in order to be ready to learn the instructional goals, not just simply what the student knows already. These sets of subskills have already been identified through the instructional analysis process. Now we must know where our target population fits on the learning hierarchies so we can determine just where instruction must begin. This knowledge can be gained many ways:

- By pretesting. This is a real advantage of computer-based instructional systems. Pretesting and placement in the instruction can be accomplished by computer. Pretesting also creates a database

— NATHAN M. SMITH JR., MARY I. PIETTE, AND BETTY DANCE —

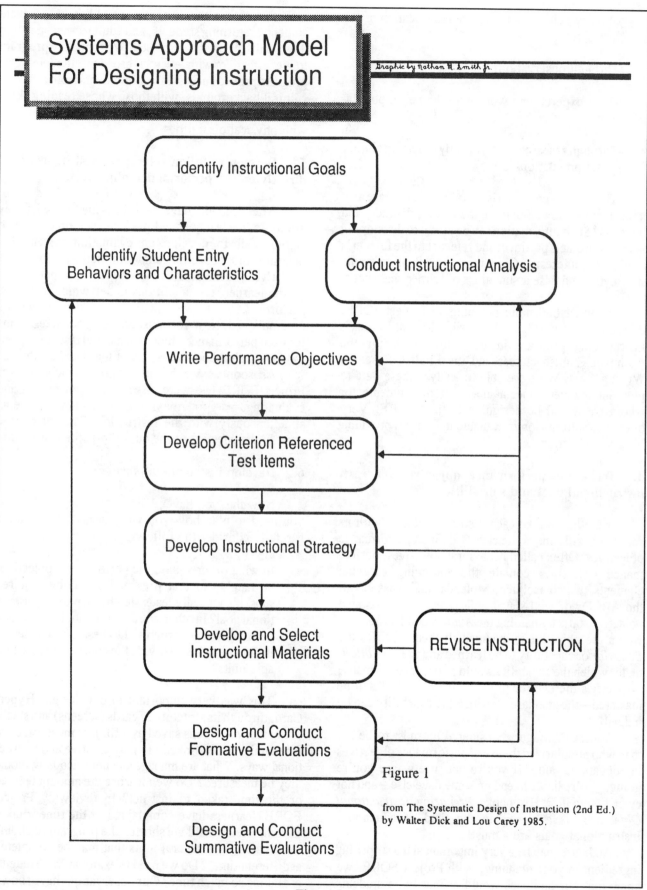

Systems Approach Model For Designing Instruction

Graphic by Nathan M. Smith Jr.

Identify Instructional Goals

Identify Student Entry Behaviors and Characteristics

Conduct Instructional Analysis

Write Performance Objectives

Develop Criterion Referenced Test Items

Develop Instructional Strategy

Develop and Select Instructional Materials

REVISE INSTRUCTION

Design and Conduct Formative Evaluations

Design and Conduct Summative Evaluations

Figure 1

from The Systematic Design of Instruction (2nd Ed.) by Walter Dick and Lou Carey 1985.

Figure 1

of entry behaviors for future modification of the instruction.

- Through observation.

- From experts who work with the target population.

- Through research performed by others on similar target populations.

The general characteristics of the learners are also important to know. What are their likes, dislikes, and interests? Such information can be useful to developing instruction that is pertinent and relevant to the learner's needs and interests. Care must be taken to avoid stereotypes and false assumptions of learner characteristics.

When we began our planning for Project FORE, these data were readily available since Merrill Library's instructional program included tests both for the freshman English classes and the English Research Writing class. We were able to analyze these data to pinpoint the very special needs of the students for whom we would be designing Project FORE. Very often, this information is available in libraries providing library instruction.

4. Write the performance objectives for each instructional goal and subskill.

It is vital to take each instructional goal with its set of subskills and write clearly defined performance objectives. Often called behavioral objectives, performance objectives contain the following essential elements, which Heinich, Molenda, and Russell call the ABCDs of well-stated objectives: "A well-stated objective starts by naming the *Audience* of learners for whom the objective is intended. It then specifies the *Behavior* or capability to be learned and the *Conditions* under which the capability would be observed. Finally, it specifies the *Degree* to which the new skill will be mastered—the standard by which the capability can be judged".[4]

Robert F. Mager, considered by most to be the man who popularized the use of performance objectives in education, said, "If you're not sure where you're going, you're liable to end up someplace else—and not even know it."[5] His book, *Preparing Instructional Objectives*, is a classic in the field of education. Instructional goals are a must!

Audience may be a very important and a surprising ingredient in your planning. With Project FORE, we knew that our audience would primarily be students from the English Research Writing class. We also recognized that the program would help graduate students, returning students, and adult learners needing these skills. We were surprised. We found the program to be effective with even a broader clientele. Our program proved successful with students from different cultural backgrounds, with those whose reading skills were less advanced, and it was accessible to students with physical disabilities.

5. Develop criterion referenced test items based directly on the performance objectives.

After students have been informed of what they are to do as clearly stated performance objectives, it is only fair to develop an evaluation system that measures those specific behaviors. In the performance objectives you have stated the behavior to be performed by the learner, the conditions under which it will be performed, and to what degree or quality it must be accomplished. Now you must create a pool of test items for each performance objective that will test the student for the mandated behaviors, under the stated conditions.

As soon as we began designing the units for Project FORE, we were also thinking of testing and evaluating. A good maxim is to design test items simultaneously with the instruction. The instruction must fit the question or the question fit the instruction!

6. Develop instructional strategy.

Now that you have planned what you will teach, you need to plan how you will teach it. You should carefully consider the following:

- In what order should the performance objectives be taught, so that presentation of the required subskills logically leads step-by-step to the instructional goal? In other words, how should the course be organized or structured to best facilitate learning? How will you divide the course into manageable units?

This was very important in our design. Hyper-Card, through its structure of cards (screens) and stacks (a number of screens saved as a file), is most effective when units can be linked in many creative and instructional ways. What are manageable units and how should they be measured? Do we measure the amount learned or the time taken to instruct? In reviewing Project FORE, learners have complained of the time it takes to complete. Should we shorten the program or should we divide it into several units that may be completed at different times? Do we need to examine why students are taking so much time? Our observations have shown that many students insist on taking written notes

— NATHAN M. SMITH JR., MARY I. PIETTE, AND BETTY DANCE —

throughout the program. This is not necessary. It may be that our introductory materials need to emphasize the nature of this type of instruction.

- What pre-instructional activities will be included? How will you motivate the learner? How will you make the instruction relevant to the students' needs and interests? Too often, we neglect to provide materials that will motivate a student to try a new program, or we do not provide instruction to simply access the program.

With Project FORE, we have developed materials that support and guide a student during the review. Our introductory screens are designed to attract and motivate. The program opens with a very attractive view of the campus and the library. Sounds and movement, together with graphics, provide many of the motivational features of a Metro Goldwyn Meyer production. We provide a very attractive introduction, but we still need to provide motivational/promotional handouts for students.

- How will the instruction be presented? Lecture? Simulation? Slide-tape? Computer-assisted instruction? On-the-job training? Books or other print materials? Videotape? Interactive videodisc? Or, even a combination of these? All too often, instructional designers pick the presentation medium first.

We selected a hypermedia format for Project FORE. The opportunity to simulate library processes and to offer the user opportunities to practice were the very special features we needed to successfully teach library use.

- How will the learner be tested? Will you have entry-level tests? Pretests? Embedded test items in the instruction? When and how will the learner take the posttest?

- What types of remediation activities will be needed? Enrichment activities? How will you determine when these should be given?

As designers for Project FORE, we dealt with such questions as: What kinds of practice will the student have? How will feedback be given? We found that we could investigate new and innovative ways in which practice and feedback could be offered. Practice can include challenging games, simulated experiences rather than the usual multiple choice tests. Sound has a wonderful feedback quality. Project FORE may at times greet a student who is in error with a statement such

as "You must have goofed up somewhere. Try again." This is nonthreatening and adds new interest and charm.

These points must be carefully considered and planned into your course of instruction. Remember too that learning theory indicates that effective instruction contains these instructional events:

- Gaining attention and motivating the learner.

- Informing the learner of the performance objective.

- Stimulating recall of prerequisite learning.

- Presenting the stimulus material.

- Providing learning guidance.

- Eliciting performance.

- Providing feedback about performance correctness.

- Assessing the performance.

- Enhancing retention and transfer.[6]

7. Develop and select instructional materials.

Let's focus on developing CAI. When developing CAI, you need to keep in mind its advantages, disadvantages, and also know the research on applying learning theory and design principles to CAI. Literature varies in its assessment of the effectiveness of computer-assisted instruction as compared to other instructional methods.[7] Most reviews were positive toward CAI. The margin between CAI and the other methods was narrow in nearly all the reviews. Perhaps the margins were narrow because computers were used to mimic the instructional method they were being compared with, rather than using the computer to its greatest advantage. Hypermedia programs do not need to resemble a book. They should be used to develop programs that will take advantage of this media's very special attributes or advantages. Hypermedia programs must recognize the disadvantages and try to counter them.

Advantages:

- Depending on the authoring software, CAI can include graphics, sound, text, and animation—it can be "hypermedia". Well-designed hypermedia instruction can help students whether their learning preferences are aural, visual, or kinesthetic. Often, instruction that is designed to exercise multiple modalities is the most effective instruction.

- It is capable of keeping and analyzing records accurately.

- It can provide an interactive learning experience.

- It can give appropriate and timely feedback.

- It allows for individualization of instruction.

- It can allow the student to control the pacing and sequence of the instruction.

- It can itself adjust the content of the lessons to fit the student's needs, or it can allow the student to adjust the content.

- It can eliminate some personal factors such as fear of ridicule from peers, subconscious prejudices, and others, often encountered in traditional classroom settings.

- Most students have a very positive attitude toward using computers.[8]

- Well-designed computer-assisted instruction substantially decreases the amount of time required for students to complete instruction.[9]

There are disadvantages and these should be considered, perhaps even countered in designing in the environment. The disadvantages most often mentioned are listed below.

Disadvantages

- There is often reduced contact between the student and the library staff.

- It diminishes the number of personal interactions between the student and peers or teachers.

- Frequently, appropriate software is nonexistent.

- The cost of the equipment is typically high versus the benefits of using it.

- Hardware configurations often limit the range and depth the instruction can take.

- Authoring systems limit the range and depth of instruction, and limit the range of ways instruction can be presented. However, this disadvantage is rapidly disappearing as more powerful authoring tools become available.

- They are subject to the glitches/problems that computers and other audio-visual programs can develop.

- With Project FORE, the technology to network the program is still not as powerful as needed.

- The technology is developing faster than programs can be developed. Project FORE changed and improved as there were improvements in Hyper-Card and as new software enhancements appeared. SuperCard was just being announced as we were designing, and Version 2.0 of HyperCard appeared just after we finished.

With these factors in mind, we felt that Project FORE could effectively use the advantages of CAI programs while overcoming some of the disadvantages. Equipment was available in our computer centers. Students would have easy access and this would not necessarily be a new venture. In fact, we recognized that many students were already sophisticated computer users who would prefer to work in this environment. We also felt that a review such as we envisioned would offer the students empowerment. They would feel more confident about beginning their research and would in turn be less hesitant about approaching the reference desk. In some ways, the human interaction might be more positive. Throughout the program, we offered strong messages of encouragement, requesting that the students consult a librarian. We were very deliberate in our selection of pictures of the library and the librarians, realizing that we could add charm and touches of humor through the pictures we selected. Most of all we were concerned that the instruction be such that learning would indeed take place. We tried to recognize and apply learning theories. We valued and incorporated instructional design, methods of feedback, innovative testing, screen displays, and human interface. We were committed to use the advantages of this medium to its fullest while minimizing and anticipating the disadvantages.

Application of Learning Theories to CAI: The Use of Behavioral Theories.[10]

Behavioral learning theories and principles—antecedents, behavior, and consequences—are also considerations in designing and development. Each is briefly outlined.

Antecedents. First, analyze the learners. What general characteristics do they have (age, grade level,

— NATHAN M. SMITH JR., MARY I. PIETTE, AND BETTY DANCE —

job/position, cultural background, and socioeconomic factors)? What learning styles do they exhibit? Determine their specific entry competencies (mastery of prerequisite skills, mastery of target skills, and attitudes). Begin the student at a section of the program appropriate to his/her level.[11] Analyze the learning environment. What resources are available? What possible distractions are there? Sequence the CAI from least difficult to most difficult. Provide prompts to help students select the correct answers, but eventually fade the prompts as they are no longer needed. The goal is for the student to give a correct response without being prompted.

Behavior. State the objectives, or target behavior, as specifically as possible. Build complex skills out of simpler responses by using shaping and chaining. Design the CAI so that skills can be remediated until mastered. Evaluate the student's responses to the program, and have the program branch to needed remediation, or skip to more difficult level skills.

Consequences. Provide immediate, specific feedback to reinforce correct responses. Use corrective feedback for incorrect responses. The quantity of reinforcement is not significant. Reinforcement must be geared to the student's needs, and be perceived as satisfying. Reinforcement should be timed to promote a continued interest in and retention of the material. Skinner stresses the importance of reinforcing each response—"continuous reinforcement" for the acquisition of new behavior and "intermittent" reinforcement, after groups of responses, for maintenance of behavior.[12] Determine the effectiveness of the program and revise as needed.

Methods of feedback to consider when designing CAI.[13]

Feedback is important to both behavioral and cognitive theories. Feedback can be given in two ways: immediate or delayed. M. David Merrill teaches that immediate feedback is best when instruction is being given; delayed feedback is best when testing a student's knowledge of the instruction.

Based on these methods, feedback can be broken down further. Feedback can be

- given item-by-item upon the completion of each question or student response,

- learner controlled, or in other words, the student can call for feedback when s/he feels s/he needs it,

- given at logical content breaks,

- given at the end of a module of instruction,

- given at the end of the session,

- given when the student wishes to break out of the program,

- time-controlled; the system responds to the student depending on the amount of time spent on a problem or module, or

- given at a much later time, when the student re-enters the program.

Project FORE provides quizzes at the end of each module. There is immediate feedback on each question. The quizzes change in format as the program proceeds, moving from the quick response to case studies, which prompt more conceptual thinking. Throughout the instruction, students are asked to respond to shorter questions as a quick learning device.

Using principles of cognitive psychology when designing CAI.

"To be effective, a tool for learning must closely parallel the learning process...."[14] Cognitive psychologists have created a construct of learning and memory that consists of the environment impinging upon the senses (receptors and sensing registers), then being handled by short-term memory, which then can be coded into long-term memory.[15] The following three aspects of the cognitive learning process are primary considerations when designing CAI.

1. **Short-term memory.** Design programs that recognize short-term memory and its limited storage capacity. Capacity can be increased by "chunking" or clustering the pieces in meaningful ways. In order to keep information in the short-term memory, which is limited to about a thirty-second duration, it must be rehearsed or refreshed constantly. Design CAI programs, which present limited numbers of ideas at a time, chunk them together in meaningful ways, and continually review them. Supplement the limited capacity of short-term memory by making large amounts of information easily accessible to the learner.

2. **Long-term memory.** In order to be entered into long-term memory, information must be coded, organized, or structured in some way. Organizational patterns are referred to as schema, which are sets of ideas that are cross-referenced to each other. Each idea is a connecting point to which other related ideas can be attached. Schema are analogous to scaffolding; the

more connecting points you create, the more information can be added on. Once placed in long-term memory, information is there permanently. Forgetting is only a problem of retrieval. The ability to retrieve information increases when retrieval is practiced. CAI programs should have advanced organizers that build upon previous, related knowledge, which prompt the learner to connect new ideas with previously learned ones, and give the opportunity from time to time to retrieve the ideas. This could be presented in the form of self-testing and practice. Practice should let students solve problems in a variety of contexts.[16] Make relevant, previously learned information available simultaneously with the new information, so that connections can be made between the two sets. Represent information both verbally and pictorially.

In Project FORE, we sought graphics that would visually represent or reinforce the concepts presented. The attributes of scholarly journals were presented by a "scholar." We endeavored to include in our text mnemonic devices and metaphors which would indeed connect, relate, and build schema for the learner. Figure 2 offers examples of the graphic/mnemonic screens. This particular screen comes in two formats representing both genders. Because our learning environment is visual, gender issues must be considered.

3. The learner's use of cognitive strategies.

The methods we use to code information into long-term storage are called cognitive strategies. Some cognitive strategies are scanning, searching, questioning, comparing, contrasting, chunking, hypothesis generation, decision making, among others. Design CAI programs that teach or model cognitive strategies when presenting new ideas to the learner.

Each unit of Project FORE outlines what will be presented and then summarizes and reinforces what is presented through textual reviews, examples, and interactive quizzes. Throughout the unit, there is recall of previous instruction and final case studies involve the student in using many of the concepts presented. The intent is to allow the student to practice internalizing and using all the detail and the concepts as a total strategy. Too often, students remember the details but have been offered no practice in using and integrating the material taught.

Considerations on designing screen displays for CAI.

Using all the learning principles mentioned earlier will not do much good if no thought has gone into the planning of the screen displays and the management of the program. Such planning can facilitate learning

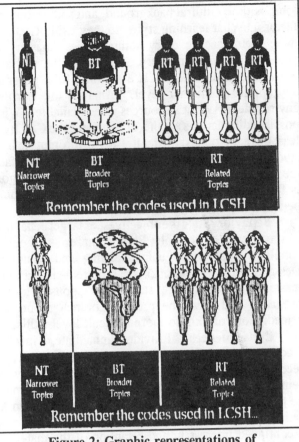

Figure 2: Graphic representations of LCSH's symbols....

and be aesthetically pleasing. M. David Merrill has researched and written extensively in this area of CAI design. Listed below are some points he and others feel are important to consider:

Instructional strategies

- Make sure that objectives to be accomplished are clearly described.

- Don't use the screen as a book, merely turning pages of text.

- When teaching a generality, always give many examples and practices.

- Avoid rote learning.

- Focus attention with devices that relate examples to generalities. Be sure to point out important characteristics of graphs, pictures, and the like.

- Encourage active mental processing. One way to do this is by asking rhetorical questions (rather than multiple choice answers). This engages the

— NATHAN M. SMITH JR., MARY I. PIETTE, AND BETTY DANCE —

student in a conversation. Feedback should not be in the right/wrong format, but respond to input as a person in conversation would.

- Don't jump into practice until you've given some expository examples.

- Allow the user to correct entries at any time.

Project FORE uses rhetorical questions in several instances. While learning to use the online computer, the student will find that the library has absolutely no books or information on "UFOs." The question then is "What do you do now?" There is a pause—the student is allowed some time to think, and then is presented with some alternatives. The graphics that accompany the scene do illustrate some of the frustration students experience when this occurs. Of course the answer is using correct subject headings. Do not overlook the conversational quality that hypermedia offers. Our textual instruction became immediate and conversational since we realized that students could interact and respond.

Display techniques

- Avoid scrolling screens. It is very difficult to keep your place and too easy to get confused when using a scrolling screen.

- Text should not disappear from the screen until some response from the student indicates that he is finished.

Provide a way to repeat the presentation if the screen is a dynamic presentation where things appear and disappear,

- Use dynamic displays. These are displays in which the timing of text presentation and/or attention focusing devices (flashing, inverse text, graphics, sound, animation, color) are used. (These are the very positive attributes of hypermedia!)

- Dark letters on a light screen are easier to read, and seem more natural to most students.

- Avoid a crowded screen. Leave lots of space, and erase unneeded information.

- Avoid long lines of expository text. Use short, concise, natural statements. Placing each statement on a separate line is helpful.

- Do not justify text on the screen.

- Information in all upper-case letters is hard to read.

- Sometimes, varying the text style can provide emphasis or indicate different types of messages. Don't overdo this one, however!

Human factors

- Give the student a way of navigating through the program. S/he should be able to review, preview, or repeat portions or pages of the material. If s/he reviews information, give him or her a way of returning to the original place without repeating all the information in between.

- Give the student some way of tracking in the program, perhaps a map or some other location indicator.

- Allow the student to adjust the sequencing of the presentation. (A menu will allow this.)

- Allow the student to adjust the speed of the presentation.

- Make student input as simple as possible. Limit the typing required.

- Provide some way of warning the student when a potential problem exists.

- Permit the students to choose the number and difficulty of examples they practice.

- Give students a way to skip sections of material they feel they already know. Provide a way to bypass instructions.

- Provide a way for students to quit an activity, but inform them of the consequences, if any, of their actions. Furnish a way for the student to restart the program in the place where s/he left off.

- Arrange that the records of any individual are retained in a confidential manner.

- Always provide clear, accurate instructions. The user should always know when and how to respond. Let the student know all the options available. Perhaps this could be done through a help screen pulled up by a certain key-press, or the click of a button. Planning for guidance—help screens, should be a part of each module. Help screens should specifically address the problem and should not be long explanations of the system.[17]

Navigation was a primary problem in our first trial runs with Project FORE. Students were not accustomed to the mouse as a directional vehicle. We now require the student to practice travelling through the Macintosh icons, pointing with the mouse and learning what to expect. This unit quickly and pleasantly familiarizes the user with this environment. By introducing this exercise, the student becomes more at ease with the program.

8. Design and conduct evaluations.

In his article *Instructional Product Verification and Revision: 20 Questions and 200 Speculations*, Thiagarajan devised a two-pronged, inexpensive and effective approach to evaluation. One prong is learner verification and revision, or LVR. This is where you have a small group of learners use and evaluate your instructional product. The other prong is EVR, expert verification and revision. Select experts in content, language, programming, learning theory, audience characteristics, and so on, and have them evaluate your product.

Project FORE improved through a multi-tiered formative evaluation process. Our first and most severe critics were ourselves. As each section of the program developed, both the programmer and librarian worked through each module. CAI expert Dr. J. Steven Soulier at Utah State University would evaluate and critique the program from time to time with constant reminders of instructional soundness and design. Our work was no secret. We asked, invited, and called upon our library and teaching colleagues to examine our work.

The next level of evaluation was LVR, then finally EVR. A warning! Evaluation is difficult. It was not easy to send out our work for criticism and evaluation. As designers we knew of the hours of thought and planning. It did seem threatening. We, however, wanted to have a sound evaluation, to be sure to have more than kind words. We constructed questions and guidelines for our experts informing them of the purpose of the program and its goals. In programs of this nature, the final product is never only one person's achievement but the result of a team of very thoughtful experts and learners working together. Through this layered process of evaluation and revision, Project FORE was fine tuned until it achieved the objectives we had set for it. A full account of our initial evaluation is outlined in "Evaluating a Hypermedia Library Instruction Program" *Research Strategies*, 9 (Spring 1991): 87-94. Another excellent review of evaluation is Neuman's article on designing library instruction in *College and Research Libraries*.[18]

9. Revision, revision.

When you revise, you may have to return to many of the previous steps and rework them. Though often a long and tedious process, it is the refiner's fire that will separate the gold from the dross. Your instruction will emerge finer than it was before. Remember, when many people evaluate your product, you will receive many opinions, often conflicting ones. You must carefully weigh each and choose those that will improve your product the most.

10. Implementing the program.

Implementation plans are often forgotten when discussing innovative programs. Yet the success of a new endeavor will depend on communication. Handouts should be designed to advertise and describe the program. The purpose should be clearly stated as well as who should use the program. Instructions on accessing and quitting should be clearly outlined. Printed materials should be developed for teachers using the program. These materials would include the following: the kind of equipment needed, installation instructions, a telephone number to call, the goals, and the target audiences. Student manuals and instructions are a must. This may be a time when planners should take on the role of merchandisers and market managers. A good product will need good promotion.

When Project FORE was initially planned, we had envisioned an instructional program that would be paperless. Students would report to a computer and learn basic library skills and then continue on to the library where librarians would continue to guide and inform. It was to be a rather "Utopian" world in which manuals would not have to be written and revised. Any updating would be a "mere" change in programming or additional units. This was not the case. First, we recognized that we were introducing radical changes to the library instruction program. These changes would impact students and faculty. Already overburdened English instructors would need to revise their syllabi to include this change. They would be needed to encourage, advertise, and promote the program. We would have to advertise. First a series of memos were developed and sent to all English instructors. We were grateful that the program itself had been designed with the help and assistance of the writing program director. This was a plus for our program with the department. Instructors were invited to come in and become familiar with the program. Finally, flyers were designed to advertise the program to the students. After our

— NATHAN M. SMITH JR., MARY I. PIETTE, AND BETTY DANCE —

evaluation, we felt that we had an outstanding product to "sell."

Yet other kinds of instructional materials were also needed. We developed a short, brief description of the program and its purpose for student helpers in the computer centers. If these students were aware of the importance and purpose of this program, they would be able to help, encourage, and promote it with students arriving with their assignments. We did not want English students arriving at the computer centers only to discover that the center staff could not locate the program. The center's staff was also warned they might meet nervous students new to the computer world. We asked for their help in smoothing out anxieties. We had worked closely with the computer center's manager in creating the program and so once again, we had an ally.

Finally we created a manual covering the same material in Project FORE. After the interactive, graphic world of HyperCard, it seemed prosaic but we recognized the need. Some students had already expressed a need for "something to review" after they had completed Project FORE. It seemed only fair to offer this alternative. We developed guides that allow the student to take notes or just respond in writing to the program. These guides were also a means of our testing the students' completion of the unit and evaluating their learning. Students also received a review handout upon completing the unit. Were we to plan or develop a program of this nature again, implementation plans would be recognized as equally important as evaluation. We recognize that programs like Project FORE supplement and enrich instruction but they do not stand alone.

11. A summative evaluation.

Collect data on how the students use the program, and any problems they encounter. Keep test scores, and all other pertinent data. Attitude surveys may be helpful. After a suitable period of use, design and conduct a formal summative evaluation. A summative evaluation's purpose is to let interested parties measure the worth of an instructional product. It is performed by a third party or outside organization who has no vested interest in the product.

With this in mind, we were delighted to be able to ask a new staff member, who had not been involved in the development of Project FORE, to conduct an initial summative evaluation of the results of the first year. The report of the evaluation follows. It must be noted here that a summative evaluation becomes a formative one, as the instructional product is revised and new versions released to the public. This initial evaluation does show that students are learning better with this program. Our concern is with the small

numbers who are taking advantage of the program. Our efforts now will be directed to making the program more accessible in all computer centers and in the writing centers and to make sure that it is free of programming or networking problems. We will respond to their evaluations. We will need to initiate other types of evaluative measures, which will reflect attitude changes and behavior changes. Ideally, a long-range program should be planned to measure retention.

Evaluation of Project FORE.

A statistical analysis on Project FORE was run using SPSS, the Statistical Package for the Social Sciences. This discussion is broken down by the two quarters in which the program has been used. During the break between fall and winter quarters, the programmer made minor changes eliminating some "bugs" and improving access speed.

The analysis is based on students enrolled in English Research Writing classes. Each is expected to participate in the library instruction module of the class, then take a follow-up library test. Scores on the test are factored into their overall grades. The students are allowed to take the test as many times as they wish in order to improve their scores. All scores used in the statistical analysis are the students' first efforts. For the fall quarter, a total of 575 students participated in the program. Of this number, 173 students, or 30 percent, used Project FORE; the remaining 402 (70 percent), did not use Project FORE. During winter quarter, 511 students participated in the library testing program. A total of 194, or 38 percent, used Project FORE while 317, or 62 percent, did not use Project FORE. A memo was sent to faculty teaching these classes noting the higher scores that students reviewing Project FORE received. Knowing the improved results, we hoped they would encourage their students to try Project FORE.

In order to analyze the difference in mean scores for students using Project FORE and those not using Project FORE, a t-test was used. For fall quarter, the mean score for Project FORE students was 91.88 as compared to 86.95 for the non-FORE students. Winter quarter results were similar: Project FORE mean scores were 90.75; non-FORE scores were 86.22. These results clearly indicate that students using Project FORE to learn use of library skills scored higher on the follow-up test than those not using Project FORE (see figure 3).

Another t-test included all students who completed Project FORE. Mean scores for fall quarter of the students who indicated that they had previous library experience by taking English 101(n=71) were compared to the scores of those students who had not taken

	Project FORE		Non-Project FORE	
	Fall	Winter	Fall	Winter
Student Participants	173 30%	194 38%	402 70%	317 62%
Mean Scores	91.88	90.75	86.95	86.22
Percent 1st Time Passes	93%	90.7%	84.8%	81.7%
Percent Scoring 100	41%	33.5%	20.1%	21.8%

Figure 3

English 101(n=97). The overall results showed that the mean scores of non-English 101 students were slightly higher (92.00) than those of the students who had previously taken English 101 (91.82). For winter quarter, the results were different. The non-English 101(n=106) scores were 89.77, as compared with the English 101(n=85) scores of 91.96. In this case, previous library experience proved to yield higher scores than use of Project FORE. Figure 4 illustrates these results.

A final t-test was administered to compare scores of students with no previous library experience (non-English 101, but who completed Project FORE) with the scores of students who did not use Project FORE for library skills. For fall quarter, 97 students were in the non-English 101 group, and 402 were in the non-Project FORE group. Means for the non-English 101 group were 92.00; means for the non-Project FORE group were 86.95. Winter quarter results were similar. The non-English group(n=106) had mean scores of 89.77 as compared to the mean scores of the non-FORE group(n=317) of 86.22. Both of these results would indicate that use of Project FORE, even without having had previous library experience, produces better scores than not using Project FORE (see figure 5).

Cross tabulations were run on the scores of students using Project FORE and those not using Project FORE. The lowest scores (28, 34) were obtained by two students not using Project FORE during fall quarter. Of the students utilizing Project FORE, 41 percent scored 100, while 20.1 percent of students not using FORE scored 100. Ninety-three percent of the students using FORE passed with a score of 80 or better, while 84.8 percent non-FORE students passed. For winter, again the lowest scores (20, 26) came from the non-FORE group. For the FORE group, 33.5 percent scored 100; the non-FORE group had 21.8 percent score 100. The percentage of passes for Project

FORE participants was 90.7; for non-FORE students, 81.7 percent (see figure 3).

Comments were made on the survey sheet regarding the program. The most frequent complaint for fall quarter was that the program was too long. Other problems encountered were that the program locked up in certain places, and that it was difficult to access and to exit. Positive comments were "it was very easy and fun to work with" and "it suggested good ideas." Another student mentioned that "I feel like I can get started" after going through the program. After the changes between fall and winter, comments from the winter quarter students again centered around the program being too long. There were not as many problems with the program locking up after the revisions. Among the positive observations, one student commented "it was great!" and another said, "cool graphics—I loved it. I went back just to look."

Conclusion

The purpose of this paper is to introduce librarians to design, evaluation, and implementation principles for instructional products in computer-based/hypermedia instruction and to relate some of the experiences we as designers had with Project FORE. It will be recognized once again that we cannot endorse enough the principles of design, systems analysis, and evaluation that we have described.

We would also like to convey our excitement about the possibilities of this new instructional environment. Most librarians will recognize that our instructional opportunities are unique, some of us do not have classrooms or required instructional programs and yet we must somehow instruct! The power of this environment, which is attractive and that can meet the library user's needs at a time when that need is most obvious, makes this environment one that can be particularly attractive for library instruction.

— NATHAN M. SMITH JR., MARY I. PIETTE, AND BETTY DANCE —

Completed Project FORE				
	Fall		Winter	
	Number	Mean	Number	Mean
Non-English 101	97	92.000	106	89.7547
English 101	71	97.8169	85	91.9647

Figure 4

No Previous Library Experience with Non-FORE				
	Fall		Winter	
	Number	Mean	Number	Mean
Non-English 101	97	92.000	106	89.7547
Non-FORE	402	86.9552	317	86.2240

Figure 5

- **The caution we raise** is that librarians should not attempt to build these programs by themselves. We will have to reach beyond the library, to form teams of expertise including the disciplines of instructional technology, education, and computer programming.

- **The suggestion we offer** is that we communicate. We need to form interest communities to share, report, and work together.

- **The excitement we suggest** is that we are not finished. We need to examine many programs and look for creative uses of this new environment. We need to come to grips with new styles of learning.

Can we go on to offer good, well-designed programs that can touch bases with new experiential instruction in which the learner is allowed to learn inductively? Can we break away from linear presentation and, to paraphrase Mecklenberger, revolutionize our library instruction so that we "break through stereotypes and exceed normal expectations of what 'school' (or library instruction) can be."?

NOTES

1. James A. Mecklenberger, "Education in the Information Age: The New Revolution. The Technology Revolution Comes to Education," *Business Week* 3191 (10 December 1990): 22ED.

2. R.F. Mager, *Goal Analysis* (Belmont, CA: Fearon Publishers, 1972), 7-11.

3. See Robert M. Gagné, *The Conditions of Learning and Theory of Instruction*, 4th ed. (New York: Holt, Rinehart, & Winston, Inc., 1985) and Robert M. Gagné, Leslie J. Briggs, and Walter W. Wager, *Principles of Instructional Design*, 2d ed. (New York: Holt, Rinehart, & Winston, Inc., 1988).

4. R. Heinich, M. Molenda, and J.D. Russell, *Instructional Media and the New Technologies of Instruction*, 3d ed. (New York: Macmillan, 1989), 38.

5. Robert F. Mager. *Preparing Instructional Objectives*, rev. 2nd ed. (Beemont, CA: Pitman Learning, 1984), v.

6. Gagné, Briggs, and Wager, 177-197.

7. For a varied sample see the following sources: B. Champion, *Computer Assisted Instruction and Bibliographic Instruction: Preliminary Data on the Use of PLATO in the BI Program of the Humanities and Social Sciences Library*,

University of Alberta, 1986, ERIC Document Reproduction Service no. 284 576; J.D. Hooks, *Teaching Library Skills to Academically Unprepared College Freshmen*, 1986, ERIC Document Reproduction Service no. 296 740; D. Kimmage, *Integrating CAI into an Undergraduate Library Skills Course*, 1986, ERIC Document Reproduction Service no. 290 492; K.A. Johnson and B.S. Blake, "Evaluation of PLATO Library Instructional Lessons: Another View," *Journal of Academic Librarianship* 16, no. 3 (July 1980): 154-158; D. Madland and M.A. Smith, "Computer-Assisted Instruction for Teaching Conceptual Library Skills to Remedial Students," *Research Strategies* 6, no. 2 (Spring 1988): 52-64; S.M. Rawlins, "Technology and The Personal Touch: Computer-Assisted Instruction for Library Student Workers," *Journal of Academic Librarianship* 8, no. 1 (March 1982): 26-29; S. Stebelman, *Evaluation of Self-Paced Library Instruction at the University of Nebraska-Lincoln Libraries*, 1980, ERIC Document Reproduction Service no. 197 742; and S.W. Zsiray, Jr., "A Comparison of Three Instructional Approaches in Teaching the Use of the Abridged Readers' Guide to Periodical Literature," *Journal of Educational Technology Systems* 12, no. 3 (1984): 241-247.

8.   See Madland and Smith, 52-64; D. Nipp, *In-House Library Production of Microcomputer Software for Freshman Orientation*, 1985, ERIC Document Reproduction Service no. 271 117; and M.E. Skinner, "Attitudes of College Students Toward Computer-Assisted Instruction: An Essential Variable for Successful Implementation," *Educational Technology* 28 (February 1988): 7-15.

9.   Skinner, 7-15.

10.   L. Poppen and R. Poppen, "The Use of Behavioral Principles in Educational Software," *Educational Technology* (February 1988): 37-41.

11.   R. Heinich and M. Molenda, and J.D. Russell, *Instructional Media and the New Technologies of Instruction*, 3d ed. (New York: Macmillan, 1989), 34.

12.   Poppen and Poppen, 37-41.

13.   J.V. Dempsey and S.U. Wager, "A Taxonomy for the Timing of Feedback in Computer-Based Instruction," *Educational Technology* 28 (October 1988): 20-25.

14.   R.B. Kozma, "The Implications of Cognitive Psychology for Computer-Based Learning Tools," *Educational Technology* 27 (November 1987): 20-25.

15.   Gagné, Briggs, and Wager, 177-197.

16.   C. Dudley-Marling and R.D. Owston, "Using Microcomputers to Teach Problem Solving: A Critical Review," *Educational Technology* 28 (July 1988): 27-33.

17.   See J.K. DeJoy and H.H. Mills, "Criteria for Evaluating Interactive Instructional Materials for Adult Self-Directed Learners," Educational Technology 29 (February 1989): 39-41 and M.D. Merrill, "'Don't Bother Me with Instructional Design—I'm Busy Programming!': Suggestions for More Effective Educational Software," *Computers in Human Behavior* 4 (1988): 37-52.

18.   Delia Neuman, "Designing Library Instruction for Undergraduates: Combining Instructional Systems Design and Naturalistic Inquiry," *College and Research Libraries* 52, no. 2 (1991): 165-175.

REFERENCES AND RECOMMENDED READINGS

Bitter, G., and K. Gore. *The Best of Educational Software for Apple II Computers*. Berkeley: Sybex, 1984.

Champion, B. *Computer Assisted Instruction and Bibliographic Instruction: Preliminary Data on the Use of PLATO in the BI Program of the Humanities and Social Sciences Library, University of Alberta*. 1986. ERIC Document Reproduction Service no. 284 576.

DeJoy, J.K., and H.H. Mills. "Criteria for Evaluating Interactive Instructional Materials for Adult Self-Directed Learners." *Educational Technology* 29 (February 1989): 39-41.

Dempsey, J.V., and S.U. Wager. "A Taxonomy for the Timing of Feedback in Computer-Based Instruction." *Educational Technology* 28 (October 1988): 20-25.

Dick, Walter, and Lou Carey. *The Systematic Design of Instruction*. 2d ed. Glenview, IL: Scott, Foresman and Co., 1985.

Dudley-Marling, C., and R.D. Owston. "Using Microcomputers to Teach Problem Solving: A Critical Review." *Educational Technology* 28 (July 1988): 27-33.

Flouris, G. "The Use of an Instructional Design Model for Increasing Computer Effectiveness." *Educational Technology* 29 (January 1989): 14-21.

Gagné, Robert M. *The Conditions of Learning and Theory of Instruction.* 4th ed. New York: Holt, Rinehart, & Winston, Inc., 1985.

Gagné, Robert M., Leslie J. Briggs, and Walter W. Wager. *Principles of Instructional Design.* 2d ed. New York: Holt, Rinehart, & Winston, Inc., 1988.

Heinich, R., M. Molenda, and J.D. Russell. *Instructional Media and the New Technologies of Instruction.* 3d ed. New York: Macmillan, 1989.

Hooks, J.D. *Teaching Library Skills to Academically Unprepared College Freshmen.* 1986. ERIC Document Reproduction Service no. 296 740.

Johnson, K.A., and B.S. Blake. "Evaluation of PLATO Library Instructional Lessons: Another View." *Journal of Academic Librarianship* 16:3 (July 1980): 154-158.

Joint Committee on Standards for Educational Evaluation. *Standards for Evaluations of Educational Programs, Projects, and Materials.* New York: McGraw-Hill Book Co., 1981.

Kaufman, R., and F.W. English. *Needs Assessment: Concept and Application.* Englewood Cliffs, NJ: Educational Technology Publications, 1979.

Kemp, Jerrold E., and Don C. Smellie. *Planning, Producing, and Using Instructional Media.* 6th ed. New York: Harper & Row, 1989.

Kimmage, D. *Integrating CAI into an Undergraduate Library Skills Course.* 1986. ERIC Document Reproduction Service no. 290 492.

Komosky, K. "Educational Computing: The Burden on Insuring Quality." *Phi Delta Kappan* 66 (1984): 224-248.

Kozma, R.B. "The Implications of Cognitive Psychology for Computer-Based Learning Tools." *Educational Technology* 27 (November 1987): 20-25.

Madland, D., and M.A. Smith. "Computer-Assisted Instruction for Teaching Conceptual Library Skills to Remedial Students." *Research Strategies* 6:2 (Spring 1988): 52-64.

Mager, R.F. *Goal Analysis.* Belmont, CA: Fearon Publishers, 1972.

Mecklenberger, James A. "Education in the Information Age: The New Revolution. The Technology Revolution Comes to Education." *Business Week* (Industrial Technology Edition) 3191 (10 December 1990): 22ED.

Merrill, M.D. "'Don't Bother Me with Instructional Design—I'm Busy Programming!': Suggestions for More Effective Educational Software." *Computers in Human Behavior* 4 (1988): 37-52.

Merrill, M. David, and Robert D. Tennyson. *Teaching Concepts: An Instructional Design Guide.* Englewood Cliffs, NJ: Educational Technology Publications, 1977.

Neuman, Delia. "Designing Library Instruction for Undergraduates: Combining Instructional Systems Design and Naturalistic Inquiry." *College and Research Libraries* 52:2 (February 1991): 165-175.

Nipp, D. *In-House Library Production of Microcomputer Software for Freshman Orientation.* 1985. ERIC Document Reproduction Service no. 271 117.

Piette, Mary I., and Nathan M. Smith, Jr. "Evaluating a Hypermedia Library Instruction Program." *Research Strategies* 9:2 (Spring 1991): 87-94.

Piette, Mary I., and Nathan M. Smith, Jr. "Hypermedia and Library Instruction: The Challenge of Design." *Reference Services Review* 19:4 (1991): 13-20.

Poppen, L., and R. Poppen. "The Use of Behavioral Principles in Educational Software." *Educational Technology* 28 (February 1988): 37-41.

Rawlins, S.M. "Technology and the Personal Touch: Computer-Assisted Instruction for Library Student Workers." *Journal of Academic Librarianship* 8:1 (March 1982): 26-29.

Reigeluth, Charles M., ed. *Instructional-Design Theories and Models: An Overview of their Current Status.* Hillsdale, NJ: Lawrence Erlbaum Associates, Publishers, 1983.

Reigeluth, Charles M., ed. *Instructional Theories in Action: Lessons Illustrating Selected Theories and Models.* Hillsdale, NJ: Lawrence Erlbaum Associates, Publishers, 1987.

Skinner, M.E. "Attitudes of College Students Toward Computer-Assisted Instruction: An Essential Variable for Successful Implementation." *Educational Technology* 28 (February 1988): 7-15.

Snelbecker, G.L. *Learning Theory, Instructional Theory, and Psychoeducational Design.* New York: University Press of America, 1985.

SPSS/PC+ V 2.0. *Base Manual for the IBM PC/XT/AT and PS/2.* Chicago: SPSS Inc., 1988.

Stebelman, S. *Evaluation of Self-Paced Library Instruction at the University of Nebraska-Lincoln Libraries.* 1980. ERIC Document Reproduction Service no. 197 742.

Sugranes, M.R., and others. "Computer Assisted Instruction Remediation Program for Credit Course in Bibliographic Instruction." *Research Strategies* 4:1 (Winter 1986): 18-26.

Thiagarajan, Sivasailam. "Instructional Product Verification and Revision: 20 Questions and 200 Speculations." *ECTJ* 26:2 (1978): 133-141.

Zsiray, S.W., Jr. "A Comparison of Three Instructional Approaches in Teaching the Use of the Abridged Readers' Guide to Periodical Literature." *Journal of Educational Technology Systems* 12:3 (1984): 241-247.

— NATHAN M. SMITH JR., MARY I. PIETTE, AND BETTY DANCE —

THE PORTAL AND THE GATEWAY:

LIBRARY TECHNOLOGY IN THE FRESHMAN

SURVEY CLASS AT THE OHIO STATE UNIVERSITY

Fred Roecker and Thomas Minnick

THE GATEWAY

There was tremendous excitement at The Ohio State University Libraries, especially in the Office of User Education, when bibliographic instruction (BI) was to be included in the curriculum of OSU's University College (UVC) Freshman Survey classes beginning in 1978. The opportunity to reach more than 10,000 students every year was a significant step toward achieving the mission of the User Education Office: to educate the university's undergraduate students to become successful users of library information.

Those first UVC/BI classes during the fall of 1978 showed the immensity of the task of the Office of User Education to provide bibliographic instruction to OSU's students. The 23 volunteer library instructors reached 8,500 freshmen in 198 teaching sessions during that first fall quarter. It was evident that to achieve our goals for UVC would require a major effort on the part of the libraries' facilities and staff to ensure quality instruction and relevant assignments. Without significant attention to this program, the bibliographic instruction component could easily be dropped from the UVC curriculum.

CONSIDERATIONS FOR THE UVC BIBLIOGRAPHIC INSTRUCTION CLASSES

Five questions summarized the general concern felt by Virginia Tiefel, head of the Office of User Education and coordinator of the UVC/OSU Libraries program:

Roecker is User Education Librarian, and *Minnick* is Assistant Dean, University College, The Ohio State University, Columbus, Ohio.

1. What should be taught?

One of the original concerns in giving bibliographic instruction to all of these students was deciding what library skills should be presented during a one-time, 50-minute class. This class might be the only contact some students would have with a librarian, with training in information seeking, and using basic reference materials. How could the BI session be constructed to cover the most vital information, keep it under 50 minutes, and be interesting and entertaining to a classroom with 40-150 undergraduate students?

2. What impact will this program have on patrons and staff?

Once a BI program is presented to 10,000 students and a library assignment given, the libraries must be prepared to welcome 10,000 new users through their doors and assist students with their searching. How many times could reference librarians and staff answer the same questions about how to use the online catalog? Could the print indexes and other materials stand up to all the page turnings? How would other patrons feel about the study and research areas being flooded with huge numbers of novice users?

3. Were there enough BI instructors now and for future needs?

During the fall of 1978 several librarians taught 35 BI classes for the UVC program. If there were to be fewer volunteers in the future, it would mean an even heavier teaching load on the undergraduate librarians and the User Education Office. How many more classes could the User Ed and the undergraduate librarians take on?

4. Would the volunteers' teaching skills and overall presentations be consistent and effective?

The User Education Office, undergraduate librarians, and volunteers must deliver the goods in their presentations to justify UVC's commitment to BI. Each hour of class was too valuable to be given to non-relevant or poorly organized presentations.

5. How could librarians build on these introductory skills to enable students to become successful users of library information?

With only this one, short BI session the students could hardly be considered proficient information seekers. Additional instruction would be needed in the use of CD-ROM, the online catalog, and course-related

searching. With fewer than 100 librarians at OSU, there was concern in the User Education Office about maintaining the existing programs while expanding BI courses to meet other information-seeking needs for all 53,000 students.

By 1980 an additional 10,000 students were receiving other course-related BI classes. The combination of UVC classes and course-related BI demonstrated that to keep up with the growing demands for existing and new user education programs, a new solution was needed.

BIRTH OF THE GATEWAY TO INFORMATION IDEA

It occurred to Virginia Tiefel that a computer system might be developed to ease the basic UVC library instruction load, and provide on-demand follow-up instruction and information access to build on the initial library skills presented in UVC classes. Tiefel envisioned a computerized BI/information access system that would provide consistent delivery of instruction, could handle huge numbers of students, would have the potential for easy modification to reflect UVC or course-related assignment changes, could protect paper indexes from damage by supporting searching in electronic indexes, and would keep the interest of students by using computers and emerging technology.

Geared to the undergraduate or novice library user, the computer was conceived to act as a personal advisor that students could consult to locate and access library materials. Tiefel pictured a system from which a student could organize a search strategy, identify relevant materials regardless of format, search available CD-ROM's and the online catalog, then locate the materials by examining library floorplans and campus maps. In this scenario, the final step in the research process would be to consult the librarian for more in-depth, specialized information that was not identified on the computer. The student would be able to perform independent information seeking, while the librarians would be freed from basic resource questions and able to use their skills as specialists to locate more specific research materials.

In 1987 Tiefel was able to move ahead and develop this computer project . Working with a team of other librarians, she submitted a formal grant proposal to the Fund for the Improvement for Post-Secondary Education (FIPSE), a U.S. Department of Education agency. "FIPSE bought into an idea, for which I will always be grateful," she now says. "We had no equipment, no programmers, no idea of what type of system we would use...just an idea, and they enabled us to continue."

The system was conceived to be a "one-stop-shopping" computer for all research needs, bringing together a variety of electronic and paper information sources in a single computer workstation so users would not have to find library information on one computer, search the catalog on another, or read CD-ROM's from yet another.

The project was named "The Gateway to Information."

PHASE I: THE MISSION AND THE MISSIONARIES

An immediate hurdle presented itself when an initial literature search revealed there were no existing BI computer systems currently available that could be modified or even examined for ideas. There were library orientation systems with library information, rules, floorplans, and hours, as well as some subject-specific computer programs to identify materials in various disciplines. A few CD-ROM networks had been created with menu-access to various disks, but nothing had been done on the proposed scale of The Gateway to guide users to relevant sources, create front-ends for databases, and provide critical-thinking information. In addition, many of the technical tools and workstations configurations needed to create and implement the goals of The Gateway simply did not exist.

With FIPSE money and in collaboration with the Libraries Office of Automation, The Office of User Education began to create the system. One programmer was hired full-time, two student programmers were enlisted, and eight Macintosh IIcx computers and Imagewriter printers were purchased along with supporting HyperCard software. (The Macintosh computer had been decided upon as the workstation because its HyperCard software allowed simplified programming and permitted easy changes to the narrative text on the screens.) Technical and design committees of librarians and staff were formed, and with the support of Dr. William Studer, director of The University Libraries, work on The Gateway began.

The Gateway's primary function agreed on by its designers was to assist undergraduate or novice library users in identifying, locating, and evaluating relevant research materials regardless of the format. Central to achieving these goals was a focus on an organized "search strategy." This concept of selecting and narrowing a topic, then moving from broad, general sources of information to specific data materials, had been taught in the UVC classes for 9 years. Using this search strategy as a basis, the project began to take shape.

PHASE II: PROTOTYPE TESTING AND MODIFICATION

Two years later in 1989, an incomplete prototype of The Gateway was made available to library faculty and staff for their testing and comments. This version contained encyclopedia and periodical index information, as well as library profiles, hours, and floorplans. The first user testing was conducted with selected undergraduate students supervised by the User Education staff under controlled circumstances. Subjects were asked to locate information on The Gateway in the few areas that had been completed.

Results of these tests led to many changes. Arrow icons, familiar to HyperCard users for turning to the next page, were a puzzle to the users despite a screen of instructions. Students could understand using box icons with words in them, so the arrows used for turning pages were replaced with boxes marked, "Back" and "More." Working a mouse was not a problem even for first-time users, but reading more than three lines of text was. The screens were re-designed to permit skimming of information and to sizably reduce the amount of text on each screen.

Innovations in the programming allowed access to the LCS and *The Electronic Encyclopedia* by Grolier. Both were mounted on the local area network for OSU called SONNET (System of Neighboring Networks). A patron could now identify print materials, search a CD-ROM, and access the LCS catalog from a single workstation. One of the first goals, to create a one-stop workstation, was being realized.

Two workstations were placed in the Main Library for public use in January 1990. These two workstations were only available for a few hours every day. A Gateway developer from User Ed or the Library Automation Office was present with each user to listen to comments and assist with any problems. Once a user completed a search, they were invited to fill out an evaluation form and comment on any aspect of the project.

Using these comments, changes were implemented in content and programming. The main menu became a graphic representation of the search strategy map that was taught in the UVC classes (see figure 1). This new screen was created to encourage total access to a variety of sources beyond the online catalog. Other screens were constantly being re-worked for clarity, with links added to permit movement between related information sources.

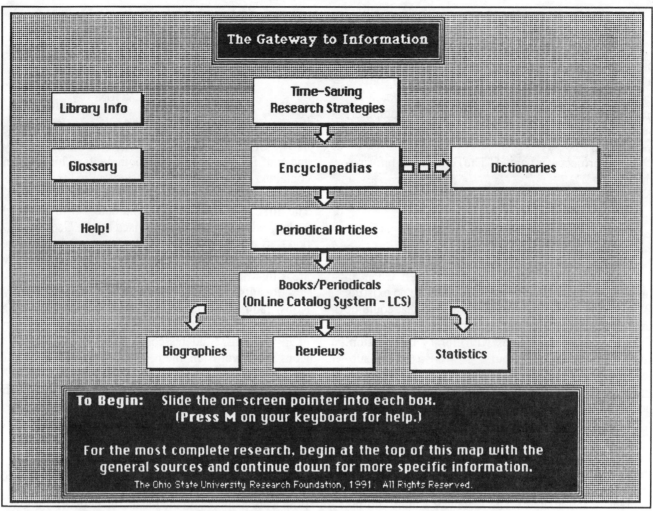

Figure 1: Gateway Search Strategy Map Screen

Six months later in June 1990, two more Gateway workstations were added to the Main Library. All four computers were now left unattended to test the reliability of the program and to see if students could use the system without instruction or supervision. Based on the positive user response and reliability of the programming, two additional workstations were placed in the Undergraduate Library in January 1991, bringing the total to six Gateway workstations on the OSU campus.

RECEPTION TO THE GATEWAY
AT OHIO STATE

Over 1,000 evaluations were collected between July 1990 and May 1991. From the start of testing, evaluations have been positive. Given the simplified LCS searching, the students (and faculty) immediately were drawn to The Gateway as an alternative to the difficult language of the original LCS system.

Initially, users liked The Gateway for its front-end to LCS and the library floorplans. But it was in April 1991 after 11 CD-ROMs were mounted (appendix 1) that the users' evaluations reflected the new success they were having with their searching. These CD-ROM databases were being heavily used. Keyword searching in these databases almost always produced citations to articles on their topics.

During the first testing most of the evaluations came from graduate students and some faculty. But in the months of April and May 1991, with the addition of the CD-ROMs, the demographics changed. Undergraduate student use of The Gateway rose from 45 percent from July 1990-March 1991 to 66 percent from April-May 1991. The target audience was using the system (see figure 2).

By this time 75 percent of patron evaluations indicated they were "completely or mostly successful" with their searching, while usage of LCS on The Gateway fell from 76 percent to 61 percent. Patrons were finding relevant information in other areas in addition to the online catalog. In addition, 87 percent

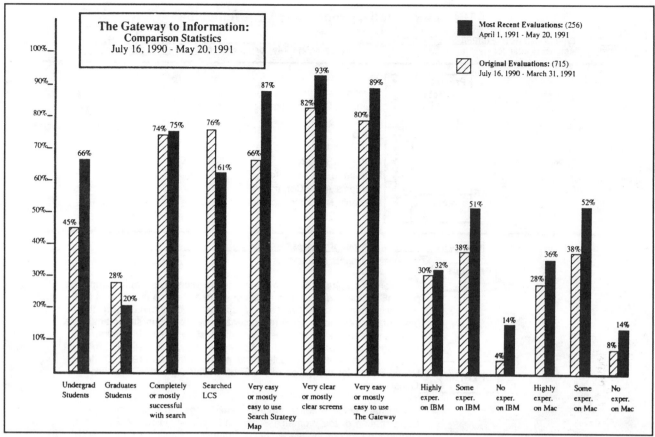

Figure 2: Graph of Evaluation Statistics

felt the Search Strategy Map was "very or mostly easy to use" and 93 percent felt the screen layouts were "very or mostly clear." Overall, 89 percent felt The Gateway was "very or mostly easy" to use and 81 percent said they "would use The Gateway again."

THE PORTAL (UVC) AND THE GATEWAY

In the spring of 1990, the first UVC class was required to use The Gateway to Information to locate library materials required in their assignment. Because testing was still in the first six months and the equipment was available only on a limited basis with an observer present, the eleven students made 1-hour appointments to use The Gateway.

These students needed to find three relevant source materials for a given topic, choosing from an encyclopedia, magazine, or journal article, a book, or a statistical source. They had to retrieve these items, evaluate them for relevancy, and then assemble them into an annotated bibliography (see appendix 2).

From Gateway workstations, UVC students began the assignment by reading a full-text encyclopedia article from the *Electronic Encyclopedia* to identify basic information and to narrow their topic (see figure

3). The Gateway also suggested other print encyclopedias that corresponded to their subject. Next they identified relevant articles and read abstracts in *Readers' Guide Abstracts* or any of the other indexes on CD-ROM found on The Gateway (see figure 4). Here, too, they could also evaluate print indexes, which were shown to be relevant to their subject, by examining the information card linked to each title, containing location, call number, description, and publication year (see figure 5).

Books from the online catalog were easily located via many routes including subject searching or by author-title searching. The latter was particularly useful for finding materials previously identified from the bibliographies of the encyclopedia or periodical articles. Finding the full-text article locations was simplified in LCS by a pop-up window to check if the user needs "All," "Current," or "Specific" volumes of the title. This allowed users to determine which of OSU's 24 libraries held the exact volume that contained the article. Specialized statistical sources were also readily available, each title again complete with locations and descriptions of contents.

The results from these classes were very positive. Some students who did not know that OSU had a Women's Studies Library were able to identify materi-

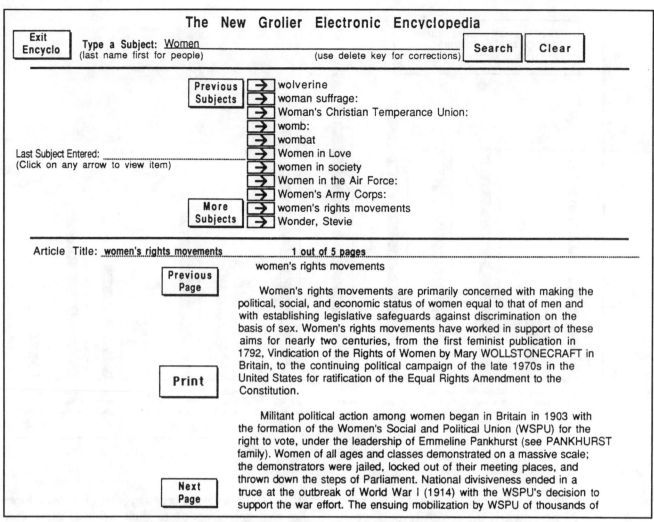

The New Grolier Electronic Encyclopedia

Exit Encyclo

Type a Subject: Women
(last name first for people)

(use delete key for corrections)

Search   Clear

Previous Subjects

Last Subject Entered: _____
(Click on any arrow to view item)

More Subjects

→ wolverine
→ woman suffrage:
→ Woman's Christian Temperance Union:
→ womb:
→ wombat
→ Women in Love
→ women in society
→ Women in the Air Force:
→ Women's Army Corps:
→ women's rights movements
→ Wonder, Stevie

Article Title: women's rights movements   1 out of 5 pages

Previous Page

Print

Next Page

women's rights movements

Women's rights movements are primarily concerned with making the political, social, and economic status of women equal to that of men and with establishing legislative safeguards against discrimination on the basis of sex. Women's rights movements have worked in support of these aims for nearly two centuries, from the first feminist publication in 1792, Vindication of the Rights of Women by Mary WOLLSTONECRAFT in Britain, to the continuing political campaign of the late 1970s in the United States for ratification of the Equal Rights Amendment to the Constitution.

Militant political action among women began in Britain in 1903 with the formation of the Women's Social and Political Union (WSPU) for the right to vote, under the leadership of Emmeline Pankhurst (see PANKHURST family). Women of all ages and classes demonstrated on a massive scale; the demonstrators were jailed, locked out of their meeting places, and thrown down the steps of Parliament. National divisiveness ended in a truce at the outbreak of World War I (1914) with the WSPU's decision to support the war effort. The ensuing mobilization by WSPU of thousands of

Figure 3: Electronic Encyclopedia Screen for Search on "Women"

als in this collection, print a floorplan and campus map to locate the building, check the library's hours, and proceed to the stacks without needing to ask for assistance (see figure 6).

A typical UVC student, with little library experience and armed with just a topic for an annotated bibliography, used The Gateway to Information to successfully identify an interesting sub-topic from a broad subject, and examine encyclopedias (including one full-text CD-ROM version with articles that could be read from the terminal), periodical indexes (including eight that could be searched), numerous books from the LCS online catalog, and statistical sources. The student even located the corresponding libraries, hours, and floorplans to guide her to the print materials selected and had printed any screen she needed, including maps, for future reference.

The UVC student found something else of equal importance: no instruction from librarians was needed to identify these materials or learn how to use The Gateway. No worksheets, pamphlets, or user manuals have been created for The Gateway. "If ever students

cannot find information located on The Gateway because they could not understand how to use the system," said Virginia Tiefel, "we will create new screens and pathways to help them. We will not need to provide workshops or paper materials to instruct users. The Gateway must be able to stand alone."

Three other UVC classes have since taken part in the testing of The Gateway for their library assignment with equal success. With six unattended workstations available, they no longer need to make appointments or need to have direct supervision. They have become independent users of information.

ONGOING DEVELOPMENT

The Gateway to Information project has established an important position for itself in The University Libraries at The Ohio State University. Over a thousand students, faculty, and staff have evaluated it in the early stages and now continue to use it for research on a regular basis. UVC classes have tested it and been so

— FRED ROECKER AND THOMAS MINNICK —

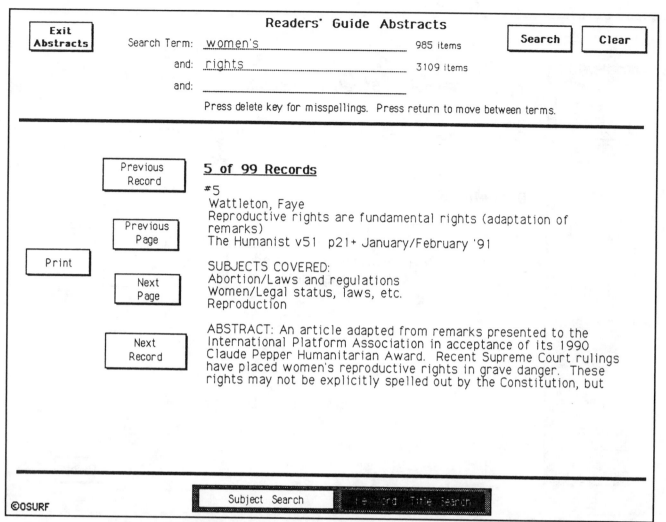

Figure 4: Search Screen from *Readers' Guide Abstracts* "Women's Rights"

successful that a new User Education sub-committee was recently formed with the charge "to plan and implement the use of The Gateway into the UVC program."

OSU librarians are also contributing to the development of the project. Four special information sections have been created to highlight materials more specific than the general reference sources currently available on The Gateway. Advanced students in the fields of communications, women's studies, Latin American studies, and business can be led to specialized handbooks, journals, bibliographies, and others in these fields. Thus a student in communications can now narrow that broad field down to interpersonal communications and be guided to the *Small Group Behavior* journal or *Language and Language Behavior Abstracts* index. Librarians now see The Gateway as a way of providing electronic pathfinders to assist patrons in finding relevant materials independently.

A notebook function is now being tested to allow users to save the results of searches or any Gateway screens to a file for viewing, downloading, or printing.

Simplified electronic mail access, direct access to the other CD-ROM databases on the SONNET network (which do not have Gateway front-ends yet), and links to remote catalogs from other campuses are all under consideration for development.

Because The Gateway operates on a microcomputer, which could be used for word processing, the English department at OSU has expressed an interest in having Gateway workstations installed in their writing labs. This would allow students to research a paper, write a draft copy, check electronic sources, read full-text articles, load bibliographic reference materials, and eventually download the results to create a final paper, all without leaving the English writing lab and its Gateway computers.

In addition, the administration and computing centers at The Ohio State University recognize The Gateway's value to the campus. They have determined that the new replacement terminals for the worn-out LCS Telex terminals must be able to support The Gateway program. Over 50 new workstations for The

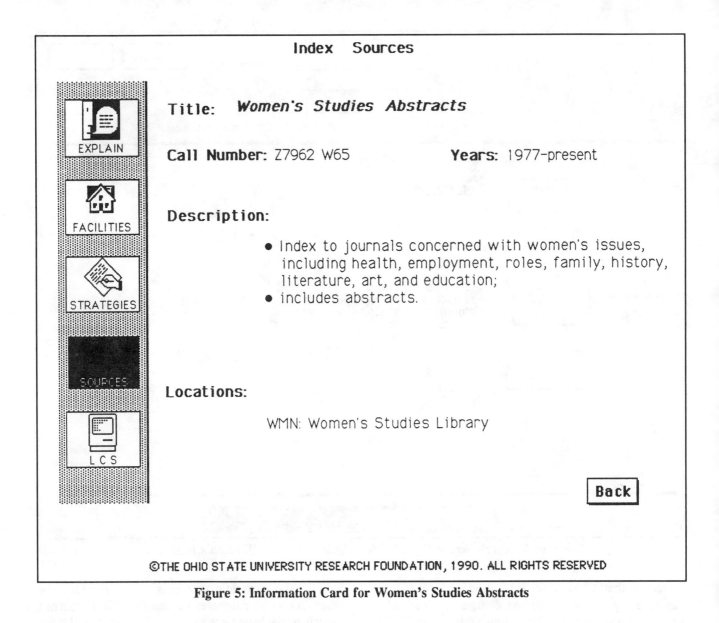

Figure 5: Information Card for Women's Studies Abstracts

Gateway will be available on campus by the end of 1992.

CONCLUSIONS

By creating The Gateway to Information, the initial steps have been taken to provide widespread quality library instruction and information-seeking skills to the general student population. Each Gateway workstation not only provides bibliographic instruction but also serves as a consistent, simple tool for accessing a variety of materials regardless of format. In addition, it encourages critical thinking from users to evaluate relevance of the materials. The workstation, which requires no workshops or support materials, has taken form and has been accepted by the novice and advanced users alike.

The Gateway to Information has demonstrated its tremendous potential to change the manner in which undergraduate students approach research and libraries. It is a valuable tool used to address the growing needs of the UVC/University Libraries program and the other challenges of an information society. By reducing barriers to information and de-mystifying the libraries and their collections, The Gateway allows even novice library users access to the most relevant materials available, regardless of format. The Gateway to Information has proven itself to be the new first step to information retrieval.

— FRED ROECKER AND THOMAS MINNICK —

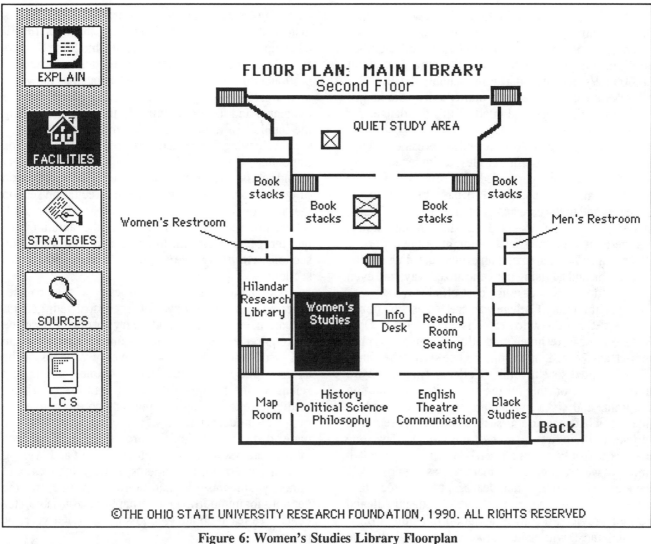

Figure 6: Women's Studies Library Floorplan

THE PORTAL

I want to start by thanking you for allowing someone who is not a librarian to spend some time up here at the podium. There are times, however, when I feel like an honorary librarian. When I started as a freshman at Ohio State in 1960, I was a raw 18-year-old who paid for late evening submarine sandwiches and the occasional beer by working as a library page, shelving books, opening the periodical room early every weekday, and, all at the minimum wage of $.85 per hour, oiling the leather bindings in the rare book collection.

I remember with special fondness Mrs. Haynesworth who was in charge of the Periodical Room. Behind her desk were the stacks where, at Ohio State in the early 1960s, you had to go to find "THE GRILL," a locked area where we kept the pornography, or what in someone's best judgment was then regarded as pornography: the elegant Japanese bride books, the works of Henry Miller, and a host of other memorable

items. It was Mrs. Haynesworth who decided that we needed to do an inventory of "The Grill," and who assigned the job of completing it to me. This, I must say, was a job that gave real definition to the term "library instruction," and a job I carried out with infinite patience and care. I have never really been sure which needed that inventory more—the Periodical Room or me. But since then I have been a constant user of libraries, and I hope a friend to them as well.

In addition to the foregoing thank you, I must also start by explaining the apparent redundancy of our title: "The Portal and The Gateway: Library Technology in the Freshman Survey Class at Ohio State." My job at Ohio State is to serve as the assistant dean for advising in University College—a unit that has analogies at a growing number of institutions but, which at Ohio State, is unique in many ways. In the late 1960s, when the prognosticators foretold an infinite period of expansion for Ohio State, someone was thoughtful enough to be concerned about our freshmen. We were approaching the enrollment level we have now—about

42,000 undergraduates in Columbus, with another 3,500 on our regional campuses, and enough graduate and professional students to bring the total Columbus enrollment above 55,000 and on all campuses to about 60,000. We are the land grant school, the Big Ten school, the comprehensive multiversity, the major research institution—and in all of this the danger for freshmen is obvious.

About 25 years before "retention" became the buzz word that it has in academic circles, enlightened faculty and administrators persuaded the rest that if some professionals were appointed to pay attention to the concerns and to the care and guidance of lower division students, those students—and ultimately the university, and perhaps even the society—might be the better for it. They also pointed to certain efficiencies in handling orientation and advising in a centralized way, and even managed to make a case for cost efficiency.

So University College was created as "the portal of entry" for all new lower division students at Ohio State—all new freshmen, and all freshman and sophomore transfer students. From the late sixties they have been admitted to University College, from 1972 we have been responsible for the universities' orientation program, and since our beginning we have taught a one-credit orientation course that students are required to take in their first quarter of enrollment. That one class is the only one we teach. And, let me admit it quickly, we are not faculty members as we do it. We have a dean, two assistant deans, a college secretary responsible for academic actions like dismissal and petitions review, a staff of about 30 full-time professionals, most with a doctorate, about 70 half-time graduate students, and clerical staff to make up a total college roster of about 130. Our collegewide enrollment is largest in the autumn, usually about 16,000 students, and we serve their needs annually for about $2.3 million, which we think is a bargain, especially since it allows the faculty to dedicate themselves that much more to teaching and research. (We are also, incidentally, the National Clearing House for Academic Advising.)

An important element in our work is the course we teach. We call it "University Survey" or University College 100. At many schools it is known simply as the Freshman Survey course. Like Evan Farber and the folks at Earlham who have been doing bibliographic instruction for about 25 years, we've been at our collective task for a quarter century. We continue to try to do it better, but we're convinced that for the foreseeable future, we will be relying heavily on this class as our principal means of introducing students to the notion and the reality of the university. That is, simply put, the objective of the course: to introduce students *to the university*, its policies, its procedures,

its resources (you see where libraries come in), its historical traditions of liberation through liberal education, and its local traditions at Ohio State University. So we deal with matters as mundane as how to use touchtone registration and as elevated as the value of literature, history, science, history of art, foreign language, and foreign culture, in forming and freeing the intellect of those who make up our community.

Achieving this objective is a big job. Consider for a moment, the dimensions of our task. Each student attends class twice each week, once in a lecture section of up to 115 students, and once in a recitation section that may be as few as 5 or as many as 45. We teach 80 lecture sections each week in the autumn, our quarter of greatest enrollment, and 180 recitation sections. *Annually*, we teach more than 150 lecture sections.

Curriculum is a major focus of this course, especially in these days of reconstructed general education requirements, and we try not only to describe the requirements of each curriculum but also to explain and justify them. So we offer twenty versions of the course—one version for business, one for arts and sciences, one for dental hygiene, one for veterinary medicine, one for engineering, and so on, across the range of student interests, including a version for undecided students. And we provide tailored versions of these classes for honors students, adult and evening students, international students, student athletes, and minority students—in addition, of course, to the versions for unmodified, or perhaps unclassifiable, students. We teach about 10,000 students each year, or try to.

The many various sections of the course differ in audience, and therefore in specific ways related to audience. But there is a core of information shared by all the sections, and the textbook represents that persisting core in detail. We talk about our own college and its services, we talk about the university regulation system and the grading system, we discuss the *Code of Student Conduct* and spend a lot of time on plagiarism, as well as student rights, such as the right to privacy and a confidential record. We talk a little about career planning (more in some sections than others) and we talk about study skills and time management (more in some sections than others). We spend a good while on the university resources available to support and occasionally distract students, and this, of course, is the point at which we bring in the OSU Libraries.

Virginia Tiefel, whose name is one to conjure with on our campus, came to Ohio State a baker's dozen years ago and started us on the right track. In fact, she built the terminal, designed the train, and developed the initial steam. The library instruction program has changed a lot in the 12 or 13 years we have been at it. Let me say a little about how.

We used to have one library assignment worth 15 percent of the grade in the class. Students read the chapter in the *Guidebook* (maybe), came to a class where they heard a guest lecturer and received an assignment, went to the library to work on our on-line system and then to find the items they had identified through a search strategy, and turned in the assignment in a week or ten days. There was some grumbling from students—when isn't there? But our libraries developed the videotape, "Library Superstars," which I hope some of you know, and they polished the presentations and the assignment. The librarians, with a team of student workers, were responsible for grading that assignment. We were really pleased with the program: students found their ways to the library in hugely increased numbers, and they learned how to locate materials within the Library of Congress classification system and without a card catalog.

And as the course improved, and the library instruction program improved, we decided to set higher goals. Within the last three years the library component has greatly expanded. We still spend only one class period out of twenty on the libraries, but I think we accomplish twice as much and do it more effectively. Students still read the *Guidebook* chapter (we hope), and we still pass out the first assignment. We have added a little more information to that assignment, since students now do it without a librarian's presentation. Students still get a week or so to complete it, and the librarians still oversee the grading.

This first assignment calls for students to read and analyze an editorial on a news topic. We used to select random topics for that editorial, and students had a range of 15 or 20 to select from. We still provide about that many, but now the topics focus on a unit of our course called "Contemporary Issues." In each section of University Survey, we try to open a dialogue on at least three major issues that are, as we see it, important in the university: equality of race, equality of gender, and AIDS. A fourth topic that we address less formally is substance abuse. (Our intention, by the way, is not to be "politically correct." Basically, we tie these in to the University's hope and expectation that in our community, all inquiry will proceed without threats, without denigration, with respect for individuals and their points of view, with a rational basis for judgment. My own belief in that way of proceeding derives from the European intellectual tradition, and I am a white male. But I don't think these are narrowly Eurocentric or racist or chauvinist ground rules.) In short, we have tied the first assignment directly to the content of part of the course, which has made it less of a merely academic exercise. We have also found that students

complete this exercise about as well without the librarians' lecture as they used to do with it. Many students had said they found the earlier lecture was too fundamental, and our experience suggests that they may have been right (see appendix 3).

Now students hear directly from a librarian after they have gotten back the first assignment, which is 10 percent of their grade, and before they get their second assignment, which is an additional 15 percent of the grade. That is, their library work counts as 25 percent of the grade in this course. The librarian's lecture emphasizes the materials learned in the first assignment, talks some about library services in general, and then introduces the second assignment, which is to complete a brief annotated bibliography, in MLA form, on a topic related to their first assignment, and so both assignments tie to the subject matter content of the class. This pleases our instructors because it integrates the course and assignments while providing some genuine exercise in library skills. It also puts the librarians in a position of expertise on issues where students really need them, and students really do need them for advice and help on the annotated bibliographies. Some students, by the way, still grumble, but I can say with assurance that all students who get a "C" or better in our course have made a serious stab at compiling an annotated bibliography by the eighth week of their first quarter at Ohio State (see appendix 2).

Two added notes: First, the librarians do not do the grading for the second assignment. Instead, they train a cadre of honors undergraduates who work well and come cheap. We pay them, and our instructors are grateful for the help. We also assure more uniform standards, which is always a matter of concern when dealing with 150 sections a year.

Second, and this one really pleased the library staff: We used to grade the course satisfactory/unsatisfactory. We put a lot of thought into making it a meatier experience and 18 months ago asked our Faculty Council on Academic Affairs for permission to grade on the traditional "A" to "E" scale. I was part of the group that presented the request, first to a subcommittee and then to the Council itself, and I was able to report to Virginia Tiefel and her colleagues that the element of the class that most clearly persuaded the faculty members of the council that we should be allowed to use grades from "A" to "E" was the fact that 25 percent of the class grade was determined by library assignments measuring library skills.

As you may well imagine, in implementing this program since 1978, we have faced a lot of challenges. It is a tremendous challenge just to manage the class. Guest speakers for 150 sections have to be identified and told where to be at what time. Students' papers need to be graded in a timely way so that this phased pattern can work. We cannot deliver 8,000 students to the Undergraduate Library in a two-week period, and so we need to stagger (and that's sometimes how it feels) the assignments and lectures. In fact, we're used to that, and we balance not just the librarian's lectures but five guest lectures in each section.

A second challenge is to manage all this and still stay friends. Virginia Tiefel and I have lunch each quarter, and I meet with the volunteer librarians (did I mention these were volunteers?) for tea and shop talk every December, when the worst is over. Members of my staff get turf conscious from time to time—they don't willingly let me come in as a guest lecturer very easily. And librarians have on rare occasions shown a little turf consciousness themselves. Academic collaboration can be harder than marriage, largely because once two units are linked in so intimate a project, there are no ground rules for taking separate vacations. We are bedfellows by choice, and for a greater good, but there have been mornings . . . .

A third challenge, alluded to already at this conference, had been to know, and then help librarians and instructors understand, just what the general level of library—or information retrieval—skills of our students really is. Remember, also, that generally university faculty members and grad students who teach had to develop decent library skills at some point before they entered the classroom. They may not remember how much they didn't use to know. We struggle with the question of what is reasonable for us to expect them to accomplish in the time available. And I might note that it is harder to come to judgment on this when you're dealing with 90 instructors and 35 guest lecturers.

A fourth challenge is to assure quality delivery of the course in its totality and of the library unit in particular. Someone noted yesterday that faculty have not usually taken courses in how to teach, and that we have found to be true. Nor have many librarians. I think that Anne Lipow was absolutely on target when she said yesterday that library schools need to include instruction on teaching (and, I would add, teaching experience) to the curriculum of prospective bibliographic instructional staff. Moreover, it is harder to be an effective guest lecturer than it is to be an effective teacher for the entire quarter. The classroom teacher can bomb several days each term and still come out ahead. Moreover, students know by instinct that what they hear from the person who assigns the grade is more important than what they hear from anyone else.

A fifth challenge is for our library staff to deliver, now that we have the program started. We do stagger the lectures and the timing of assignments, but we are nonetheless sending wave after wave of students, pen and assignments in hand, to the library, where I am told the librarians occasionally have other things to do as well. This issue is complicated by a persistent fact of student behavior: manage them however you try, students frequently wait until the last minute to do their assignments.

The Gateway promises to help with some of these challenges, and is remarkable in its own right. But it will add a challenge or two, which I will end with.

The ways we seek information often control the information that we find, as well you know. Similarly, the ways we arrange and label and deliver information all affect the information that we get. When we do this arranging and sifting with linear electronic devices and systems, sometimes we solidify that information and may misrepresent it. It starts out rounded and ends up hard edged—all denotation, no connotation. Our delivery can yield least-common-denominator information. The "objective world of information" (as someone recently called it) is not entirely objective, and not entirely susceptible to arranging and sorting. Sometimes a little bit of chaos is really not so bad, since, it reminds us of the lurking nature of things, and since it is often the generative source of new ideas. This is not to argue against HyperCards or microdots, but it is to suggest that when we teach students to seek information, we sometimes need to remind them to wander.

Finally, it is a challenge to remember what all of this is for. I studied "Bibliography and Methods of Research" under Richard Altick, who insisted that in literary studies, bibliographic inquiry—indeed, historical inquiry—needs always to keep in mind that its purpose is to illuminate the work of literature that generated it. Yes, it is a worthy goal to provide information as an end in itself. And yes, information and library skills are means to a further end—education, indeed lifelong learning. But William Blake would add, if he came to a LOEX conference: "Would to God that all the Lord's people were prophets!" If he did come to a LOEX conference and I had the good luck to hear him say that, I would think he meant that information is a means to wisdom, and that it doesn't hurt for faculty members and librarians to keep that in mind.

— FRED ROECKER AND THOMAS MINNICK —

Appendix 1

List of CD-ROM databases found on The Gateway to Information (June 1991)

Applied Science and Technology Index

Biography Index

Book Review Digest

Business Periodicals Index

Electronic Encyclopedia

Essay and General Literature Index

Humanities Index

Microsoft Bookshelf Dictionary

Newspaper Abstracts OnDisc

Readers' Guide Abstracts

Social Sciences Index

> The Ohio State University
> # LIBRARIES

Undergraduate Library
205 Sullivant Hall   1813 N. High Street
614-292-2075

Name_____

Instructor_____

UVC Annotated Bibliography Assignment

An annotated bibliography is a list of sources -- each summarized -- which could be used as the basis of a research paper.

For this assignment, the following requirements should be met:

1. **Use one of the following general topics:** AIDS, Race Discrimination, Sex Discrimination, Substance Abuse, Women's Issues.

   Narrow the focus of your topic. For example, you might select "Substance Abuse" and choose to focus on "Alcoholism." An encyclopedia article will help narrow your topic.

2. **Find three different types of sources on your topic.** You have five types of sources from which to choose: an encyclopedia, a popular magazine, a newspaper, a scholarly journal, or a book.

3. **Write annotations (brief summaries) for all three items.** Use complete sentences. Keep notes on a separate paper so your assignment will be neat and legible.

4. **Use MLA (Modern Language Association) bibliographic format** (as shown in the sample references). Additional examples of this style are available in the library.

5. **Turn your assignment in to your adviser.**

Using The Gateway to Information

For this assignment you <u>must</u> use the new library resource computer, "The Gateway to Information." These computers are located in the Main Library and Undergraduate Library.

The Gateway helps you to:
- choose and narrow your topic;
- read full-text encyclopedia articles;
- identify and search magazine, newspaper, and journal indexes for articles;
- search LCS quickly and easily;
- identify other relevant materials, such as statistical sources;
- locate campus maps and library floor plans

Identify and find the locations for all your materials. When you have identified and copied the relevant information on each item you need, leave The Gateway workstation and locate the full-text versions of the items in the library to complete your assignment.

Fill out an evaluation form located by The Gateway terminal to give your comments on this computer project. Deposit the form in the basket near the workstation.

(Begin Assignment on Next Page)

1

Indicate your topic: _____

     (Note: You may want to look at an encyclopedia article first to narrow your topic.)

     Read the instructions for each question. Remember you are to complete three (3) of five (5) choices.

     Reshelve the reference books when you finish so the books are available for the next student. The last two pages list the reference books you may use and their shelving location in the Undergraduate Library.

Sample reference and annotation: **Journal article**

Kenney, Alan. "Teen Pregnancy: an Issue for the Schools." Phi Delta Kappan 68 (1987): 728-736.

          Although teenage pregnancy has decreased, attention is focused on it today because more pregnant teens remain in school. Discrimination based on pregnancy or parenthood would deprive schools of federal funds. School counseling, health clinics, and child care services are being provided in some schools in addition to courses in parenting, child development, and sex education.

_____

1. Find an encyclopedia article. Use an encyclopedia from the attached list; many of these encyclopedias are described in your University Survey Guidebook. pp. 35-36.

Sample reference:
Dratman, D. Peter. "Acquired immune deficiency syndrome." World Book Encyclopedia. 1988 ed.

Write your reference and annotation here:

2

2. Find a popular magazine article.
     a. Use a magazine index to find an article on your topic. See the attached list; each index is described in your <u>University Survey Guidebook,</u> p. 38.
     b. After consulting an index, you may search LCS to locate the periodical. Remember to search the **title of the magazine,** not the title of the article.

Sample reference:
Smith, John. "Portents for Future Learning." <u>Time</u> 21 Sept. 1981: 65.
     (Note: 21 is the date in September, not the volume; 65 is the page number; no volume number is listed.)

Write your reference and annotation here:

3. Find a scholarly journal article.
     a Use a scholarly journal index to find an article on your topic. See the attached list; each index is described in your <u>University Survey Handbook,</u> p. 38-39.
     b. After consulting an index, you may search LCS to locate the periodical.

     Remember to search the title of the magazine, not the title of the article.

Sample reference:
Brown, B.S. and Beschner, G. M. "AIDS and HIV infection - implications for drug abuse treatment." <u>Journal of Drug Issues</u> 19 (1989): 141-62.

Write your reference and annotation here:

3

     — FRED ROECKER AND THOMAS MINNICK —

4. **Find a statistical source.** Use a statistical source from the attached list; some of these are described in your University Survey Guidebook. p. 42.

Sample reference:
"Selected characteristics of readers--percent distribution: 1983." Statistical Abstract of the United States: 1988. Washington, D.C.: U. S. Government Printing Office, 1987. 215.

        (Note: 215 is the page number.)

Write your reference and annotation here:

5. **Find the LCS catalog record for a book on your subject.** You DO NOT have to get the book to complete this question.

        Look at the Library of Congress Subject Headings to identify the correct subject heading used in LCS. Do a subject search on LCS. (Use the yellow LCS brochure to review the steps of a subject search.)

        Select any book on your topic and **look at the catalog record for a description of the book.** This will indicate any special features included in the book. Near the bottom of the catalog record are listed the subject headings, shown as SUB, assigned to this book. This is a good method of identifying other subject headings to search in LCS.

Sample reference:
Brown, Thomas. JFK, History of an Image. Bloomington: Indiana University Press, 1988.

        (Note: You may want to consult the MLA stylesheet handout for the correct bibliographic form if you book differs substantially for the sample reference. Copies of the stylesheet handout are available at the Reference Desk.)

Write your reference here:

Instead of writing an annotation, look at the catalog record and answer the following questions.

a. How many pages does this book have? _____   b. Does it have an index? (Yes/No) _____

c. Does it have a bibliography? (Yes/No)   _____

d. What subject headings are assigned to the book? _____

e. What other special features, if any, does this book have (e.g. illustrations, maps, etc.)? If none are listed, write "not applicable." _____

4

Reference Books for Use with UVC
Annotated Bibliography Assignment

Encyclopedias
General Encyclopedias

Title	Call Number	Location in Undergrad
Academic American Encyclopedia	AE5A231987	Encyclopedia Case
Collier's Encyclopedia	AE5C61986	Encyclopedia Case
Encyclopedia Americana	AE5E2971985	Encyclopedia Case
Grolier's Electronic Encyclopedia	(CD-ROM)	Gateway Workstation
The New Encyclopedia Americana	AE5E351986	Encyclopedia Case
World Book Encyclopedia	AE5W921988	Encyclopedia Case

Specialized Encyclopedias

Title	Call Numbers	Location in Undergrad
Congressional Quarterly Almanac	JK1C745	Index Table 3
Encycl. of American Economic History	HC103E52	Reference Collection
Encyclopedia of Bioethics	QH332E52	Reference Collection
Encyclopedia of Crime and Justice	HV6017E521983	Reference Collection
Encyclopedia of Education	LB15E47	Reference Collection
Encyclopedia of Philosophy	B51E49	Reference Collection
Encyclopedia of Religion	BL31E461987	Reference Collection
Encyclopedia of Social Work	HV35S67	Reference Collection
Encyclopedia of World Art	N31E41	Reference Collection
McGraw-Hill Encyl. of Science and Tech.	Q121M31987	Reference Collection
World Encycl. of Political Syst. & Parties	JF2011W671987	Reference Collection

Other appropriate encyclopedias, handbooks or source books:

AIDS

AIDS and the Law	KF3803A54A351987	Reference Collection
AIDS (Opposing Viewpoints)	RC607A26A34421988	Reference Collection
The Almanac of Science and Technology	Q158.5A471990	Reference Collection
Am. Medical Assoc. Encyl. of Medicine	RC81A2A521989	Reference Collection

Race Discrimination

Dictionary of Race and Ethnic Relations	DA125A1C351988	Reference Collection
Encyclopedia of Black America	E185E551984	Reference Collection
Intl. Handbook of Human Rights	JC571I5871987	Reference Collection
The Negro Almanac	E185N3681989	Reference Collection
The State of Black America	E185.5N34	Circulation Desk

Sex Discrimin. & Women's Issues

The American Woman 1988-89	HQ1420A61988	Reference Collection
The American Woman 1987-88	HQ1420A61987	Reference Collection
Sex Discrimination and the Law	KF3467S4	Reference Collection
Women's Action Almanac	HQ1115W64	Reference Collection
Women's Studies Encyclopedia	HQ1115W6451989	Reference Collection

Substance Abuse

Disease Prevention/Health Promotion	RA427.2D571988	Reference Collection
Encyclopedia of Alcoholism	HV5017E51982	Reference Collection
Encyclopedia of Drug Abuse	HV5804O241984	Reference Collection

5

Periodical Indexes

Magazines	Location In Undergrad
Infotrac Academic Index (CD-ROM computer)	Near LCS terminals
Reader's Guide to Periodical Literature	Index Table 2 (also G'way)
	Index Table 1
Scholarly Journals	Index Table 1
Applied Science and Technology Index	Index Table 1 (also G'way)
Art Index	Index Table 1
Business Periodicals Index	Index Table 1 (also G'way)
Education Index	Index Table 1
General Science Index	Index Table 1
Humanities Index	Index Table 1 (also G'way)
Public Affairs Information Service Bulletin	Index Table 1
Social Sciences Index	Index Table 1 (also G'way)

Statistical Sources

Title	Call Numbers	Location in Undergrad
Statesman's Yearbook	AY754S8	Reference Collection
Statistical Abstract of the U.S.	HA202	Ref. Coll. and Circ. Desk
World Almanac Book of Facts	AY67N5W9	Reference Collection

(Note: You may also use volumes of Statistical Abstract or the World Almanac from the last 5 years. They are shelved by call number in the circulating collection.)

Other appropriate statistical sources:

AIDS

Disease Prevention/Health Promotion	RA427.2D571988	Reference Collection
Health. United States	RA407.3N28	Reference Collection
A Matter of Fact	AG6M27	Reference Collection
State of Black America	E185.5N34	Circulation Desk

Race Discrimination

Country Reports on Human Rights Prac.	JC571C6945	Reference Collection
Face of the Nation	HV35S671987Suppl	Reference Collection
A Matter of Fact	AG6M27	Reference Collection
State of Black America	E185.5N34	Circulation Desk

Sex Discrimin. & Women's Issues

The American Woman 1988-1989	HQ1420A61988	Reference Collection
The American Woman 1987-1988	HQ1420A61987	Reference Collection
Face of the Nation	HV35S671987Suppl	Reference Collection
A Matter of Fact	AG6M27	Reference Collection

Substance Abuse

Disease Prevention/Health Promotion	RA427.2D571988	Reference Collection
Illicit Drug Use, Smoking and Drinking...	HV4999Y68J641988	Reference Collection
A Matter of Fact	AG6M27	Reference Collection
Sourcebook of Criminal Justice	HV6787S73	Reference Collection

UEd/ Spring 1991

6

The Ohio State University
LIBRARIES
Undergraduate Library
205 Sullivant Hall   1813 N. High Street   614-292-2075

Name: _____
Class: _____
Instructor: _____

UVC LIBRARY ASSIGNMENT

The purpose of this assignment is to help you understand the research process that you will use when gathering information for papers and projects. A logical approach to finding and using information involves devising a plan, or search strategy, and then selecting, as you proceed, information relevant to your task.

ASSIGNMENT IN A NUTSHELL

1. **Read and analyze an editorial** on a news topic. Pick up the editorial at the Undergraduate Library.

2. **Practice a basic search strategy** for finding information on this topic. You will:

   - **Identify an encyclopedia** or reference handbook that might provide general background information on your topic. **Consult your *UVC Guidebook* for the encyclopedia list.**

   - **Select and use a periodical index** to find an article in a magazine or journal that relates to your topic.

   - **Identify the valid subject term to use when searching LCS,** the Libraries' computerized catalog.

   - **Use LCS to find a book** that might provide information on your topic.

   - **Use LCS to find the location of the magazine identified earlier.**

3. **Evaluate this source** in terms of whether it supports or refutes the position taken in the editorial. This may involve visiting another OSU library to read and analyze the magazine article.

Read the directions carefully. Write your answers to questions 1-10 on this form.

NOTE: Each person's search strategy will be unique. As a result, each person's completed assignment should also be unique. **Be sure to work on the assignment by yourself.**

• • • • • • • • • • • •   **Assignment questions begin on the next page.**   • • • • • • • • • • • • • •

-1-

EDITORIAL:

Bring this assignment to the Undergraduate Library and select an editorial that interests you from the display rack in the Library. **Only editorials in the Undergraduate Library display may be used.**

TOPIC ANALYSIS: DEFINING YOUR RESEARCH QUESTION

The important first step in any research project is defining the information need. Examine the scope of your topic and decide what questions must be answered. Begin this assignment by reading and analyzing your editorial. Answer the following in one or two sentences.

QUESTION 1:   What is the topic of this editorial?

                          What position does the editorial writer take on this issue?

CHOOSING RELEVANT INFORMATION SOURCES:

This section of the assignment covers different types of information sources you may use when researching a topic.

A. BACKGROUND INFORMATION: REFERENCE HANDBOOKS AND ENCYCLOPEDIAS

A general overview of a topic or issue can help you to understand it more fully before searching for more specific information. An overview can also help to narrow or focus a broad topic.

Look at the list of <u>specialized</u> encyclopedias in your *UVC Guidebook* (pp. 35-36). Extra copies are at the Circulation Desk. Read the information presented there and **choose one source** that might provide general backgound information on your topic. Although several sources may seem useful, indicate only one below. **You do not need to examine this reference work.**

QUESTION 2:   Write the title of a specialized encyclopedia from the list.

B. FINDING INFORMATION IN PERIODICALS

To locate magazine articles on a topic, especially one that is current, you must use subject indexes to magazines and journals. These subject indexes are called periodical indexes.

Choose a periodical index that is likely to provide information on your topic from the list that follows.

-2-

ALL ARE LOCATED IN THE UVC MATERIALS AREA, NEXT TO THE EDITORIAL DISPLAY
RACK. ANSWER ALL QUESTIONS, USING ONLY THE VOLUMES LISTED.

QUESTION 3:   Circle the letter next to the title of the index you chose. Also circle the volume number
                used.

    a. *Readers' Guide to Periodical Literature* (covers news, opinion, popular
        magazines; many are located in the Undergraduate Library); vols. 46, 47, 48.

    b. *General Science Index*   (covers life and physical sciences); vols. 9, 10, 11.

    c. *Social Science Index* (for psychology, sociology, politics); vols. 12, 13, 14.

    d. *Education Index* (covers educational topics); vols. 37, 38.

    e. *Business Periodicals Index* (for business related topics); vols. 28, 29.

QUESTION 4:   Under what subject heading (search term) did you find relevant material listed?
(Refer to topic mentioned on editorial. Avoid however, headings that contain specific names or places
found in the editorial.)

Scan the titles of articles on your topic. Judging by the titles of these articles, choose a brief article which
looks as if it will either support or refute the position of the editorial. Answer all parts of the question below.

QUESTION 5:   a. Title of article:

                b. Author (if given):

                c. Complete title of magazine or journal in which this article appears . Remember to
                    check the list of journal title abbreviations in the front of the index volume.

                    _____

                d. Volume: e. Pages: f. Date:

C. SEARCHING LCS FOR BOOKS ON A TOPIC: SUBJECT SEARCH

To find books which provide longer, more detailed analyses of your general topic, use the Libraries'
computerized catalog, LCS. First, **identify the subject terms or language used by this system for
your topic.**

LCS uses subject terms in the *Library of Congress Subject Headings* books. Look at these large red books
to find the correct search term for your topic. Copies are shelved in the UVC MATERIALS AREA and
NEAR COMPUTER TERMINALS.

-3-

QUESTION 6:   What word or phrase should you use to search LCS for information on your subject?

(HINT: look for the word or phrase which is the same as your editorial topic. Be specific. If a term is printed in bold type, it is a valid search term).

D. LCS SUBJECT SEARCH:

Follow all of the directions below to complete an LCS subject search on your topic. (If the terminal makes a clicking noise when you touch the keys, press RESET to unlock the keyboard.)

1. Tell LCS what kind of search to perform   TYPE: sub/

   Then type the subject term you found for QUESTION 6.   EXAMPLE: sub/acid rain

   (HINT: Omit punctuation; use only lowercase, not capital, letters.)

2. Press the ENTER key once, lightly, when you have finished typing. Then wait for the system to respond. Do not press ENTER twice. This causes the keyboard to lock.

3. Your subject term will display at the top of the list on the screen. Look at the instructions that are located at the LOWER RIGHT corner of the display.

   To open the LIST OF TITLES on a subject,   TYPE: tbl/

   Then add the LINE NUMBER to the far left of the term.   EXAMPLE: tbl/1

   Press ENTER.

4. Now look at this list of titles and choose one that relates to your topic. Again there are useful instructions at the LOWER RIGHT corner of the display.

   To open the LOCATION RECORD for the book you choose,   TYPE: dsl/

   Then add the LINE NUMBER to the far left of the title.   EXAMPLE: dsl/2

   Press ENTER.

QUESTION 7:   What is the call number of the book? (HINT: look at the top of the screen).

What is the title of the book?

What is the library location code? (HINT: look under the word LOCATION). List all location codes for your book. The yellow *LCS Brochure* contains a list explaining these codes.

-4-

E. LCS TITLE SEARCH

You have finished an LCS subject search. Now you will search LCS to locate the magazine or journal that you looked up eariler in the periodical index (QUESTION 5).

1. Tell LCS what kind of search to perform.   TYPE: tls/

   Add the title of the MAGAZINE (not the article title).

   Then add a QUALIFIER at the end to limit the search to
   magazine (serial) titles.   EXAMPLE: tls/fortune/ser

   (HINT: Spell out all title words completely. Do not abbreviate.)   Press ENTER.

2. A list of serial (magazine) titles which match some of the letters you typed will display on the screen. Sometimes this list is lenghty. Scan each page of the list until you find the magazine title that is exactly the same as the one you typed. **Be sure that the title you choose has the system code OSU preceding it.** Ignore the dates on this screen.

3. Sometimes several titles exactly match the one you typed. To find the right record, examine the first record that matches in the manner described below.

   Open the LOCATION RECORD: TYPE: dsl/

   Add the LINE NUMBER to the far left of the title.
   Then add a QUALIFIER indicating the volume you need.
   (See QUESTION 5 for volume number.)   EXAMPLE: dsl/2,v=44

   Press ENTER.

4. Look at the information displayed on the new screen. **Does the volume and year shown match the information you found in the periodical index (QUESTION 5)?** If so, you have located the correct LCS record for your magazine title and can answer QUESTION 8 below.

   (HINT: Be sure to look at all pages of the LCS record you have displayed. Use the white PD= key on the right side of the keyboard to turn pages.)

5. **If volume and date information on the screen does not match what you listed in QUESTION 5,** you should examine other possible matching titles in the same manner. Press the white PG1 key on the right side of the keyboard to return to the list of titles. Choose another line number and try again.

See the PROBLEM SOLVING GUIDE on the last page of this assignment if you cannot find the correct LCS record. Ask library staff for help as needed. To complete this assignment, you must go to the library that owns your magazine to read and evaluate the article.

QUESTION 8:   What is the call number of the magazine?   (HINT: look at the top of the screen).

                 What are the library location codes for the volume you need? List all codes.
                 Be sure to look at all pages of the display.

-5-

EVALUATING INFORMATION SOURCES:

To read the article you just searched for on LCS, to to the library location that owns the volume of the magazine. See the PROBLEM SOLVING GUIDE below if you were not able to determine where the magazine is located. If your magazine is at UND (Undergraduate Library), go to the Periodicals Area (near the editorial display rack). This area is arranged alphabetically by title of the magazine.

Read the article (skim if lengthy), and evaluate its relevance to the editorial topic.

QUESTION 9:   Circle the letter next to the appropriate answer below after reading the article.

      a. Article supports the position of the editorial.
      b. Article refutes the position of the editorial.
      c. Article is not relevant to the editorial (it neither refutes nor supports).

QUESTION 10:   Summarize below, in two or three sentences, the content of this article.

You have finished this assignment. Please return it to your UVC Instructor.

PROBLEM SOLVING GUIDE

The title of the magazine you need is not listed on LCS:

If the Libraries does not own the magazine you need, you must go back to the periodical index and select a new article in a different magazine. Check with Library staff to be sure the magazine is not owned by OSU Libraries before proceeding.

The magazine volume you need is not listed on LCS:

LCS lists only bound (hard cover) volumes of magazines. If your volume is recent, it may not have been bound yet. For those volumes that are not recent, the library may not have received those issues. Please check with library staff before proceeding.

The magazine volume you need is listed as "missing" or "checked out":

Are there other copies of this volume listed on LCS when you search with the volume qualifier? If not, you must select another article in a different magazine. Go back to the periodical index, change your answers to Question 5 and search LCS for the new magazine.

The article you need is torn out of or missing from the magazine volume:

The library may have a duplicate copy of this issue on microfiche or microfilm. Check with library staff to determine if other copies are available. If not, you must go back to the periodical index to select another article in a different magazine.

The Ohio State University
LIBRARIES

The Gateway to Information
History and Description

History of the Project The Gateway to Information was conceived in 1986 by the Library User Education Office at The Ohio State University to meet the basic library research needs of undergraduate students.

Goals/Target Audience The primary purpose of the project is to assist Freshmen, all other underclassmen, and those patrons unfamiliar with the OSU libraries to choose and narrow their research topics and identify and locate relevant indexes, encyclopedias, books, and other special materials. Evaluation of materials and critical thinking are major components of The Gateway. A search strategy map is used as the menu screen to show the overall approach to extensive research.

Funding The project received four grants, three from the U.S. Department of Education (2 Title II-D grants and one from the Fund for the Improvement for Post-Secondary Education [FIPSE]), and one additional grant from the William Randolph Hearst Foundation. The Ohio State University Libraries have also been very supportive, as have University Systems and the Center for Teaching Excellence.

Testing The Gateway has been tested on select target groups since October 1989. In January 1990, two public workstations were placed in the Main Library LCS area and opened daily for brief, supervised periods. By August 1, 1990, the two workstations were available unsupervised whenever the library was open. Two more workstations were added in the Main Library in September and two in the Undergraduate Library in January 1991.

Creation of Screens The Gateway to Information is the result of many committees and consultants under the overall leadership of Virginia Tiefel, Director User Education. The primary information was gathered by both public and technical service librarians at OSU, then combined into the existing form by Nancy O'Hanlon, Head of Reference in the Undergraduate Library. Technology is coordinated by Susan Logan from the Library Automation Office and is under the direction of John Salter, Senior Programmer for The Gateway project. Evaluations and demonstrations are conducted by Fred Roecker in the User Education Office, and who also serves as public liaison for questions and problems. Four consultants from outside OSU and three consultants on campus have given expert advice throughout the entire project.

Immediate Plans The primary goal, as outlined in the original grant proposals, is to have 8 workstations available in the Undergraduate and Main libraries. This will be accomplished in 1991. We will continue to add CD-ROM databases, including *Newspaper Abstracts OnDisc, Microsoft Bookshelf*, and *LCSH*.

Future Plans Once the primary goals have been accomplished, development of The Gateway narrative will be undertaken to highlight special materials in popular subject areas (i.e. Communication, Business, English, Latin American Studies, etc.). The possibility of placing the Gateway in other locations (i.e., other OSU libraries, dorms, etc.) will be also explored. Expansion to make The Gateway more usable for graduate students will also be undertaken.

Remote Searching At this time, due to costs of site licensing for databases and local area networking technology requirements, we are not actively pursuing dial-up access from homes, offices, etc. We hope this service will be available eventually, but at this time it is not our highest priority.

Appendix 4 (continued)

What Can You Find in The Gateway?

To Get Started Press the "F1" key to return to the "Search Strategy Map" screen from any Gateway screen. For those not familiar with the Macintosh mouse, press the "M" key on the keyboard from this first screen for help. Move the on screen cursor / finger into any button or box by sliding the computer mouse along the desktop. Click the mouse button (the rectangle on top of the mouse) once on any arrow box or button to select an action.

General Search Strategy For the undergraduate, library novice, or basic researcher, the Search Strategy Map outlines the relevant materials available at OSUL. Clicking on "Timesaving Research Strategies" will lead a user through a comprehensive search to identify and locate resource materials.

Encyclopedias The *Electronic Encyclopedia* is the full-text version of the *Academic American Encyclopedia*. Other special and general encyclopedias may be located by selecting a broad topic from the list found in "Encyclopedias" and letting The Gateway suggest relevant encyclopedias for that topic. General encyclopedias are also available, all with a description, call number, and location at OSUL.

Periodical Indexes Search Wilson indexes and *Newspaper Abstracts OnDisc* by clicking on the Periodical Articles button and then the "Electronic Indexes" arrow. This will bring up the list of CD-ROM discs searchable from the Gateway terminal. Clicking on any choice will allow a user to connect to that database and search it for citations and abstracts (as in the case of *Readers' Guide Abstracts* or *Newspaper Abstracts*). One can also locate relevant indexes by selecting a broad subject from the list and then indicating whether you want a newspaper / magazine index, journal index, or citation / abstract index. The Gateway will bring up relevant indexes, a descriptions of contents, their call numbers and locations.

Books Search LCS via The Gateway. No need to type in the three-letter search codes of "TLS,""ATS," "DSL," etc. Just select your method of searching LCS, wait for the cursor to appear on the blank line and type in your search. The Gateway will guide you through the screens, allowing you to click on the selected sources for titles, locations, catalog records, etc. One may even search by "Call Number" and "Series," and have periodical searches automatically qualified by volume and year.

Special Sources Sources for biographies, reviews, and statistics are all identifiable and searchable via the "Search Strategy Map" screen. *Biography Index* is available on CD-ROM for searching from the "Periodicals" and "Biographies" sections.

Library Info Hours, floorplans, campus maps and collection profiles for OSU libraries are available via the "Library Info" button on the "Search Strategy Map" screen.

Circulation Info Information on OSUL book fines, sanctioning procedures, how to save a book, etc. are available in the "Library Info" section on the "Search Strategy Map" screen.

Miscellaneous Info A glossary of library terms used in The Gateway, how to read a citation, how to use a computer mouse, etc. are found in the "Help" and "Explain" sections.

For more information, contact:
Fred Roecker, User Education Librarian
326 Main Library, The Ohio State University
Columbus, OH 43210-1286
(614) 292-6151

User Ed: 4/26/91

Gateway to Information - Evaluation 4
July 16, 1990 - March 31, 1991

(Public evaluation forms recorded: 715)

| Fresh | 48 (7%) | Junior | 101 (14%) | Grad | 197 (28%) | Lib. Fac/Staff | 19 (3%) | NonLib Staff | 14 (2%) |
| Soph | 66 (9%) | Senior | 107 (15%) | Other | 53 (7%) | NonLib Fac. | 30 (4%) | No Answer | 66 (9%) |

	General Info	LCS Search	Library Info	Search Strategy	Evaluate Gateway	Other/ Blank
Purpose for searching Gateway?	370 (52%)	321 (45%)	30 (4%)	34 (5%)	189 (26%)	48 (7%)

	Complete Success	Mostly Successful	Neither	Not at all Successful	No Opin or Blank
Rate your success?	207 (29%)	321 (45%)	57 (8%)	77 (11%)	61 (9%)

	Strategies	Sources	LCS	Facilities	Explain
Where did you search?	245 (34%)	387 (54%)	540 (76%)	180 (25%)	60 (8%)

	Very Easy	Mostly Easy	Neither	Not at all Easy	No Opin or Blank
Ease of Search Strategy Map?	279 (39%)	195 (27%)	22 (3%)	14 (2%)	209 (29%)

	Very Clear	Mostly Clear	Neither	Not at all Clear	No Opin or Blank
Clarity of screens?	388 (54%)	197 (28%)	13 (2%)	14 (2%))	102 (14%)

	Very Easy	Mostly Easy	Neither	Not at all Easy	No Opin or Blank
Ease of use of Gateway?	333 (47%)	237 (33%)	22 (3%))	27 (4%)	94 (13%)

	Highly Experienced	Some Experience	No Experience	No Opin or Blank
Your experience with computers?				
IBM	218 (30%)	271 (38%)	31 (4%)	190 (27%)
Macintosh	198 (28%)	271 (38%)	56 (8%)	190 (27%)
Other	115 (16%)	86 (12%)	29 (4%)	475 (66%)
Computer Mouse	204 (29%)	190 (27%)	39 (5%)	268 (37%)

The Gateway to Information
Selected Quotes and Comments - 1990

Sample of topics searched on the Gateway to Information

Reflexology
Greek theater
Women in politics
Waste water pollution
Medieval period dress and customs
Information on Thomas Edison
I asked for specific periodicals on linguistics
Gum chewing/Bubble gum
Ohio's interest in trade with foreign countries

Meteorological instruments
Reunification of Germany
Booking binding
I was looking for a good novel to read.
I need general data on 12 authors.
Social Welfare
Buried Child by Sam Shepard
Suicide as portrayed in TV; it's effect on viewers
Lithuanian independence

Comments from students and other patrons
Easy as pie.
It is fast, easy to follow, and requires little knowledge of computers.
I found this useful because it offered suggestions.
Screens are intelligently laid out and really easy to learn to use.
This thing takes your hand leads you right down the path.
I have never used a computer. This system is very user friendly.
I had no idea how to begin and it help me begin the process.
Very helpful. I am in information heaven.
This was incredible!! What a time saver.
Gateway helped me to located the index so that I may look up specific information.
I could see exactly what I was doing and I knew my status all the time.
Everything was explained on the screens. I didn't really have to guess if it was what I really wanted.
Gateway is user friendly and informs users of its operations in an understandable manner.
Sat down to play with Gateway and found it informative and fun to use.
I found a couple of indexes I wasn't aware of.
Excellent way of learning to use the system. You don't really have to learn, you are carried through your task.
Everything you could want is at your finger tip!
These maps/floorplans are simply fantastic. I can even find the men's rest room.
Found everything I wanted initially and more information I realized I needed.
Gateway provided me with several good indexes to periodicals to help establish a solid paper topic.
I'm addicted; great visual format.
Really easy to use - please get more of these.

Comments from Library Professionals

"The 'Gateway' is an ambitious undertaking to build a networked instructional user interface for undergraduate students to learn about, and actually use, a variety of information retrieval tools, including the OSU online catalog, CD-ROM database, and other large files which reside on or off campus. I felt like I was seeing the future and it worked!
Brian Nielsen, Northwestern University

"What do I think of [the Gateway] project? At the least, that it's important; at the best, that it's of historic significance....Up to now, [the Gateway] has been a vision of futurists. This project could show us how to make it a reality....It is without a doubt the most exciting development in library instruction I've seen. Its potential---for librarians, for teachers, for students-- is enormous.
Evan Farber, Earlham Library

"The quality of the project staff, the teamwork, the work done thus far in organizing the program, and the review/testing process you have followed are all impressive."
Judy Sandler, University of Delaware

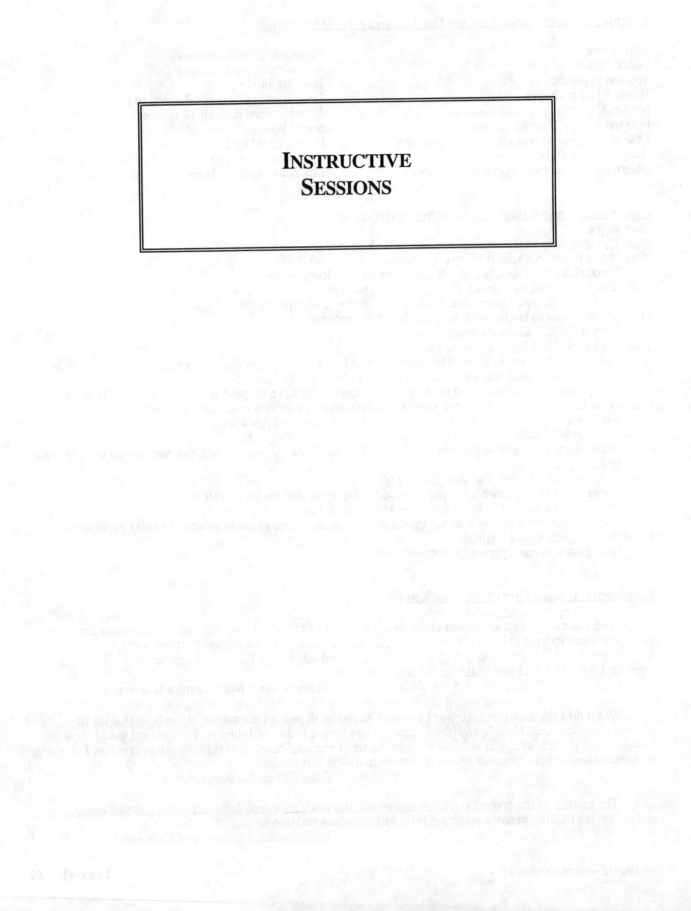

INSTRUCTIVE
SESSIONS

INFORMATION TECHNOLOGY AND CURRICULUM DESIGN:
NEW APPROACHES FOR LIBRARY AND FACULTY PARTNERSHIPS

Betsy Baker, Head of Reference
Marilee Birchfield, Instructional Services Librarian
Norm Weston, Curriculum Innovation Librarian

Although support for faculty teaching and research will continue to be the primary mission for any university library, the means for providing this support are changing. New information technologies are promising to "break down the walls" of the library. There are two critical areas impacted by the rapid proliferation of new information technology: faculty development and the undergraduate curricular experience.

Faculty members unexposed to recent developments such as integrated bibliographic systems, CD-ROM publishing, computer networking, full-text databases, and electronic text manipulation are obviously often at a loss in taking advantage of them, and thus cannot easily incorporate them into their own teaching practices. The need to give faculty opportunities to learn about new technologies in a supportive environment, and in ways that are immediately applicable in their areas of teaching and research, is increasingly being recognized as an important educational issue.

Librarians from the Reference Department at Northwestern University are garnering their experience and knowledge working with integrated technological solutions to library problems, and through a well-regarded user education program, are moving the Library into the main-stream of University curriculum development efforts. Projects are currently underway to explore the potential of specific information technologies to enrich and expand not only the teaching and research capabilities of faculty, but the undergraduate learning experience as well. To this end, the Library is actively involved as a test site for the Library of Congress' American Memory Project; in integrating LEXIS/NEXIS instruction into journalism, business, and political science courses; and in creating a Curriculum Innovation Laboratory which will provide computer software resources and telecommunication links for faculty to use and explore in a supportive environment.

Drawing upon these experiences, within a panel discussion format, Betsy Baker, Head of the Reference Department, will open discussion by outlining the underlying philosophy of such efforts as well as on the importance of library visibility and outreach efforts to the initiation and expansion of such projects. Norman Weston, the Curriculum Innovation Project Librarian, will focus on the professional and educational benefits to be gained by librarians working with faculty in shaping the content and design of courses. And, Marilee Birchfield, Instructional Services Librarian, will discuss the personal element of librarians being challenged to be part of on-going change.

Instructive session 1 (Baker, Birchfield, and Weston): part 1 - Abstract

Points of Conversation

‡ Community and Connectivity

‡ Program with a small "p"

‡ Co-Creating the curriculum

‡ User education as an institutional value

‡ Communication within a personal comfort zone

‡ Education is communication

‡ Education is democracy

‡ All learning is personal

‡ Technology for creating communities

Instructive session 1 (Baker, Birchfield, and Weston) cont.: part 2 - Points of Conversation

Connecting Libraries to Curriculum: A Reading List

Conceptions of Curriculum

Dewey, J. (1931). The way out of educational confusion. Cambridge, MA: Harvard University Press.

Gabelnick, F. et al (1990). Learning communities: Creating connections among students, faculty, and disciplines. New directions for teaching and learning. San Francisco: Jossey-Bass.

Greene, M. (1978). Landscapes of learning. New York: Teachers College Press.

Pinar, W.F. (Ed.) (1975). Curriculum theorizing: The reconceptualists. Berkeley, CA: McCutchan.

Schubert, W.H. (1986). Curriculum: perspective, paradigm, and possibility. New York: Macmillan.

Libraries and Scholarship

Baker, B. (forthcoming). "Teaching information retrieval: Making connections with our users." Library Trends.

Dain, P. (1990). "Scholarship, higher education, and libraries in the United States: Historical questions and quests". In Dain, P. & Cole, J.Y. (Eds.) Libraries and scholarly communication in the United States. Beta Phi Mu Monograph, no. 2. New York: Greenwood Press.

Weigand, W.A. (1990). "Research libraries, the ideology of reading, and scholarly communication, 1876-1900". In Dain, P. & Coles, J.Y. (Eds.) Libraries and scholarly communication in the United States. Beta Phi Mu Monograph, no. 2. New York: Greenwood Press.

Weiskel, T.C. (1988). "University libraries, integrated scholarly information systems (ISIS), and the changing character of academic research. Library Hi-Tech, 6(4), 7-27.

Building Partnerships

Baker, B. and Birchfield, M. (1990). "Bibliographic instruction: Bringing the faculty on board." In O'Brien, B.A. (Ed.) Summary of Proceedings, Forty-fourth Annual Conference of the American Theological Library Association. Evanston, IL: American Theological Library Association.

Pasterczyk, C.E. "Checklist for the new selector." College & Research Libraries News, 49(7), 434-435, July/August 1988.

Schrage, M. (1990). Shared minds: The new technologies of collaboration. New York: Random House.

The Librarian as Practical Researcher

Schon, D. (1983). The reflective practitioner: How professionals think in action. New York: Basic Books.

Schwab, J.J. (1969). "The practical: A language for curriculum." School Review, 78, 1-23.

Instructive session 1 (Baker, Birchfield, and Weston) cont.: part 3 - Bibliography

NORTHWESTERN UNIVERSITY LIBRARY
User Education Goals and Selected Recommendations

The following goals and recommendations are from the Northwestern University Library User Education Task Force Final Report, December 1989.

Members of the task force were: Betsy Baker (Chair), Kathleen Bethel, Marilee Birchfield, Leslie Bjorncrantz, Deborah Campana, Robert Lesh, Stephen Marek, Natalie Pelster, Gary Slezak, Susan Swords Steffen, Norman Weston, Mary Case (ex officio), Adele Combs (ex officio).

The report is available from LOEX. The report has also been submitted to ERIC and is currently under review for acceptance.

Goal 1: User education must be clearly articulated as an institutional value.

1. User education must be philosophically supported and endorsed by the Library administration.

2. The Library administration should promote user education to the central administration and the faculty through its involvement in the Undergraduate Dean's Council, University Senate, University Library Committee, and campus-wide committees.

3. Emphasize the educational function of the Library in the Library's mission statement.

4. Foster a sense of responsibility within each division for the provision of instruction in a way appropriate to each division.

5. Unless specifically excluded, involvement in user education should be a component of all professional position descriptions at Northwestern University Library.

Goal 2: Create a more varied instruction program than what is currently offered to meet more fully the needs of our diverse clientele.

Goal 3: Enhance and expand Northwestern University Library's current programs of outreach to faculty.

The purpose of educational and outreach services for faculty is two-fold. Faculty members need instruction in new developments in information retrieval and bibliographic research for their own projects. Furthermore, in their role as teachers, they exert a profound influence on the way the library is used and viewed by students. Experience has shown us that students will use library resources in their courses only if encouraged to do so by their instructors and will care about learning how to draw upon library resources if they can see how it can enhance their studies. Instruction to faculty, therefore, is necessary for student instruction to take place.

Scholarly research and bibliographic research do not necessarily coincide. It is widely recognized that many scholars have become quite independent of library research in their work. The "invisible college," the narrow number of highly specialized scholarly journals, and professional conferences that furnish faculty with the tools they require in their research are contributing factors to this phenomenon. In the sciences, faculty have come to rely upon laboratory and clinical or field research.

Instructive session 1 (Baker, Birchfield, and Weston) cont.: part 4 - Goals and Recommendations

In the humanities, scholars often base their research on the analysis of texts, a method of research bypassing library research. As a whole, faculty interest is highly specialized within a narrow field, and, therefore, their knowledge of the bibliographic tools used in general research and in other fields is limited. They may also remain unaware of new developments in information technology that may be of use to them and, more importantly, to their students. Through active outreach, librarians can make faculty aware of the value of library instruction for their students and of new possibilities for locating and retrieving information.

Recommended Action Plan:

1. Establish Library-wide faculty liaison responsibilities with all departments, schools, and programs.

    A faculty liaison program provides strong ties between librarians and faculty. A liaison program has been initiated on a limited basis in the Reference Department. Librarians from a number of other departments have also established relationships with schools and departments. A review of liaison assignments should be undertaken in cooperation with the Collection Management Division to assure contact with all academic programs of the University.

2. Modify the Library Impact Statement to include service and user education implications of curriculum changes.

    Through the Library Impact Statement we can urge departments and schools to consider the library user education needs they may have as new courses or programs are established.

3. Implement a faculty seminar program, using the University of California model.

    The Faculty Update Program at the University of California, Berkeley, remains the best model for informing faculty about new developments in information retrieval and bibliographic research. Research update seminars on CD-ROM, online searching, and information management software should be given top priority at Northwestern University. The feasibility of offering seminars on interdisciplinary topics should also be pursued. A workshop to assist NU instructors in designing their class library research projects should also be offered. Teaching assistants may be included in some of the seminars. A separate program of outreach to teaching assistants is proposed in the fifth recommendation under Goal 2.

4. Produce a brochure designed specifically to describe the user education program.

    The text should address common faculty questions about the purpose and probable outcomes of user education. Include the user education mission statement, description of user education activities, and some statements by faculty who have included library instruction in their courses.

5. Use campus publications and newsletters to communicate Library news to faculty.

    In the past, the Library's newsletter, Channels, proved to be a highly visible means of communication to faculty. It provided a unique forum in which librarians could describe trends in publishing and scholarly communication in such a way as to exert clear leadership on campus in these important areas. Reinstituting Channels would reflect the importance the Library places on communication with its teaching and administrative colleagues. Other campus publications, such as the Northwestern Observer, are highly read by faculty and would also prove to be valuable vehicles for communication.

6. Continue and expand the existing packet of information distributed to new faculty members.

    The existing packet of information that is distributed to new faulty members should include, in addition to the letter of welcome from the University Librarian and the Library Handbook, materials that are specific to the discipline/research area of the new faculty member. Material that describes the innovative uses the Library has made of technology, such as brochures on using LUIS (including dial-access instructions), literature on access to local area catalogs, and resource sharing material should be included.

Instructive session 1 (Baker, Birchfield, and Weston) cont.: part 4 - Goals and Recommendations (continued)

7.   Continue and expand the Library's Faculty Day Program.

The Library's Faculty Day program has proven to be a successful way to welcome and instruct new faculty. Expansion of this program to branch and departmental libraries should be explored.

8.   Work toward including faculty use of library user education activities in their courses as a criterion in Undergraduate teaching awards.

A series of awards for excellence in undergraduate teaching has been proposed by the University. With the emphasis placed upon student research by the Undergraduate Experience Report, recognition of use of library research in teaching would be consistent with the goals the University is promoting in Undergraduate education.

Goal 4: Integrate advances in information technologies into library user education programs.

Goal 5: Improve coordination and communication of user education library-wide.

Goal 6: Enhance the use of space to further the educational function of the Library.

Goal 7: Promote and recognize staff initiative in user education programs.

Goal 8: Promote evaluation in all aspects of the user education program.

Instructive sesion 1 (Baker, Birchfield, and Weston) cont.: part 4 - Goals and Recommendations (continued)

NORTHWESTERN UNIVERSITY LIBRARY
1935 Sheridan Road

Dear

Strengthening relationships with academic programs is a key recommendation from a two-year planning process in the University Library. The Reference Department has had a long standing user education program and is now pleased to work toward stronger faculty/library collaboration. As such we have initiated a liaison program from the Reference Department to academic departments. The liaison for your department is 4~, 6~. The reference/user education liaison is in addition to and compliments the existing relationship library bibliographers have with faculty. Of course, all of us in the Reference Department are available to answer your reference questions over the telephone or at the desk.

Specifically, each department now has a reference librarian who will serve as a resource person to support its reference and instruction needs. To clarify our user education goals, we have prepared a mission statement, a copy of which is enclosed for your information. The particular focus of the liaison program is to provide consultation on student assignments which make use of library resources. The importance of providing opportunities for students to engage in critical thinking and information retrieval was underscored in the Undergraduate Experience report.

Faculty in your department will soon be receiving correspondence from their Reference Department liaison describing relevant information services. It would further our efforts if you could include your liaison on any department mailing lists.

We are hopeful that this liaison program will prove to be an effective means for linking developments in information technology with course planning and teaching.

Sincerely,

Betsy Baker (1-2174)   Marilee Birchfield (1-8961)
Head, Reference Department   Instructional Services Librarian

Instructive session 1 (Baker, Birchfield, and Weston) cont.: part 5 - Letter

Mission Statement for User Education

The purpose of Northwestern University Library's user education program is to provide members of the Northwestern University community with the information handling abilities appropriate for their individual levels of scholarship and for the support of their ongoing research interests. Information handling skills range from basic awareness of the value of information to knowledge of communication networks and complex systems for information retrieval that exist within and cut across disciplines. The ability to make sound decisions about the appropriate use of information is a key facet of information literacy.

Efforts to promote information literacy must actively strive to provide individuals with the ability to 1) recognize the role, power, and value of information; 2) understand standard systems of organization for information within disciplines; 3) retrieve information from many systems and in various formats; 4) evaluate and synthesize information; and 5) manage personal information collections.

While students, faculty, and administrators of Northwestern University are of primary concern, the service responsibilities of a research library extend beyond the immediate university community to other scholars and, to some degree, the general public. As with all other services, these non-affiliated user groups should receive some level of assistance.

Instructive session 1 (Baker, Birchfield, and Weston) cont.: part 6 - Mission Statement

— BETSY BAKER, MARILEE BIRCHFIELD, NORM WESTON —

19th National LOEX Library Instruction Conference
Working with Faculty in the New Electronic Library
B. Baker, M. Birchfield, N. Weston -- Northwestern University

Northwestern University Library
Staff Announcement No. **1312**
August 9, 1990

Fostering Curriculum Innovation
Through the Use of New Information Technologies

The Library has undertaken an interdepartmental pilot program entitled "Fostering Curriculum Innovation Through Faculty Seminars on New Information Technologies," or, more informally, the Curriculum Innovation Project. The Project Director will be Brian Nielsen, with Betsy Baker serving as Assistant Project Director. Norman Weston will act as Curriculum Innovation Project Librarian, working closely with Marilee Birchfield, Instructional Services Librarian, and other staff in Reference and elsewhere to develop seminars designed to introduce faculty to various new computing technologies.

The goal of the Curriculum Innovation Project seminars is to integrate computing technologies into faculty research and ultimately into the University curriculum. The Project will integrate two user-oriented functions of the Library: (1) promoting the use and dissemination of new information technologies both within the Library and in the Northwestern teaching and research community at large, and; (2) actively pursuing the faculty outreach component of the Library's user education efforts.

An Information Technology Demonstration Laboratory in Room 1214 (opposite the Reference Conference Room) will be established for faculty and their students to preview, experiment with, and use microcomputer software on both IBM and Macintosh machines. Funding for this laboratory is coming from University budgetary resources, not internal to the Library. Areas of exploration in the lab will include textual manipulation software, online searching, bulletin boards, electronic mail, CD-ROM technology, hypertext, and online and local catalog access.

One notable element of the Project will be to foster faculty interest in and use of the Library of Congress "American Memory Project." Northwestern Library's Marjorie Iglow Mitchell Media Center has recently been selected by the Library of Congress as one of eight sites to beta-test for LC the "American Memory Project" workstation and database. In this segment of the Curriculum Innovation Project, Norman Weston will be working closely with Stephen Marek, Head of the Mitchell Media Center, other Media Center staff, and staff in the Advanced Technology Group of Academic Computing and Network Services. Efforts will be undertaken to integrate use of these tools into the NU curriculum. The American Memory Project itself (including a Macintosh computer, CD-ROM drive, laser disk player, laser printer, and video monitor) will be located in the Media Center's interactive laserdisk lab.

The impetus for the Curriculum Innovation Project stems from the Report on the Undergraduate Experience recommendations calling for the improvement of the teaching and learning environment at Northwestern. Norman Weston's current work with the student information system, recently dubbed "NUINFO," has helped pave the way for the Library to work toward integrating new information technologies within its other programs of general service to the University. We feel that this project will contribute substantially to modeling the kinds of learning experiences and supportive structures for faculty to become more familiar with these technologies.

Brian Nielsen
Assistant University Librarian
for Branch Libraries and
Information Services Technology

Betsy Baker
Head of Reference

Instructive session 1 (Baker, Birchfield, and Weston) cont.: part 7 - Curriculum Innovation Project

Especially for Faculty . . .

Northwestern University Library Presents

Demonstrations of Information Technology
&
Personalized Introductions to Library Collections and Services

October 17 and 18
3:00 p.m. to 5:00 p.m.
Reference Conference Room
Level 1, Main Library

Learn about:

- Information Technology Demonstration Laboratory
- Library online catalogs via the Internet
- PsycLIT & Academic Index on CD-ROM
- LEXIS/NEXIS commercial databases
- Interactive Laserdisk Lab
- OCLC and RLIN databases
- LUIS Online Catalog
- ILLINET Online

Visit and meet staff from:

Africana	Music Library
Art	Newspaper/Microtext
Collection Management	Preservation
Core Collection	Reference
Curriculum	Reserve
Government Publications	Science-Engineering Library
Interlibrary Loan	Special Collections
Management Services	Transportation Library
Map Collection	University Archives
Media Center	

*An informal wine and cheese reception will be held each day
at 4:30 in the Ver Steeg Faculty Lounge (Level 3, South Tower).
Join us to meet with librarians who are key to your teaching and research needs.*

Instructive session 1 (Baker, Birchfield, and Weston) cont.: part 8 - Promotional Flyer

Evaluation: Our Program, Ourselves

by

Polly Frank and Lee-Alison Levene
Mankato State University

Introduction

Librarians who have taught in an instruction program for any length of time have a pretty good sense of what stamina means. It is a challenge to stay fit intellectually, psychologically, physically and politically. For many instruction librarians, the demand for B.I. service at their libraries is growing at the same time funding for library materials and services is falling away. "Trim the fat!" is the academic chant. Like all other public services we chose to develop, librarians must be willing to publicly proclaim and defend the value of our library instruction programs. To do so requires an honest examination of the B.I. services provided and a willingness to consider how librarians can respond to the changing needs of our faculties and their universities.

At Mankato State we are in the process of evaluating a twenty-year-old bibliographic instruction program that began with one full-time bibliographic instruction librarian and one half time graduate assistant. For many years instruction stood as a separate unit, librarians taught one-shots and shared responsibilities with the Media Education Department for a one credit library orientation class.

Twenty years later this picture has changed. We no longer teach the one credit class because of the demand for course-related instruction. Bibliographic instruction is now a unit within reference with a coordinator and twelve instructors. Of these twelve, four instructors are referred to as hard core, carrying a half-time assignment in B. I. The remainder are lovingly referred to as soft core instructors, carrying much lighter and, often times, more specialized teaching assignments. In addition our program, like many, has redirected its focus as a result of changing demands and technology. After so many years, the time and atmosphere was ripe for evaluation.

Evolution of Evaluation

In the spring of 1989, the instruction librarians responded to the Dean's challenge to begin an evaluation of the library instruction program. Simultaneously, there were forces moving on campus toward some form of peer review for faculty. The library's group of instructors thought that it was time to step back and examine the instruction program as a whole, take an honest look at what we were doing, consider where we should be headed, and provide an opportunity for librarians to individually investigate their teaching effectiveness.

With the help of the University's Institutional Research Service, we began our program evaluation by first determining who would be our critics and then deciding what we wanted each group of critics to evaluate. We sought the opinions of faculty, students, and our peers, implementing the evaluation process in stages.

Our evaluation process began with student input. Examining student evaluation forms used by other faculty on campus helped us mirror what had been done by others while forming questions more suitable for one-shot, course related instructional

Instructive session 2 (Frank and Levene): part 1 - Presentation

sessions. In developing the evaluation form, we sought agreement, as we knew ownership of the form by all the B.I. librarians was important. Aggregate scores of student evaluations provided by the University's Institutional Research Service have given us a snapshot of the instruction group's teaching effectiveness.

Our next step in the evaluation process was to query the faculty we had served through our instruction program. A preliminary survey was distributed with the assumption that faculty would reveal questions and problems that we could investigate further . (Attachment A) We looked for recurring themes in faculty responses and took action to address these issues. A year later, faculty were queried again incorporating the concerns expressed in the first survey. We also asked their opinions on other potential instruction services.

Next, we surveyed faculty who had not used our service to find out why. Was it reasonable? Were there classes that would benefit from B.I.? What would make our service more appealing? The prospect of surveying 225 faculty, about half of all non-users, was intimidating. However, we knew this survey could offer other clues as to whether or not we were addressing the real needs of the university with the resources available.

Peer Coaching Development

Along with program review, the librarians noticed a growing interest on campus in peer review. We found in the literature and in the practices of faculty on campus that peer review could be interpreted in a number of ways. The librarians favored some form of peer review that was developmental. Our administration would support whatever we chose but wanted us to observe each other in the classroom.

We sought the assistance of Mankato State's Center for Faculty Development for our peer review process. With their guidance, we approached the College of Education faculty to learn about their teacher-mentor program. In this program, selected high school teachers with ten or more years of experience mentor beginning instructors. One teacher-mentor taught us how to develop a framework for peer coaching and review peer coaching sessions. We learned how to provide specific feedback and openly address fear issues. The teacher-mentor explained methods used to keep track of classroom observations and how to report to ur partners.

Next, we took a look at peer review processes used by two other departments on campus. Although their emphasis was not as developmental as ours, we learned:

• There is no one way to do peer evaluation or peer review.

• If you are not tenured or are less than a full professor some sort of participation in the peer review process adds weight to your tenure or promotion documents.

• It is important to be able to chose who observes you in your classroom.

Our instruction group tried to use the best of what we learned from the teacher mentor, and the two departmental contacts. We decided to use the concept of peer coaching, a developmental approach, rather than peer evaluation. The instruction librarians had strong feelings about issues of trust that hinged on someone coaching them rather than grading them. From our meetings we learned that librarians should decide what documents, whether they are student evaluations or peer coaching comments, to place in their faculty development file. The selective inclusion of these

---

Instructive session 2 (Frank and Levene) cont.: part 1 - Presentation (continued)

— POLLY FRANK AND LEE-ALISON LEVENE —

documents helps provide demonstrable teaching effectiveness .

Skit Summary

   A peer coaching skit presented one picture of the process. The setting: The director of an academic library just read an interesting article on bibliographic instruction program evaluation and the use of peer coaches. She informs all of the instructors that peer coaching is a terrific idea and they are to get with the program THIS WEEK.

   In the skit, the first meeting of the coaching team raised typical issues encountered in planning, observing, and reviewing peer coaching sessions. The peer coach modeled appropriate and inappropriate feedback and body language while the observed instructor exhibited a variety of typical responses--fear, confusion, a concern for setting limits. Following the skit, the problems portrayed were discussed with the session attendants. Additionally, the presenters shared their personal experiences with peer coaching.

Conclusion

   At Mankato State we are well into the process of evaluating our program and ourselves. We have twice surveyed the faculty who have used bibliographic instruction and sampled the faculty that have not. The librarians have used student evaluations regularly for several years to judge themselves in the classroom and this year we implemented a process of peer coaching.   These processes were not developed over night or even within one academic year.   Moving toward evaluation takes time and plenty of discussion. Once we had settled on the peer coaching process, the instruction librarians had other concerns, such as trust issues and confidentiality. These concerns provided an excellent springboard into a general discussion on the role of the peer coach, parameters of peer coaching, setting limits, and choosing a partner. Our peer coaching process is a reciprocal situation where coach and instructor switch roles, sitting in on each other's classes,with the ultimate goal of improving our instruction.

   The instructors at Mankato State are not finished yet. Use of the student evaluations and peer coaching will continue. We're challenged to respond to the information we gathered from the faculty surveys. And we need to turn inward, asking ourselves, what is our mission, where are we going?

Instructive session 2 (Frank and Levene) cont.: part 1 - Presentation (continued)

LIBRARY INSTRUCTION FACULTY QUERY

What recommendations would you make for the scheduling and preplanning activities for the library instruction session?

What do you consider to be the strong and weak points of the library instruction session?

How did the library instruction session help the students complete the assignments for your class?

Instructive session 2 (Frank and Levene) cont.: part 2 - Library Instruction Faculty Query

— POLLY FRANK AND LEE-ALISON LEVENE —

Identification Number

A	B	C	D	E	F	G	H	I	J

(0)(0)(0)(0)(0)(0)(0)(0)(0)(0)
(1)(1)(1)(1)(1)(1)(1)(1)(1)(1)
(2)(2)(2)(2)(2)(2)(2)(2)(2)(2)
(3)(3)(3)(3)(3)(3)(3)(3)(3)(3)
(4)(4)(4)(4)(4)(4)(4)(4)(4)(4)
(5)(5)(5)(5)(5)(5)(5)(5)(5)(5)
(6)(6)(6)(6)(6)(6)(6)(6)(6)(6)
(7)(7)(7)(7)(7)(7)(7)(7)(7)(7)
(8)(8)(8)(8)(8)(8)(8)(8)(8)(8)
(9)(9)(9)(9)(9)(9)(9)(9)(9)(9)

MANKATO STATE UNIVERSITY LIBRARY

In an effort to assist the Library faculty in assessing the effectiveness of their presentation, we are requesting your perceptions of the Library presentation. Your responses should reflect YOUR perceptions, not those of other students. Consider each statement separately and carefully and use the scale to indicate your level of agreement with each statement.

Use NA if the statement is Not Applicable.

Your instructor will provide instructions for completing the grid at the left.

Please use a No. 2 lead pencil to completely fill the circle representing your response.

SCALE:
- SA — STRONGLY AGREE
- A — AGREE
- UN — UNDECIDED
- D — DISAGREE
- SD — STRONGLY DISAGREE
- NA — NOT APPLICABLE

1 The library presentation as a whole was excellent.

2 The content of the presentation was appropriate for the course.

3 The librarian was effective in presenting the material.

4 I was comfortable with the pace of the presentation.

5 The information I learned will help me in this course.

6 The librarian used terms I understood.

7 The approach was appropriate to the level of the class.

8 I had confidence in the librarian's knowledge of the subject.

9 The presentation was well organized.

10 The librarian was enthusiastic.

11 The librarian's voice was clear and easy to understand.

12 The librarian made good use of examples and illustrations.

13 Students were encouraged to participate in class discussions.

14 The handouts were informative and useful.

15 The visuals were clear, understandable, and added to the presentation.

	SA	A	UN	D	SD	NA
1						
2						
3						
4						
5						
6						
7						
8						
9						
10						
11						
12						
13						
14						
15						

(20) (19) (18) (17) (16) (15) (14) (13) (12) (11) (10) (9) (8) (7) (6) (5) (4) (3) (2) (1)

Instructive session 2 (Frank and Levene) cont.: part 3 - Student Evaluation Form

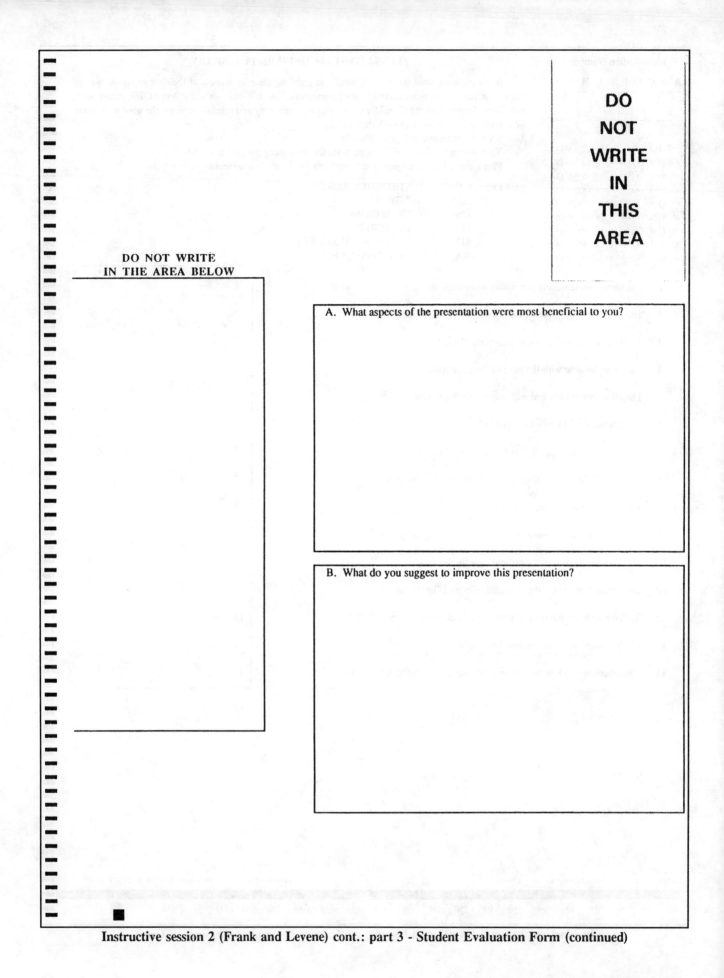

DO
NOT
WRITE
IN
THIS
AREA

DO NOT WRITE
IN THE AREA BELOW

A. What aspects of the presentation were most beneficial to you?

B. What do you suggest to improve this presentation?

Instructive session 2 (Frank and Levene) cont.: part 3 - Student Evaluation Form (continued)

The purpose of this survey is to help the Memorial Library Instruction Librarians evaluate the service we provide. Please respond to the following items with a circle or check. Return this form to Institutional Research, MSU Box 75.

1. Scheduling with library instruction coordinator

	Usually	Sometimes	Seldom	N/A
Instruction coordinator responded to my initial request for a library session within two days.	U	SO	SE	N/A
I was able to get a library session scheduled within the time frame I needed.	U	SO	SE	N/A
I was able to schedule the amount of time needed for my library class session.	U	SO	SE	N/A
Instruction coordinator was responsive to my needs and made suggestions concerning library session.	U	SO	SE	N/A

2. Planning with librarian

Librarian contacted instructor to plan library session at least three days prior to session.	U	SO	SE	N/A
Instructor's objectives for the class assignment and session were discussed.	U	SO	SE	N/A
Librarian discussed her/his objectives for the class and tailored instruction session based on the level of the students.	U	SO	SE	N/A

3. Teaching library session

Librarian taught students to select and use pertinent sources.	U	SO	SE	N/A
Librarian expressed interest in student needs and questions.	U	SO	SE	N/A
Librarian demonstrated subject expertise.	U	SO	SE	N/A
Content of library session was appropriate for the level of the students.	U	SO	SE	N/A
Teaching method used in library session was appropriate.	U	SO	SE	N/A
Amount of material covered was suited to the time allotted.	U	SO	SE	N/A
Library session was tailored to the discipline and course objectives.	U	SO	SE	N/A
Library session helped students complete research paper or other library related assignment.	U	SO	SE	N/A
Visuals used in library session were easy to see and understand.	U	SO	SE	N/A

Instructive session 2 (Frank and Levene) cont.: part 4 - Faculty Users Survey

4. What services would you like to see offered by the library instruction program?

	Definitely Needed	Needed	Not Needed
Library instruction for all incoming freshmen	DN	N	NN
Library instruction for all transfer students	DN	N	NN
Graduate seminars for students beginning graduate research	DN	N	NN
Individualized consultation for graduate students with librarians	DN	N	NN
Term paper clinics for library research	DN	N	NN
Regularly scheduled training sessions on searching CD-ROMs and external database systems	DN	N	NN
More brochures explaining how to use various resources in the library	DN	N	NN

Please list additional brochures needed

_____   _____

_____   _____

	Definitely Needed	Needed	Not Needed
Computer assisted instruction for basic library research	DN	N	NN
Computer assisted instruction for direction to library collections and services	DN	N	NN

Other:

5. How did you find out about the library's instruction service?

College_____

Years at Mankato State University   1-3   4-6   7-9   10 or more

Comments:

Please return
To: Institutional Research, MSU Box 75

Instructive session 2 (Frank and Levene) cont.: part 4 - Faculty Users Survey (continued)

The purpose of this survey is to help the Memorial Library Instruction Librarians evaluate the service we provide. Please respond to the following items with a circle or check. Return this form to Institutional Research, MSU Box 75.

1. **Are you aware of the following instruction services?**

   Assistance in developing library-related assignment---------------------------------- Yes   No

   Library instruction during class time-- Yes   No

   General tour of the library (first five weeks of the quarter)------------------------ Yes   No

   Basic demonstration of the online catalog (first five weeks of the quarter)--------- Yes   No

   Library tours for special groups--- Yes   No

   Demonstrations of new library computer technology (for faculty members)------- Yes   No

   Brief bibliographies and pathfinders in special subject areas----------------------- Yes   No

   Library instruction publications on how to use the online catalog,
   CD-ROMs, and external databases---Yes   No

2. **Which of the following explain why you do not use the library's bibliographic instruction service? Please check all that apply.**

   ____ No time

   ____ Was not aware of service

   ____ Do not regularly teach classes that require students use the library

   ____ Students are given instruction in the use of the library in my class

   ____ Students should learn to use the library on their own

   ____ Most students have learned to use the library before they get to my class

   ____ Students should take the one credit Library Orientation class to learn to do
          library research

   Other:

3. **How would you rate your students' abilities to:**

	Very Good	Good	Poor	Very Poor
Find their way around the library----------------------------	VG	G	P	VP
Use appropriate library resources to find materials for term papers or research projects----------------------------	VG	G	P	VP

Instructive session 2 (Frank and Levene) cont.: part 5 - Faculty Non-users Survey

4. What services would you like to see offered by the library instruction program?

	Definitely needed	needed	not needed
Library instruction for all incoming freshmen	DN	N	NN
Library instruction for all transfer students	DN	N	NN
Graduate seminars for students beginning graduate research	DN	N	NN
Individualized consultation for graduate students with librarians	DN	N	NN
Term paper clinics for library research	DN	N	NN
Regularly scheduled training sessions on searching CD-ROMs and external database systems	DN	N	NN
More brochures explaining how to use various resources in the library	DN	N	NN

Please list additional brochures needed

_____   _____

_____   _____

Computer assisted instruction for basic library research skills	DN	N	NN
Computer assisted instruction for direction to library collections and services	DN	N	NN

Other:

College_____

Years at Mankato State University   1-3   4-6   7-9   10 or more

Comments:

Please return
To: Institutional Research, MSU Box 75.

Instructive session 2 (Frank and Levene) cont.: part 5 - Faculty Non-users Survey (continued)

INTEGRATING ELECTRONIC INFORMATION SOURCES INTO AN UNDERGRADUATE COURSE ON IMMUNOLOGY: SUCCESSFUL LIBRARIAN-FACULTY COOPERATION

Margaret Adams Groesbeck
Amherst College Library

The Amherst College Library has subsidized direct faculty searching of databases through Dialog Information Services, Inc. since the fall of 1986. The author describes Amherst College's faculty end-user program. It sprang directly from faculty interest in doing their own retrieval. This support has been critical to its success. The program was made possible in large part by a senior mathematician who helped librarians win the approval - and initial financial backing - of the Dean of Faculty. In this way the Library was able to open up online searching equally to all faculty, not just to faculty who had grants to fund online retrieval. Faculty end-user access has become an important institutional commitment as well as a key library service.

Of course it has been easier to institute end-user searching in a small college with only 150 faculty members and a history of heavily subsidizing library services. The author documents that the end-user program has not been nearly as expensive as some had imagined. She also discusses the new opportunities for bibliographic instruction in the sciences which have accompanied the Library's introduction of direct access to electronic sources.

The author illustrates growing faculty-librarian cooperation in bibliographic instruction with one example. A microbiologist/immunologist who learned online searching from a librarian came to see information retrieval as a "politically" revealing and professionally useful skill to pass along to his students. In the course on immunology he teaches at Amherst College, information retrieval and evaluation became the equivalent of a laboratory. The author presents the immunologist's course description and introductory assignment. She outlines the faculty member's objectives in creating a series of online exercises, among which are: that students gain some insight into the wealth and complexity of the literature in the field they are studying; that they understand the concept of controlled vocabulary and learn to use the thesaurus for Medline; that they distinguish among kinds of publications and evaluate their usefulness; that they recognize major researchers and the journals in which they commonly publish in immunology. She underscores the close cooperation between librarians and the immunologist in realizing these goals. She reviews the evolution of the first assignment which helps the students master online retrieval. She describes the initial classroom presentation and the six hours a week of follow-up "search labs." She argues that this end-user instruction is successful because it depended on close librarian-faculty cooperation and cast the instruction as an institutional commitment akin to a new laboratory or studio - that is, as an integral part of a course - rather than simply a supplementary new library program.

Instructive session 3 (Groesbeck): part 1 - Abstract

AMHERST COLLEGE

33. Immunology. The immune response is a consequence of the developmentally programmed or antigen-triggered interaction of a complex network of interacting cell types. These interactions are controlled by regulatory molecules and often result in the production of highly specific cellular or molecular effectors. This course will present the principles underlying the immune response and describe the methods employed in immunology research. In addition to lectures, a program of seminars will provide an introduction to the research literature of immunology. Four class hours per week.

Requisite: Biology 12 and either Biology 21, 29 or 30. Limited to 24 students. First semester. Professor Goldsby.

35. Neurobiology. Nervous sys~~

level. Ioni~~

physi~~

tion;~~

tions;~~

neuro~~

labora~~

Requ~~

ited to~~

**38. An~~

cal and~~

and eth~~

of resou~~

sion mak~~

versus ho~~

ing system~~

riality an~~

per week.~~

Requisit~~

ter. Profes~~

**39. Plant ~~

that affect ~~

spectives. ~~

tion, hybridi~~

nuclear-cyto~~

struction u~~

will include ~~

molecular gen~~

of laboratory ~~

Requisite: ~~

Omitted 1990~~

**43s. Seminar ~~

from the pers~~

LEARNING & USING ELECTRONIC DATABASES

You have received copies of the editorial board of The Journal of Experimental Medicine, a leading immunology journal. Please note that your name appears beside the name of a member of the JEM editorial board on a additional sheet you have received. For the editorial board member tagged with your name, please supply the following information in the format indicated below by 9/27/90:

- Name of board member:

- Departmental affiliation:

- Institutional name and address:

- Age:

- Major Area[s] of Research:

- Complete citations [Authors-title of paper-journal name-volume-page-year] of one paper published by the board member during the past two years and one paper published between 1980 and 1982. Give some indication of the two or three journals [names] in which most of the board members work appeared during the periods specified above. Also tell how many papers were published by the board member in 1985.

Also, please provide answers to the following questions:

- How many papers were published on AIDS [the disease] in 1984, 1987 and 1989?

- Where any papers published on human T cells [lymphocytes] during 1988? If so, how many? How many of these appeared in the Journal of Experimental Medicine?

- Did Robert C. Gallo write any chapters or reviews on AIDS or AIDS-related topics during 1987? If so, provide citations for up to 3 such reviews or chapters.

Please use either a typewriter or computer-directed printer to prepare the material you submit for this assignment.

Instructive session 3 (Groesbeck) cont.: part 2 - Online Exercise

FROM PITFALLS TO WINDFALLS: DEVELOPING INSTITUTIONAL SUPPORT FOR YOUR END-USER TRAINING PROGRAM.

I. INTRODUCTION & BACKGROUND NOTES

The following paper describes the steps taken to set up a database searching facility at a small liberal arts college in south-central Pennsylvania. This was a low budget operation that was undertaken in collaboration with several important segments of the academic community. The issues and considerations involved in creating a relatively self-sufficient program are discussed. The theme of the process was to take advantage of existing resources and also deficiencies and to develop procedures that blended smoothly into the existing range of research practices.

Juniata College is a liberal arts school located in rural Pennsylvania. Affiliated with the Church of the Brethren, it has a student body of 1100 and a library with 169,000 books and 4 professional librarians (including the director). In an ironic twist of fate, the liberal arts programs are fairly weak. Traditional strengths of the college tend towards business and science programs, particularly pre-med and chemistry.

As a result of budget cuts in the late 70s, many journal titles were discontinued, including the Chemical Abstracts yearly and five yearly indexes. The 9th collective, covering literature from 1972-76 was the most current, although the biweekly copies of the abstracts themselves continued to arrive on a regular basis.

In compensation for canceling the more expensive indexes, the budget line for computer searches was enhanced. The reason behind the move was that it was cheaper to pay as the index was used. Students could arrange for a database search to locate needed materials.

And, in fact, it was a cheaper way to operate. For the most part, the remaining Wilson Indexes were sufficient to handle typical undergraduate research projects. More creative or advanced work could be accommodated by a database search.

The one glaring deficiency in the setup was in Chemistry, where there is only one main index to the literature, Chemical Abstracts. The majority of the Chemistry faculty were good library users and had several courses in which library research was part of the lab assignment. Five of the eleven faculty were computer literate and were capable of doing their own searches. One professor in particular was quite interested in online searching and did course related searches regularly. Students however, were required to have a librarian perform a search for them if they needed information more current than 1976.

The librarian found the situation unsatisfactory for several reasons. The students were not learning how to find relevant chemistry information on their own. A "magic" computer search did it for them. The creative thinking processes that develop when clarifying a research topic and translating it into library terms were being short circuited. A related problem was that while some attempts were made to develop the topic during the reference interview, the results were always limited by the librarian's ignorance of the field and the lack of clarity on the part of the student. As long as someone else sat at the controls of the computer, the students would never get any closer to negotiating chemistry literature.

II. PHASE ONE, THE TRIAL BALLOON

Ongoing discussions over the course of the year with the professor who was most interested in online searching lead to the idea of teaching students in the advanced research class how to do their own searches. She was enthusiastic about the idea and in the fall of 1988, arranged for the instruction to be given to the Synthesis class and the Advanced Research class, comprised of eight students and two faculty.

Instructive session 4 (Jaffurs): part 1 - Presentation

Students were given exercises at the end of each lecture and required to work with a partner to complete them. A sign-up sheet was posted outside the Public Services Librarian's office where the computer searches were done and the students reserved time in the evening to do their assignments.

Results of the course were encouraging. Three of the four student pairs worked well together and their learning experience was enhanced by the partner's observations. For the most part, they were mildly interested to bored with the lecture, but intrigued to totally captivated by the process of doing their own searches. One student was computer-phobic and needed extra hand-holding to get through the exercises.

The attempt to cover structure searching was overly ambitious, as the students concentrated too much on the simple mechanics of building structures. They seemed to forget the previous lecture's more important presentation about developing efficient search strategies. It would appear that structure searching is best taught as an advanced course to individuals with research projects that require that type of search (organic chemists).

Three students came back after the semester was finished to do additional searches. One student came back three times. Most of the searches they did were fairly simple, but the students said they were satisfied with the results. The single workstation in the Public Services Office was totally inadequate to handle the load. The professor was pleased. In all, it was a valuable learning experience for everyone concerned.

III. PHASE TWO, THE GRANT PROPOSAL.

In February, the librarian met with the chemistry department and discussed expanding the instruction. Were the faculty interested in learning to do online searching? Would they commit precious class time so that their students would receive training? Were they interested in integrating the instruction across the curriculum?

Much of the presentation was in terms of how faculty would benefit. After all, computer searching was rapidly becoming an important method of gathering information. The chemists were concerned about their own professional development as well as advancements in their areas of interest. The faculty were very interested and identified six or seven courses or honors sections within courses where it made sense to introduce the instruction.

Providing the envisioned instruction would require a larger facility. The choices were to find space in the library or to tie in with the computer center. Creating a facility from scratch would require lots of money and lots more training than was available to the librarians. Building on the computer center facilities would be more affordable, but would remove the search room from library premises. On the balance, the computer center was in the heart of the science building, much more convenient to the chemists. The outgoing lines would be available to anyone who could access the VAX, provided they had the proper security clearances. That had significant possibilities for future expansion of the program to other departments located across campus.

The Director of the Computing Center was supportive. A database searching facility fit in with his five year plan of providing a computer in every office and access to electronic information systems such as BitNet. He suggested two students who could write the program for security and access protocols.

A second important element of the project was the development of a workbook that would allow students to work at their own pace. STN provides many wonderful booklets and summary sheets, even a series of lecture notes. What we needed was something that presented the information in a logical sequence, building on previous chapters, focused on undergraduates (as opposed to professional chemists), and that included practice exercises to try out the concepts presented. Use of a workbook had the added attraction of making the project independent of any one single individual (including the librarian).

Instructive session 4 (Jaffurs) cont.: part 1 - Presentation (continued)

— ALEXA JAFFURS —

The third element of the project was the need for database training geared toward the faculty. The librarian did not feel confident in her grasp of chemistry, so the prospect of an official Chem Abstracts workshop was explored. "Official" instruction would have the added benefit of further committing the chemistry faculty to the idea. Although half would probably not use the training to do their own searches, they would understand better the process and strengths of database searching and could better direct their students.

With the expressed support of the chemistry department, a grant proposal asking for $4500 was submitted to an in-house funding source. The money was needed to enable five telecommunication lines capable of accessing the STN database, to pay for a workshop to introduce 12 faculty and 3 librarians to the finer arts of database searching, and to develop instruction - a workbook - for the students to use. The library would pay for the projected increase in search costs out of the computer searching line.

The first goal of the project was to provide better access to the chemistry literature. The second goal was to instruct students in good information gathering techniques (BI). A third goal was to expand the service after two years to include other interested departments or faculty. Ultimately, we hoped to see the skills filter down so that most graduating students were proficient in performing literature searches via computer. An over-arching concern was that the program be so naturally integrated into the classroom culture that it would survive and grow with minimal day to day input from any one person.

The grant was approved and the facility was set up by the middle of August. Expenditures are listed in Table One. The workshop of August 23rd proved to be the maiden voyage. Fifteen participants accessed the CA database via five phone lines. The two students who had worked on the access programming were present and had to make some minor modifications. The workbook was based on lecture notes and observations from the previous years experience and borrowed liberally from STN documentation. The most difficult part of the job was to create appropriate exercise questions. Instruction was initially offered to two advanced chemistry classes. Database searching costs came to less than $300.

IV. CONCLUSION

Successful implementation of the project was due in great measure to the enthusiasm and support of several key people: The College Librarian, the chemistry professor who initiated the first instruction sessions, and the Director of the Computing Center. All were approached as early in the planning stages as possible and participated in decision making. Development of institutional support flowed naturally from the networking process. The grant proposal was formulated based on a clear understanding of bibliographic instructional needs and goals but looked beyond the library to support other needs of the institution.

Instructive session 4 (Jaffurs) cont.: part 1 - Presentation (continued)

```
              DATABASE SEARCHING FACILITY COST BREAKDOWN

   Installation of 5 phone lines.............................$500
   5 2400 BAUD external modems................................615
   80 hours student worker time to develop access protocols...400
   Development of instruction (workbook).......................600
   STN Workshop (1 1/2 days)..................................2200

   yearly phone costs*........................................1080
   database usage*.............................................400

   TOTAL....................................................$5795

   *not included in grant funding
```

Instructive session 4 (Jaffurs) cont.: part 2 - Database Searching Facility Cost Breakdown

```
          SHORT BIBLIOGRAPHY OF USEFUL STN PUBLICATIONS*


CAS Standard Abbreviations

Frequently Posted Name Segments in the Registry File

Getting Started on the CAS Online.  - a 20 pg intro

STN Summary Sheets. - similar to dialog blue sheets

STN User Documentation Lessons 1-4b and Instructor's Notes.  --
   - designed as a series of lectures to be presented in class by
      the chemistry professor

Using CAS Online: The CA File
Using CAS Online: The Registry File
      - the above two comprise a six volume set and are the most
         detailed sources for general information on the files.

Using the Learning Files
      - similar to the above set.  very well written

*all available from STN International, c/o Chemical Abstracts
Service, PO Box 3012, Columbus, OH 43210.

ALSO:

Schultz, Hedda.  From CA to CAS Online.  New York: VCH, 1988.
```

Instructive session 4 (Jaffurs) cont.: part 3 - Short Bibliography of Useful STN Publications

Faculty/Library Interaction in
Off-Campus Instruction

Karen E. Jaggers
Northern Arizona University

Distance education at Northern Arizona University (NAU) provides a challenge to establishing and maintaining successful faculty/library interaction. This paper describes the NAU off-campus program and identifies barriers to communication including distance, compressed class schedules, teaching formats, and part-time faculty. After discussing part-time faculty, the paper describes the lines of contact established by the Cline Library Field-Services Department to overcome obstacles to communication. Support needed from administrators and faculty is addressed, followed by a brief analysis of the success of NAU's faculty contact. The paper concludes by looking at the future of the program.

Instructive session 5 (Jaggers): part 1 - Abstract

The Distance education program at Northern Arizona University provides a real challenge to establishing and maintaining successful faculty/library interaction. NAU offers off-campus instruction through continuing education classes, an off-campus center, and nine field-based sites, as well as through service and teacher education on the Navajo and Hopi reservations. Cline Library Field Services Department works directly with the nine field-based sites to provide material for field-based classes. These classes are taught across Arizona on community college campuses, public school campuses, school district offices and other suitable sites. In metropolitan areas such as Phoenix and Tucson, a large number of classes are clustered in a few locations. In other areas, such as on the Navajo or Hopi reservations, classes may be miles apart. Much faculty and student time is spent commuting.

During Spring semester,1991, 27 of the 192 off-campus faculty members are full-time faculty at NAU. The remaining 165 live in the community in which the class is taught. Often faculty from the community are affiliated with the university only for the duration of the class. Many hold full-time jobs in the community and teach for NAU part-time. It is not unusual for faculty to teach one class in the local community and another at a distance.

Off-campus faculty lack the avenues of communication available to on-campus faculty (Steffen, 1986, p. 189). Regional site coordinators set up classes, register students, and hire and orient the faculty. Since these activities take place in the field, the faculty member does not have to come to campus. Because of distance, time, and other obligations, the off-campus faculty members do not meet as a faculty, nor do they benefit from other channels of communication such as departmental meetings and committee memberships. Because of their part-time status, they feel isolated from the campus and may feel that they lack adequate information about available services.

Attempts to communicate are further complicated by class formats and the length of classes. While traditional classroom lectures predominate, courses are also offered by microcomputer and interactive video. Class length includes various compressed formats such as 8-week, 12-week, and four Fri/Sat classes three weeks apart. Starting dates for the classes also vary in order to allow students to take several classes at one time, further separating the faculty and inhibiting interaction.

Like its counterpart on-campus, the off-campus faculty is diverse. Not all are experienced library users nor have they all kept abreast of changing technologies. Some faculty are veteran users who want no help, while others are novices who really want library assistance. Some are overenthusiastic and overload the system, others are independent souls who violate or abuse the system. Communication must take each of these individual types into consideration.

Faculty members may have negative feelings toward the library. On-campus faculty make research assignments with the assumption that students have access to and will use the campus library. Faculty who were on campus before the library Field Services Department was established provided material for off-campus classes themselves. If they wished to have students read articles, they took the articles to class; if they wanted students to use particular books, they took them to class. Often the relationship between the library and the faculty was less than desirable. To have a good faculty/library interaction, faculty must become convinced that the service will work and that we will deliver.

One other thought must be kept foremost. If the faculty member is sold on the library service, the students will use it. If the faculty member feels the service will not work, the students may not use it.

The Field Services Department at NAU takes a proactive stance in communicating with faculty. The first point of contact comes through a packet of information provided by the Continuing Education Department. Along with information on reimbursement for travel, filing grade reports and other vital instructions, the packet contains a Field Services Brochure. This brochure details the library services and provides a toll-free telephone number. (Field, 1990)

Instructive session 5 (Jaggers) cont.: part 2 - Presentation

— KAREN E. JAGGERS —

As soon as the Field Services Department gets a list of off-campus faculty (in July for Fall Faculty and December for Spring Faculty), a second line of contact is established. Taking into consideration the variant starting dates and the differing class lengths, we begin with the classes which start first. If the faculty member is new to the program we make contact by mail and by telephone. Using a form letter, we list the services available and we include a bibliography prepared for the class which is being taught. The bibliography is two to three pages long and lists books and films/videotapes in our library's catalog.

The telephone call follows the letter and serves several purposes. It provides personal contact; we may never see the person face-to-face but we can interact personally. It provides a chance to ask and to answer questions. We can elaborate on how we handle reserve collections or how realistic our turn-around time may be. We can also see if a class visit is needed or if the faculty member needs resource material to aid in class preparation. Often we find the faculty member is not aware of the service or fails to consider it a viable resource.

For the field-faculty who have taught with us previously, we start with contact by mail. We know which classes have used our services in the past, and we do telephone followup on those whose classes have not requested material from us. We especially concentrate on classes taught outside the metropolitan areas of Phoenix and Tucson.

For the faculty who request a classroom presentation, we schedule a site visit. Since classes meet every week night and are taught in over thirty towns throughout Arizona, site visits are limited. The Field Services staff consists of 1.5 FTE Librarians, .5 FTE paraprofessional and 1 FTE student assistance. This staff has handled 1400 requests since July 1, 1990, 113 of which were from field-faculty. During that time we visited 25 field-based classes. In addition to having our librrians visit classes, we arrange for library instruction at community colleges provided by the librarians at those institutions. Many of our faculty work with the community college librarian and come to us only for material not available locally.

What do field-services librarians need to deal with the needs and problems of field-based faculty? First of all, experience as a librarian is essential. A thorough knowledge of the campus library needs to be supplemented by a knowledge of state and national library networks. Familiarity with the library collections in the towns and community colleges throughout the region in which classes are taught is a must since these libraries serve our students. These libraries may house a reserve collection for our classes and provide computer searches or interlibrary loan for our faculty. Before a faculty member can be referred to a local library, librarians must know what is available.

The field-services librarians must also be familiar with the programs and classes offered by the university. We ask for a syllabus and a reading list or bibliography for each class taught off-campus. We familiarize ourselves with the class descriptions listed in the general or graduate catalogs. We must know which classes are being taught, how many sections are being taught and the location of the classes. In setting up class visits, a request by one class for a visit can be expanded into a visit to several other classes meeting on the same day.

What do we need from administrators and faculty? We need support. At NAU the off-campus program is part of the campus master plan. The Field Services Coordinator is included as a resource person on an off-campus planning committee. In the library, the Field Services Coordinator has department-head status.

Departments that administer the off-campus program are supportive of the library service. The Continuing Education department verifies the teaching credentials of the faculty. They provide information about library services to the faculty and provide us with class lists and faculty addresses. The Regional Site Coordinators, who set up the classes, locate potential faculty and provide the day-to-day management of the classes, maintain close contact with the library, telling us in advance of faculty and course changes. Since the Regional Site Coordinators also teach classes, they use the service themselves. The Registrar's office provides us with lists of students and mailing labels when we request them.

What do we need from the faculty? We need a commitment to require students to use library resources and to inform them about our service. We need to be included when library assignments are being planned, especially if the assignment would be augmented by a class visit. In addition, we need the class syllabus and bibliographies or reading lists that will be used with the classes.

Instructive session 5 (Jaggers) cont.: part 2 - Presentation (continued)

How successful is library/faculty interaction? As successful as budget and staffing allow. Since the Field Services Department is still in a building stage, contact with faculty and students is geared toward promoting the existing services. After four years of growth (45%-65% increase in requests per year), staff time is devoted to locating and mailing material. Faculty contact is centered on informing the faculty of the library services we provide. As the Field Services program stabilizes and as off-campus programs expand, librarians need to become more involved in the development of courses and incorporating library assignments into them.

What do we see in the future? We see electronic networking being expanded throughout Arizona. This fall we will join the CARL system for our online catalog, enabling faculty and students throughout Arizona to search our catalog and to search ERIC and other bibliographic databases. Since the catalog will be limited to patrons with personal computers, our library foresees agreements with community college and public libraries to augment access.

Currently, faculty can correspond with the Field Services Department by toll-free telephone, fax and mail. I anticipate an electronic mail dropbox as an additional means of access.

As Northern Arizona University plans for increased cooperation with community colleges through interactive video and C-Band microwave instruction, the Field Services Department looks forward to using these technologies to interact with classes in the field. This interaction is already occuring on the NAUYuma campus. In the Yuma 2+2 program, the first two years of undergraduate classes are taught at Arizona Western College and the last two years are taught at NAUYuma on the Arizona Western College campus. Some of the classes are taught from the Flagstaff campus through interactive video. The Arizona Western College librarian, Eileen Shackelford, discusses library needs with Flagstaff instructors through the video network. As 2+2 programs expand into other areas, our field-services librarians will use this technology to meet "face-to-face" with off-campus faculty and students.

Videotaped library instruction or hypertext programs may be used in the future for bibliographic instruction and Field Services promotion. These technologies would allow uniform instruction throughout the state. Remote communications software may allow us to enhance our delivery of information to distance learners (Bell, 1991).

Although many obstacles exist in the provision of library services to off-campus faculty, none are unsurmountable. The demand for distance education programs will continue to grow placing increased demands on the faculty and the library. Through faculty/library interaction we can insure quality education in our field-based programs.

Instructive session 5 (Jaggers) cont.: part 2 - Presentation (continued)

References

Bell, Stephen. (1991). Spreading CD-ROM technology beyond the library: applications for remote communications software. OCLC Micro, 7, 16-19.

Library services for field-based programs; Cline Library. (1990). (Available from Field Services Department, Cline Library, Northern Arizona University, Box 6022, Flagstaff, AZ, 66011-6022).

Steffen, Susan Swords. (1986). Working with part-time faculty: challenges and rewards. In Lessin, Barton M. The Off-Campus Library Services Conference Proceedings (Conference Edition) Reno, Nevada October 23-24, 1986. (pp. 188-196). Mount Pleasant, Michigan: Central Michigan University Press.

Instructive session 5 (Jaggers) cont.: part 3 - Bibliography

— KAREN E. JAGGERS —

FACULTY/LIBRARY INTERACTION IN OFF-CAMPUS INSTRUCTION

DISTANCE EDUCATION AT NORTHERN ARIZONA UNIVERSITY

OFF-CAMPUS FACULTY

THE FACULTY HEARS FROM THE LIBRARY

A SUCCESSFUL FIELD-SERVICES LIBRARIAN

HOW FACULTY CAN HELP US

IS THIS PROGRAM SUCCESSFUL?

WHAT DOES THE FUTURE HOLD?

CONCLUSION

Instructive session 5 (Jaggers) cont.: part 4 - Handout

FACULTY/LIBRARY INTERACTION IN

OFF—CAMPUS INSTRUCTION

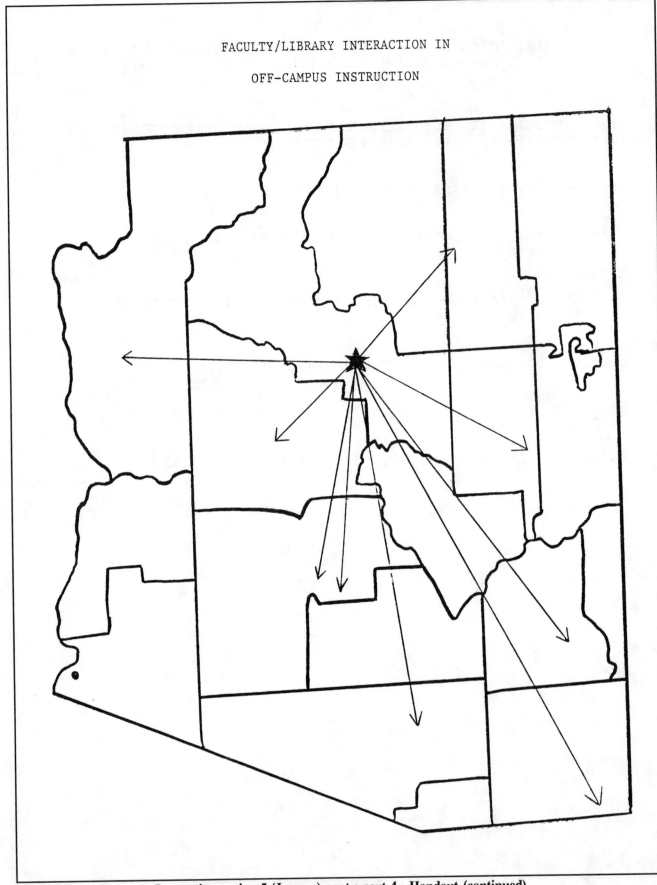

Instructive session 5 (Jaggers) cont.: part 4 - Handout (continued)

OFF-CAMPUS FACULTY

192 OFF-CAMPUS FACULTY

27 ALSO TEACH ON CAMPUS

TEACH REGULARLY OR ONLY ONE CLASS

TEACH IN SEVERAL SITES

DO NOT MEET AS FACULTY

LACK CHANNELS OF COMMUNICATION

EXPERIENCED LIBRARY USERS?

CHANGING TECHNOLOGIES

VETERAN USERS

NON-LIBRARY USERS

OVERENTHUSIASTIC

INDEPENDENT-ABUSE THE SYSTEM

NEGATIVE TOWARD LIBRARY?

IF THE FACULTY SUPPORTS THE LIBRARY SERVICE, THE STUDENTS WILL USE IT

Instructive session 5 (Jaggers) cont.: part 4 - Handout (continued)

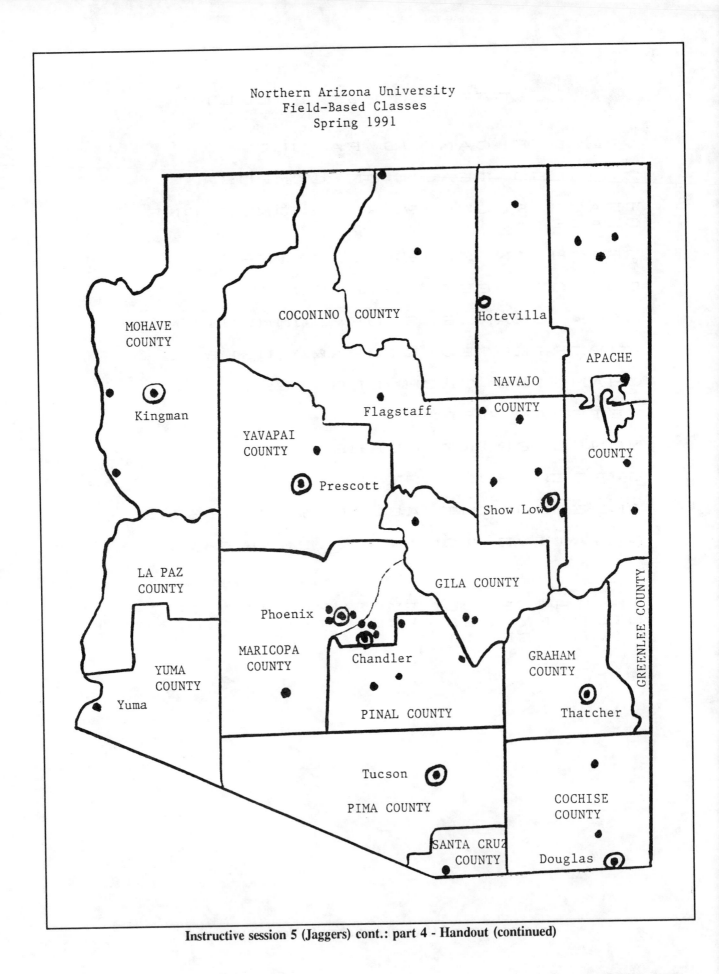

Northern Arizona University
Field-Based Classes
Spring 1991

MOHAVE
COUNTY

Kingman

COCONINO COUNTY

Hotevilla

APACHE

NAVAJO
COUNTY

Flagstaff

YAVAPAI
COUNTY

Prescott

Show Low

COUNTY

GILA COUNTY

LA PAZ
COUNTY

Phoenix

GREENLEE COUNTY

MARICOPA
COUNTY

Chandler

GRAHAM
COUNTY

YUMA
COUNTY

Yuma

PINAL COUNTY

Thatcher

Tucson

PIMA COUNTY

COCHISE
COUNTY

SANTA CRUZ
COUNTY

Douglas

Instructive session 5 (Jaggers) cont.: part 4 - Handout (continued)

LIBRARY SERVICES

TOLL-FREE NUMBER

BIBLIOGRAPHIES TAILORED TO YOUR CLASS

FREE COMPUTER SEARCHES IN ERIC AND PSYC/LIT

RESERVE COLLECTIONS

CHECKING YOUR READING LISTS AGAINST OUR COLLECTION

PHOTODUPLICATION

INTERLIBRARY LOAN

BOOK RETRIEVAL

REFERENCE ASSISTANCE

ORIENTATION

CLASS VISITS

BIBLIOGRAPHIC INSTRUCTION

FILMS AND VIDEOTAPES

TRAVELING COLLECTION

Instructive session 5 (Jaggers) cont.: part 4 - Handout (continued)

HOW FACULTY CAN
HELP US

CALL US EARLY

REQUIRE STUDENTS TO USE LIBRARY
RESOURCES

INFORM STUDENTS ABOUT THE
SERVICE

INCLUDE LIBRARIAN IN PLANNING
LIBRARY ASSIGNMENTS

SYLLABUS

READING LISTS

BOOK ORDERS

FEEDBACK

THE FUTURE

ELECTRONIC NETWORKING

VIDEOTAPED LIBRARY INSTRUCTION
OR HYPERTEXT

DEMAND FOR DISTANCE EDUCATION
WILL INCREASE

LIBRARY COOPERATION WILL
INCREASE

CONCLUSION

Instructive session 5 (Jaggers) cont.: part 4 - Handout (continued)

LIAISON PROGRAM + INFORMATION
TECHNOLOGY = GETTING YOUR FOOT IN THE DOOR

Beth L. Mark and Soo K. Lee

"Where are the scholarly journals?"

"I need a primary source on Greek education -- in a journal -- can you help me?"

"I've just spent an hour looking in Psychology Today for an article on the effects of television violence on children. Is there any other way to look?"

Each of you has been the recipient of questions like these from your students. Of course we all believe that at least a partial solution to library illiteracy is bibliographic instruction. But what do you do if your library is not like Earlham College Library with an active, course-integrated bibliographic instruction program? What if, other than freshmen tours and a written orientation, very little bibliographic instruction occurred in your library? How would you begin?

Several years ago in an ambitious attempt to address this and other problems, librarians at Messiah College (a small liberal arts college with over 2,000 students) initiated a comprehensive liaison program incorporating almost all library functions, including selection, weeding and preservation, budget-building and interpretation, nonroutine reference assistance, bibliographic instruction, online searching, and cataloging consultation. It was also recognized that liaison librarians would serve as both troubleshooters and advocates for their subject departments.

All five librarians at Messiah College, who were already sharing reference duties, as well as maintaining their primary responsibilities (acquisitions, cataloging, and administration) endorsed the program and matched themselves with the twelve academic departments, primarily on the basis of interest and academic background. After securing approval for the program from academic department chairs, we cautiously began offering faculty a variety of services, including bibliographic instruction. (For the purposes of this talk we will refer to teaching faculty as "faculty.") One or two requests for BI trickled in but most faculty members continued to be blissfully unaware of the wonderful teaching service we were offering and we did little to press the issue!

Soon after initiating the liaison program we purchased our first CD-ROM indexes (ERIC and PsycLIT) and budgeted money for free online searching for faculty. Feeling that we now had something new and exciting to offer, we sent letters to faculty in our liaison subject areas describing these technologies and offering individual and/or group demonstrations. Although the initial response was small, even in the Behavioral Sciences and Education Departments, those who came saw the potential of the new search tools for research and immediately arranged class instruction sessions.

Thus began our adventure into the world of bibliographic instruction. We found that the new information technology made many faculty members realize that they did not know everything about the library resources in their field. This in turn initiated conversation with faculty which has gone way beyond the initial CD-ROM orientations.

Over the years we have found the following strategies to be helpful and effective in communicating with faculty:

1. Communicate frequently with faculty members about materials and news of interest in their fields.

2. Identify faculty members who have already incorporated library-related assignments into their courses. (While usually interested, department chairs are often overloaded and don't have time to spend planning bibliographic instruction.)

After initiating contact with those faculty members:

a) explore the possibility of incorporating bibliographic instruction into one or two of his/her classes.

b) ask about other departmental faculty members who might be receptive to the idea of bibliographic instruction.

Instructive session 6 (Mark and Lee) part 1 - Presentation

3.   Find creative ways to introduce new information technologies to faculty. The more they know, the easier our job becomes. Be flexible with scheduling, format, etc., depending on the needs of the faculty member. For example, one librarian included an orientation to CD-ROM indexes along with departmental introductions to our new KeyNOTIS system.

4.   Use difficult assignments observed at the reference desk as an opportunity to communicate with faculty about problems students are having in the library. Often this contact results in a new or better working relationship with the faculty member and presents an opportunity to plan future BI sessions. Prior to the liaison program, we made the assumption that faculty members didn't want to hear our observations of their students' problems in the library. We have found this assumption to be entirely false.

5.   Keep communications flowing through informal phone calls and notes, even if it's only a few lines on paper or on phone mail.

6.   Break out of the library! We echo the sentiments of Frederic Messick who encouraged librarians not to be "like a reference book incarnate--to be consulted in the library on request but never to leave the building." (Messick, 1977) We try to eat lunch in the college snack bar occasionally, enjoying conversation with faculty. More than once a request or referral for bibliographic instruction has occurred over a cup of coffee.

Below are descriptions of some of the activities that have resulted from the liaison program.

Beth Mark: Education and Health, Physical Education and Recreation Departments.

The first faculty member to respond to my invitation to ERIC CD-ROM orientation has become my staunchest ally in encouraging BI in Education Department classes. We attended an Earlham College BI workshop together which heightened her interest in course-integrated BI. With a common interest in critical thinking, we now work together, constantly revising the library assignments in her classes. Departmentally, she was assigned to work with me on a sequence of library skills to be incorporated into targeted courses. This sequence will be implemented in the fall.

In the Health, Physical Education and Recreation Department I am fortunate to have a teaching colleague who is interested in critical thinking and enabling students to be independent learners. In addition to incorporating a BI session into one of his courses, he suggested that I contact a professor in a freshman level course who now dovetails his class assignment with a hands-on BI session covering periodical indexes and article evaluation.

Soo Lee: Behavioral Sciences and Nursing Departments.

Adding PsycLIT CD-ROM index has resulted in a tremendous increase in the number of BI requests. In order to meet the requests from the Behavioral Sciences Department, I decided to invest time in educating faculty members. I offered several individual and group workshops on the CD-ROM indexes we have at our library. The response from most faculty members was very positive. One faculty member was so intrigued by PsycLIT he wanted to know everything about database searching, and so I devised a three-hour customized instruction session for him. He now incorporates the knowledge he gained from that experience into his library assignments for his classes.

A psychology faculty member and I have developed a library project in which students in her Biological Basis of Behavior class are actively involved in learning research and critical thinking skills in a carefully-developed process research approach. Students are guided through the assignment, receiving feedback and approval from the professor or myself before progressing from one step to another. The process includes several steps in which students are asked to: formulate a research question using the class text and other secondary sources; develop search strategies; implement searches using the PsycLIT CD-ROM database and Medline online database; and access and evaluate the articles retrieved. The faculty member and I spend a lot of time making sure students understand the concept of controlled vocabulary and boolean logic. End-of-semester evaluations by students reflect a sense of accomplishment and a good understanding of library research and information technology.

Instructive session 6 (Mark and Lee) cont.: part 1 - Presentation (continued)

I work very closely with the Nursing Department's faculty liaison to the library. As a part of a grant she received for computer literacy, she and I have developed a four-year sequence teaching nursing students library and information skills, with an emphasis on computer applications.

The number of classroom bibliographic instruction sessions at our library has increased from two or three course-integrated sessions in 1985/86 to 43 sessions in 1990/91. Now faculty members frequently consult with us before planning a new library-related assignment or changing an old one. Reference questions have increased, but, in general, questions are better developed by the time a student comes to us. All of these indicate to us the success of our liaison program.

An unexpected benefit of the liaison program is seeing faculty/librarian relationships develop beyond BI or collection development. Information technology enabled us to get our foot in the faculty door, and we now play a significant role in the academic experience at Messiah College. This past year both of us participated with faculty in our liaison departments in presenting workshops at an all-college Colleague's Conference, a one-day conference which all faculty and staff attended.

Building on successful interactions with our liaison departments, we initiated contact with the General Education Review Committee which has now incorporated into its proposal for revision our goals and philosophy of course-integrated BI across the curriculum. The committee further strengthened our statement by adding that the library faculty "will be able to propose in which components of the curriculum--both in General Education and the academic majors--the specific [BI] program components should be established." (Messiah College General Education Review Committee, 1991)

Two faculty members asked us to join them in applying for a teaching grant in which we will further define learning outcomes and develop assessment mechanisms in two classes which have incorporated process research student projects. In the grant application, liaison librarians were identified as the means by which what we learn will be communicated to the college community. (The grant was received.)

We find ourselves in the interesting position of facilitating conversation between disciplines. Evan Farber, in his address at this conference, noted that faculty seldom talk to each other about the teaching methods they use. As liaison librarians we talk to each other and to faculty about ongoing assignments. Informal conversations with librarians and faculty often evolve into interdisplinary discussions of teaching methodology. The teaching grant and Colleague's Conference workshops described above each involved faculty members from more than one discipline. Without our liaison program, it is doubtful that we would have made so many advances with incorporating course-integrated BI into the curriculum or that we would have participated in so many professional activities with the faculty.

But every good program has its problems. The main drawback of the liaison system with an active BI program is an increased workload for the entire library staff. Helen Welch Tuttle, in an ALA debate in 1968, opposed the idea of departmental liaisons by saying that such librarians would "have to be at least quintuplets!" (Tuttle, 1969) We address this problem in the following ways:

1. Make a continuous effort to develop support staff to assume more day to day responsibilities.

2. Use each other's expertise:

   a) Media librarian's media application expertise

   b) Liaison librarians subject specialities

   c) Bibliographic instruction coordinator's teaching expertise and resource files

   d) Brainstorming/sharing sessions in which we discuss successes, failures, and possible improvements.

3. Prioritize the tasks to be done--identify which tasks can temporarily be put aside, or delegated to support staff, and which ones can not.

4. Membership in LOEX allows us to pick the brains of our fellow BI librarians across the country.

Instructive session 6 (Mark and Lee) cont.: part 1 - Presentation (continued)

If a library liaison program results in so much extra work, why do we continue with it? We believe that course-integrated bibliographic instruction is essential to the learning process of college students and that it can **only** occur with the cooperation of librarians **and** faculty. For us, the information needs of both faculty and students are most successfully met through an active liaison program.

References

Messiah College General Education Review Committee. (1991) The Messiah College general education curriculum. Grantham, PA: Messiah College.

Messick, F. M. (1977). Subject specialists in smaller academic libraries. Library Resources and Technical Services, 21, 368-374.

Tuttle, H. W. (1969). An Acquisitionist looks at Mr. Haro's bibliographer. Library Resources and Technical Services, 13, 170-174.

Instructive session 6 (Mark and Lee) cont.: part 1 - Presentation (continued)

BIOLOGICAL BASIS OF BEHAVIOR
LIBRARY RESEARCH PROJECT

Messiah College
Spring 1991
S. Nisly
S. Lee

Schedule for Project

Jan. 31	Part 1 due
Feb. 7	Part 2 due
Feb. 14	Part 3 due
Feb. 26	Part 4 due
Mar. 7	Part 5 due
Mar. 19	Part 6 due
Apr. 23	Part 7 due

NOTE: Be sure to plan ahead for this part of the Project. Inter-library loan requests may take several (even up to 3) weeks to process and receive.

Part 1

Look through Kalat (1988)* until you find an issue about which you would like to know more and on which you would like to write a research paper. (You will not actually be writing the research paper, but will do all of the preliminary steps which lead to writing a paper.) Once you have found an issue/question/topic you think you would like to explore, do the following.

I. Take notes on what Kalat has to say about your topic.

II. Now attempt to write out what question you want to ask.

SN approval to go to next part_____

REFERENCE:

Kalat, J. W. (1988). Biological psychology (3rd ed.). Belmont, Ca: Wadsworth.

Instructive session 6 (Mark and Lee) cont.: part 2 - Library Research Project

Part 2

I. What is the question you are asking at this point?

II. Using available handbooks, encyclopedias, other texts, and dictionaries, find out all you can about your question. Make detailed notes about what you learned from each source. (In some cases, you may learn nothing new. If so, say so.) Cite your sources, indicate the key word you used to access the material, and then write out in detail what you learned.

III. What question are you now asking?

IV. Are you satisfied with your question? If no, go back and do whatever part of the process you need to in order to come out with a satisfactory question.

NOTE: Hand in Part 1 again with Part 2. Please place the project in a large envelope with your name on the outside.

SN approval to go on to the
next part_____

Part 3

I. What research question are you now asking?

II. Write out a search strategy which you will use to access your question on PsycLit.

 A. Break down your research question into concepts. (Depending on your question, you may have approximately 3 concepts. A good search should have a minimum of 2 concepts.)

 Concept 1 _____(AND) Concept 2 _____ (AND)

 Concept 3 _____

Instructive session 6 (Mark and Lee) cont.: part 2 - Library Research Project (continued)

B. Consulting the PsycLIT thesaurus, locate possible subject terms. If you do not find appropriate term(s) in the thesaurus, indicate other key words, using root word(s), synonym(s), etc.

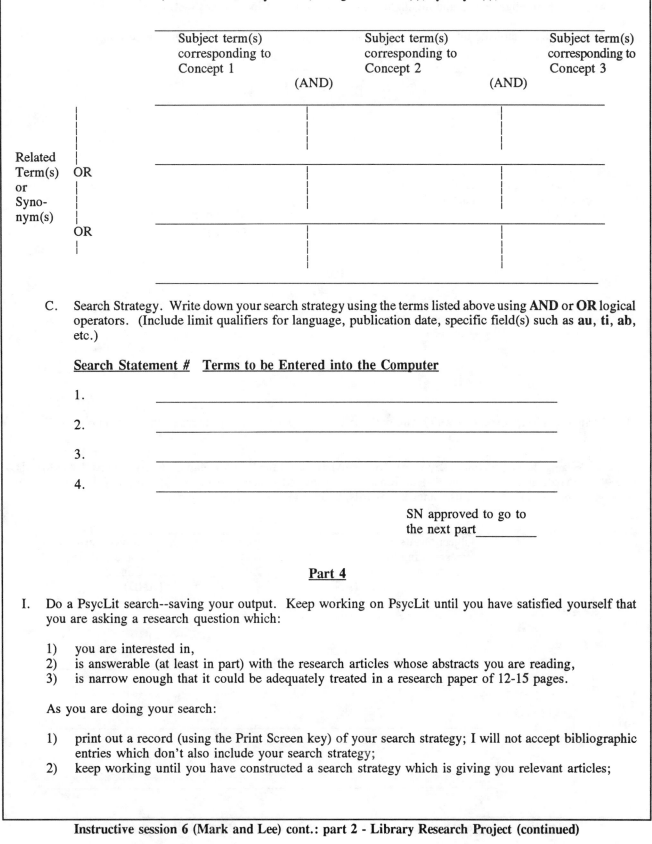

	Subject term(s) corresponding to Concept 1	(AND)	Subject term(s) corresponding to Concept 2	(AND)	Subject term(s) corresponding to Concept 3
Related Term(s) or Synonym(s)	OR				
	OR				

C. Search Strategy. Write down your search strategy using the terms listed above using **AND** or **OR** logical operators. (Include limit qualifiers for language, publication date, specific field(s) such as **au**, **ti**, **ab**, etc.)

Search Statement #   **Terms to be Entered into the Computer**

1. _____

2. _____

3. _____

4. _____

SN approved to go to
the next part_____

Part 4

I. Do a PsycLit search--saving your output. Keep working on PsycLit until you have satisfied yourself that you are asking a research question which:

1) you are interested in,
2) is answerable (at least in part) with the research articles whose abstracts you are reading,
3) is narrow enough that it could be adequately treated in a research paper of 12-15 pages.

As you are doing your search:

1) print out a record (using the Print Screen key) of your search strategy; I will not accept bibliographic entries which don't also include your search strategy;
2) keep working until you have constructed a search strategy which is giving you relevant articles;

Instructive session 6 (Mark and Lee) cont.: part 2 - Library Research Project (continued)

3) when you have combined subject terms/key words which are giving you the desired articles, print out the relevant entries (include citation, abstracts, key phrases, and descriptors);

4) use a highlighter pen and highlight what seems relevant in each abstract.

II. After having completed this search to your satisfaction, what question are you now asking?

NOTE: Please turn in the earlier parts of your project with Part 4--all in a large envelope.

SN approval to go on to next part_____

Part 5

I. What research question are you now asking?

II. Write out a search strategy which you will use to access sources for your research question on Medline or Biosis.

A. Using the same subject/key word terms you have used for PsycLit search in part 4, consult the MESH (Medical Subject Headings) or Biosis thesaurus and locate possible subject terms. If you find no appropriate term(s), use other key words, using root word(s), synonym(s), etc.

		Subject term(s) corresponding to Concept 1	Subject term(s) corresponding to Concept 2 (AND)	Subject term(s) corresponding to Concept 3 (AND)
Related Term(s) or Synonym(s)	OR			
	OR			

Instructive session 6 (Mark and Lee) cont.: part 2 - Library Research Project (continued)

B.   Search Strategy. Write down your search strategy using the terms listed above using **AND** or **OR** logical operators.   (Include limit qualifiers for language, publication date, age groups, etc.)

<u>Search Statement #</u>   <u>Terms to be Entered into the Computer</u>

1.   _____

2.   _____

3.   _____

4.   _____

Soo Lee approved to go to
the next part_____

Part 6

I.   Work with Soo Lee to do your Medline or Biosis online search. Repeat the same steps you did on PsycLIT and turn in the same output.

II.   What question are you now asking?

NOTE: Please turn in the earlier parts
of your project with Part 6--all
in a large envelope.

SN approval to go on to
next part_____

Instructive session 6 (Mark and Lee) cont.: part 2 - Library Research Project (continued)

Part 7

The final part of this project requires that you access a number of articles for which you now have abstracts. You will select the articles based on the information you have from the abstracts which seem most relevant to your research question. Once you have selected the articles, you will then need to read them and determine whether or not they are in fact relevant to your question. Use a highlighter and highlight which segments are relevant for your specific question. **CAUTION:** As you are reading each article and highlighting relevant portions, ask yourself: Am I reading and using this information in the context in which it was written?

You will need a minimum of 7 articles of which at least one must be located from each of the following sources: PsycLIT; Medline and; Bibliography from other articles.

Two of the articles you turn in may be irrelevant. Almost inevitably, in doing research, one accesses material which, when given the limited information of an abstract appear relevant, but a reading of the article itself reveals no relevance. If you access such articles, two of the seven articles you turn in may be such articles.

At the top of each article indicate:

1) whether or not the article is relevant;
2) how you located it [PsycLIT, Medline, Biosis or bibliography (include copy of bibliographic entry and cite source)];
3) how you accessed the article (ILL, other library, or Messiah library).

The following page is a copy of the form which will be used to evaluate the final project.

NOTE: Please turn in all the earlier parts of your project along with Part 7 in a large envelope.

Instructive session 6 (Mark and Lee) cont.: part 2 - Library Research Project (continued)

Grading Sheet
Research Project
PSY 250

   I.   Successful completion of Parts I-VII (90 points)   _____

  II.   Number of articles (2 points each)   _____ x 2 = _____

III.   Sources (4 points each)

      A.   PsycLit   _____

      B.   Medline/Biosis   _____

      C.   Bibliography   _____

           Subtotal   _____

  IV.   Appropriateness of evaluation
       (5 points each)

      A.   Article 1   _____

      B.   Article 2   _____

      C.   Article 3   _____

      D.   Article 4   _____

      E.   Article 5   _____

      F.   Article 6   _____

      G.   Article 7   _____

           Subtotal   _____

Total (151 possible)   _____

PERCENTAGE   _____

Instructive session 6 (Mark and Lee) cont: part 2 - Library Research Project (continued)

MESSIAH COLLEGE
LIBRARY LIAISON PROGRAM

A. Objectives of the Liaison Program:

1. Provide academic departments and administrative units with personal library contacts.

2. Assess and meet each department's needs for:

   - LRC* materials
   - funding
   - information services

3. Expedite and/or enhance communication between teaching faculty and the LRC.

B. Services Offered by Liaisons:

1. Assist with collection development in assigned department(s):

   - budget allocation and interpretation
   - selection assistance
   - weeding

2. Provide specialized reference services to faculty and   their student research assistants:

   - database searching
   - non-routine, indepth subject-related reference questions

3. Provide course-related or course integrated library instruction for departmental students and orientation for new faculty:

   - compile subject bibliographies and subject-related user guides
   - course-centered bibliographic instruction in class
   - LRC tours
   - orientation of new faculty
   - library instruction for faculty
   - upon request, consult with faculty about LRC-related class assignments; advise faculty when assignments are problematic

4. Communicate and interpret new library resources and services:

   - watch for materials and news of interest to faculty
   - maintain regular contact with department chair and faculty members
   - encourage reporting of problems, needs, etc.

5. Assist with collection organization and management:

   - cataloging consultation for subject heading and classification assignment
   - preservation of materials

*The library is part of the Learning Resources Center (LRC).

Murray Learning Resources Center
Messiah College
Grantham, PA 17027

Instructive session 6 (Mark and Lee) cont.: part 2 - Library Liaison Program

Suggested Readings*

Baker, B. (1989). Bibliographic instruction: Building the librarian/faculty partnership. In M. Pastine and B. Katz (eds.), *Integrating library use skills into the general education curriculum* (pp. 311-328). New York: Haworth Press.

Bechtel, J. (1981). Collegial management breeds success. *American Libraries, 12*, 605-607.

Carlson, D. & Miller, R. H. (1984). Librarians and teaching faculty: Partners in bibliographic instruction. *College & Research Libraries, 45*, 483-491.

Commerton, B. A. (1986). Building faculty/librarian relationships. *Bookmark, 44*, 17-20.

Gration, S. U. & Young, A. P. (1974). Reference-bibliographers in the college library. *College and Research Libraries, 35*, 28-34.

Gwinn, N. E. (1978). The Faculty-library connection. *Change, 10* (8), 19-21.

Haro, R. P. (1969). The Bibliographer in the academic library. *Library Resources & Technical Services, 13*, 163-169.

Hay, F. J. (1990). The Subject specialist in the academic library: A review article. *Journal of Academic Librarianship, 16*, 11-17.

Messick, F. M. (1977). Subject specialists in smaller academic libraries. *Library Resources & Technical Services, 31*, 368-374.

Michalak, T. J. (1976). Library services to the graduate community: The role of the subject specialist. *College and Research Libraries, 37*, 257-265.

Miller, L. (1977). Liaison work in the academic library. *RQ, 16*, 213-215.

Moran, B. B. (1990). Library/classroom partnerships for the 1990s. *College & Research Libraries News, 51*, 511-514.

Schloman, B. F., Lilly, R. S. & Hu, W. (1989). Targeting liaison activities: Use of a faculty survey in an academic research library. *RQ, 28*, 496-505.

Simon, R. A. (1984). The Faculty/librarian partnership. In Kirk, T. G. (Ed.), *Increasing the teaching role of academic libraries* (pp. 55-61). San Francisco: Jossey-Bass.

*Some references do not specifically refer to liaison programs, but contain applicable ideas.

Instructive session 6 (Mark and Lee) cont.: part 3 - Library Liaison Program (continued)

Computer Assisted Instruction: Teaching
Information Retrieval Skills Using Authorware Professional Software

Fern Russell, Faye Maxwell, Patricia Rempel, Evelyn Housch
Dr. Craig Montgomerie, Dr. Michael Szabo
Douglas Johnson, Arnold Krause, Evans Forsyth

University of Alberta

Instructive session 7 (Russell, Maxwell): part 1 - Presentation

Introduction

The Online Access to Information (OLAI) project developed at the University of Alberta uses microcomputers to teach students how to access computer-based information systems. The project is presently a joint librarian/faculty venture based on work initiated by the Department of Educational Administration. The OLAI project consists of nine modules which are accessible from a main menu (see Figure 1)

Module 1: Communicating via computers - teaches users how to connect their microcomputers to the University's mainframe computers.

Module 2: User directory - explains electronic mail and allows students to "register" in the electronic mail system.

Module 3: Message system - teaches students to use electronic mail.

Module 4: Accessing information - provides students with an overview of conventional and online information sources.

Module 5: Online catalogue - teaches students to use the Library's online catalogue.

Module 6: Advanced searching - provides an overview of the process of writing a research paper using an information literacy model.

Module 7: Online indices - teaches students to search ERIC on SPIRES.

Module 8: Online resources - teaches students to use CDROM products.

Module 9: Opinion survey - gathers data about students' opinions on CAI.

All the modules are not complete. They may be at any one of the following developmental stages:

1. The script is written by the content expert.

2. The script is coded by the programmer, using Authorware Professional as the authoring platform and following the project style guidelines.

3. The module is evaluated by the content experts and revised accordingly.

4. The module is used with a sample of students, and revisions are made, based on student responses. This step may be repeated several times.

5. Modules are considered complete when samples of users can learn from the modules on an independent basis.

Project Background

In 1989 the librarians of the Information and Reserve Centre began exploring computer-based instruction as a possible tool for library instruction, and started searching for suitable software. Storyboard was selected to develop several instructional applications. However, it was strictly a Library application, which required extensive planning, development, and training time. Informal discussions with various people about their experience with computer-assisted instruction revealed pockets of expertise on campus. It seemed logical to build from work already done rather than starting from scratch.

One pocket of expertise existed in the Education Library where one of the Education librarians was completing work on a Masters of Education degree in the Department of Adult, Career and Technology Education. As part of her course work, she was using Authorware Professional software to develop a simulation of an online catalogue search.

Also of great interest was the pioneering work underway in the Department of Educational Administration. The Department had established a project team to develop a series of computer-based lessons for its off-campus clientele; students using the lessons would learn how to use a personal computer and modem to access the information resources of the University of Alberta Library. The librarians quickly saw the potential benefit of joining the team. Both parties were interested in using computer- assisted instruction to teach information retrieval skills, albeit to slightly different

Instructive session 7 (Russell, Maxwell): part 1 - Presentation (continued)

audiences. The knowledge and skills possessed were different but complementary. The Department of Educational Administration realized it could profit from the librarians knowledge of library-based systems, and the skills they had developed in teaching end-users; the librarians in turn were grateful to have access to the knowledge and skills of the project members, including: programming, project management and CAI development skills and prior experience.

Thus began Library participation in project OLAI. It grew out of the conviction that a tremendous window of opportunity existed, and all we needed was the courage to jump through.

Developing a Proposal

Having determined that a joint venture was feasible, it became necessary to convince Library Administration to commit resources to the project. Since library involvement in the project was initiated as a grass roots effort rather than being mandated from the top down, it was necessary to win support and secure release time for the librarians involved. Fortunately, the proposal fell on receptive ears. Library Administration supported the project, even though the staffing component at the Library is barely adequate. The proposal suggested that:

1. Monies from a vacant half position would be used to second a librarian from 50% of her responsibililites in the Education Library to work on the OLAI project.

2. The librarians from the Information and Reserve Centre would be released from much of the yearly instructional burden by offering, unrevised, the bibliographic instruction program that had been offered the year before, and by hiring students to teach many of the classes.

3. No financial contribution was requested over and above the commitment of staff time. The Authorware Professional software had already been purchased through a special new initiatives fund.

Benefits of a Joint Venture Approach

The most obvious benefit of a joint venture is the pooling of expertise and skills of team members. The librarians joined an established group of individuals with specific skills. Programmers, instructional designers, content experts, and graphic artists all report to a project manager in the creation of the project. Individuals are assigned to work on specific tasks within a given time frame, capitalizing on the strengths each possesses.

In the case of project OLAI, a joint venture enabled the Library to benefit from the work done by Dr. Craig Montgomerie, who had developed the concept of the project and had developmental work on the modules. The Department of Educational Administration must also be given credit for its foresight in providing $12,000.00 for programming services along with $5,000.00 for the services of a graphic artist in a time of financial constraint.

Another benefit of interdepartmental cooperation is funding. For example, the University of Alberta provides funding for research through a Central Research Fund. High priority for this fund is attached to interdisciplinary/interfaculty collaborative research proposals that fall between the defined areas of the research agencies.

Interdepartmental cooperation also is visible in the approach taken to publication. The OLAI group decided that anything to be published would bear the names of all group members - for example, the paper published in the proceedings of this Conference will bear the names of all the participants. Needless to say, the scope of possible publication sources widens when a cooperative approach is used.

Problems with a Joint Venture Approach

Since none of the OLAI participants devote full time to the project, developmental work may proceed a a slow pace. The proposal to Library Administration set forth plans whereby library members would be able to devote approximately 50% of their time to the project, but this level of commitment was not always possible. The Education librarian was able to meet the project guidelines, since her secondment allowed her to work in a quiet area removed from her regular office. Other participants contributed

---

Instructive session 7 (Russell, Maxwell): part 1 - Presentation (continued)

somewhat less time, given the ongoing demands in their regular positions and the fact that they were readily available for consultation and phone calls in their offices.

Regular communication, which is essential in any cooperative project, can be problematic. A joint venture approach can be time-consuming, considering the amount of time required formeetings and communication among group members.

Finally, each of the stakeholders in the project has a different audience. Some of the modules developed, such as the online catalogue simulation, can be used by all parties, while other modules have a limited application. For example, the module that teaches students how to connect their microcomputers to the online catalogue cannot be offered indiscriminately as dial in access to the online catalogue is not generally available to undergraduate students. It may not be possible to meet the needs of all stakeholder groups without some modification of modules.

Authorware Professional as an Authoring Platform

Authorware Inc. released Authorware Professional for the Macintosh in 1989. It was upgraded from Authorware's Best Course of Action, an icon-based authoring tool for multimedia tutorials. The new version was chosen as the MacUser editors' choice for best best multimedia software in 1990. Authorware Professional for windows, which permits development on an IBM platform, has been announced.

For published reviews of Authorware Professional, see Littman (1990) and Mlastkowskl (1990). Some strengths are:

1. Authorware Professional is easy to use for content experts who lack a programming background. Icons located at the left of the screen representing various options are dragged into the flow line of the course (see Figure 2). As the course is being developed, it is easy to modify.

2. Powerful expansion capabilities unfold as the author acquires further levels of expertise.

3. Multimedia courseware can be developed to include graphics, animation, interaction, and simulation, along with audio, videodisc and CD-ROM control.

4. Courseware developed on the Macintosh can be transported for use on IBM computers.

There are, however, some limitations:

1. Authorware is expensive. It lists for $8000.00, but an educational professional can buy it for $995.00.

2. There are some portability problems in converting some modules to IBM format, particularly where the program is large, and where there are a number of overlapping graphics. (The transport application on the Macintosh will be replaced by Authorware Professional for Windows.)

3. Although content experts without programming experience can easily get started with Authorware Professional and prepare some basic courseware, they should be prepared to learn some programming skills including the use of functions and variables.

4. Authorware Professional gives content experts such power that they can be lulled into thinking that they can "do it all by themselves". There is a risk that people will get involved in developing lessons without the support that we have had, such as the contribution of content experts, instructional designers, project managers, programmers and graphic artists in the creation of the final project.

Where to next?

The librarians have decided to shift focus in the upcoming year from development to implementation. We plan to deliver the modules (either whole or in part) to the students in our institution even though all the modules are not complete. In the coming year we need to:

1. Develop clear, achievable goals and gain the support of Library management. The Library, along with the rest of the University of Alberta, is experiencing very tight finances; the climate that results is one of "doing more with less". The onus will clearly be on the members of the OLAI team to make a

Instructive session 7 (Russell, Maxwell): part 1 - Presentation (continued)

good case for the continuation of the project.

    2.   Incorporate the completed modules into BI programs which are already well established.

    3.   Maintain a high project visibility via conferences, presentations and publications. On the home front, we must ensure that the modules are easily accessible, train other librarians in the use of the modules, and ecourage them to introduce the lessons to our users.

Requisites to success in CAI

Requisites to success in computer-assisted instruction were outlined by Dr. Eugene Romaniuk in a March, 1990 lecture at the University of Alberta:

    1.   Establish clear goals for the project.

    2.   Communicate regularly with all involved parties.

    3.   Ensure adequate support is available. This includes financial support as well as the support of team members and other experts.

    4.   Train the staff who will have to implement the project.

    5.   Involve all areas of the institution.

    6.   Ensure that you have facilitators on the team who provide support and encouragement and keep the project moving.

Of these factors, it is interesting to note that human issues are emphasized rather than hardware, software or other technical requirements. Our experience has shown this to be true - hence the decision to overlap implementation with development.

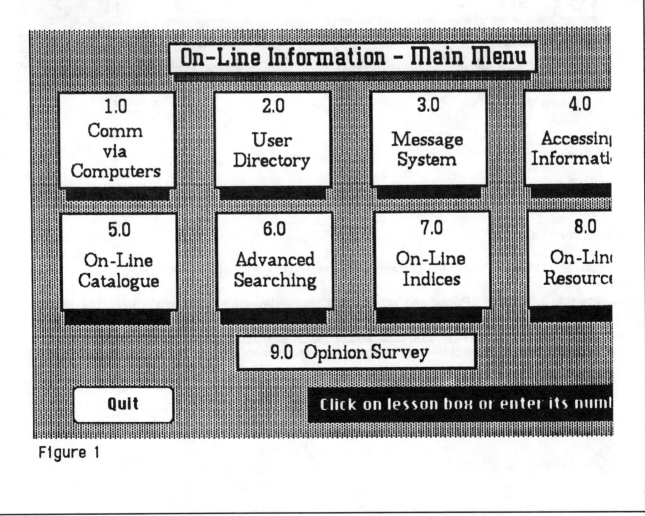

Figure 1

Instructive session 7 (Russell, Maxwell): part 1 - Presentation (continued)

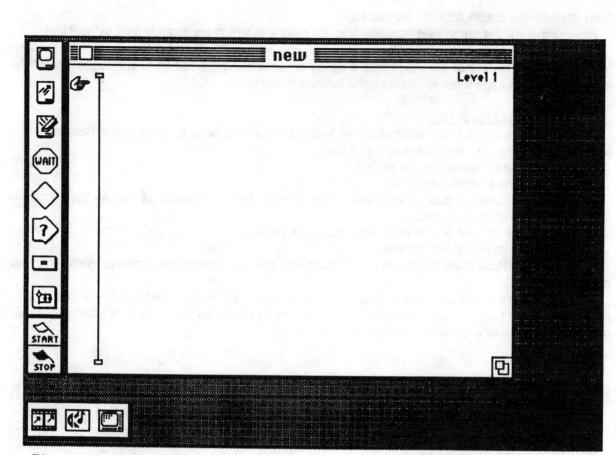

Figure 2

References

Littman, D. (1990). Putting the professor on disk. Macworld, 7(3), 107.

Miatkowski, S. (1990). Pricey and elegant multimedia development. Byte, 15(8), 114-115.

Romaniuk, E. (1990, March). Computer-based instruction: difficulties in a university setting. Paper presented for Committee for the Improvement of Teaching and Learning, Edmonton Alberta.

PART-TIME FACULTY AND THE LIBRARY

Working closely with faculty is the key to a successful user education program. Part-time faculty experience feelings of isolation and lack of connection with the institution, have no regular or consistent natural channels of communication, possess inadequate knowledge about available support services for themselves and their students, need to develop and improve teaching skills. Because between twenty and thirty percent of all faculty in higher education are employed in part-time positions, it is important for instruction librarians to understand the characteristics and needs of part-time faculty and to design outreach programs for them.

The Schaffner Library of Northwestern University works with a large group of part-time faculty who comprise the faculty of University College, the University's program for part-time adult students. They include ABD graduate students, full-time faculty from Northwestern and other institutions, and persons employed in nonacademic positions. Working closely with these faculty to meet their needs to improve teaching skills, to update their own knowledge of information technology, and locate information for their own research needs is a major component of the Schaffner Library's program of services for adult students. Librarians provide orientation for new faculty, participate actively in University College's extensive faculty development program, offer periodic information technology updates, and consult with individual faculty concerning both library assignments and their own research needs. This active outreach to faculty has resulted in a significant increase in the number of library-related assignments and thus in increased library use by University College students.

Instructive session 8 (Steffen): part 1 - Abstract

ACADEMIC LIBRARY OUTREACH TO SPECIAL STUDENT POPULATIONS

19th NATIONAL LOEX CONFERENCE - 1991

PRESENTED BY: Elaine Gawrych

OUTLINE

I. Overview

    A. Background information on Northeastern Illinois
       University.

        1.Special student services - Northeastern
            a.Proyecto Palante
            b.Project Success
            c.New Directions

II. Library instruction programs available for special
    student groups

        1.Programs offered
            a.Proyecto Palante, Project Success
            b.New Directions - Library Survival Seminars.

        2.Programs being developed
            a. Advanced Library Survival Seminars: The
               Electronic Library and Beyond

III. Establishing library programs for special student
     groups.

        1.Identify special campus programs
        2.Establish type, content and number of seminars.
        3.Promote seminars
        4.Evaluate seminars
        5.Revise
        6.Expand

Instructive session 9 (Gawrych): part 1 - Presentation Outline

PROPOSAL

19TH NATIONAL LOEX LIBRARY INSTRUCTION CONFERENCE
MAY 10-11, 1991

ACADEMIC LIBRARY OUTREACH TO SPECIAL STUDENT POPULATIONS

Submitted by:
Elaine Gawrych
Bibliographic Instruction Librarian
Northeastern Illinois University
Ronald Williams Library
Chicago, Illinois

Northeastern is a state supported, commuter institution of approximately ten thousand students. The student population is culturally diverse and includes students who are the first in their family to attend college, and adult reentry students.

The Library Instruction Program, in addition to the regular bibliographic instruction program, has developed general library tours and classes which focus on the needs of these special student groups.

This program has evolved over several years. The program includes outreach to faculty and staff who administer these special programs. This includes Proyecto Palante and Project Success, which provide support for minority students, Women's Services which provides support for adult reentry students and Veteran's Student Affairs, which supports students who are veterans of the armed forces.

General library tours are scheduled for students enrolled in these programs and "Library Survival" classes are also offered each term both during the day and in the evening. The focus of these classes is how to survive in the "New Electronic Library".

The half hour instructional session I am proposing, would discuss in greater detail outreach to faculty and promotion of this program, and information on the four part "Library Survival" classes which are taught each term. A selective guide to resources and handouts given to students who attend these tours and classes will be available.

Equipment required would be an overhead projector and the usual lectern and microphone.

Instructive session 9 (Gawrych) cont.: part 2 - Proposal

ACADEMIC LIBRARY OUTREACH TO SPECIAL STUDENT POPULATIONS
NINETEENTH NATIONAL LOEX CONFERENCE - 1991
Presented by: Elaine Gawrych
Bibliographic Instruction Librarian
Northeastern Illinois University
Ronald Williams Library
Chicago, Illinois

The emphasis of this paper is to present information on library instruction programs offered at Northeastern for special student groups and to provide suggestions on how to establish an instruction program which meets the needs of these students.

Special student groups may include foreign students, adult reentry students, and students who may need academic support services. The groups that I will be focusing on are the adult reentry students and students who need support services such as remediation in English, mathematics and reading.

Northeastern Illinois University is a state-supported commuter institution located in Chicago. Enrollment is approximately ten thousand students. Northeastern began as a teacher's college and has since expanded to offer bachelor's and master's degrees in many areas including business, counseling, education, and computer science.

The 1990-91 Annual Report and Profile of Admissions and Records indicated that 35% of the students enrolling for the 1990-91 academic year were over twenty-six years old. Many of these are first generation college students who work and attend college full time.

It is because of the large percentage of adult students as well as students who may have had limited experience in library and research skills that I established library instruction programs to meet the needs of these individuals. This program is offered in addition to the regular Bibliographic Instruction program.

There are three special programs at Northeastern: Project Success, Proyecto Palante and New Directions.

Project Success recruits and provides assistance to inner-city students who have academic potential but lack the necessary skills to meet standard admission requirements. Proyecto Palante is a support program which focuses on Hispanic students. Both of these programs offer campus orientations, counseling, and tutorial services.

New Directions: Program for Adults, is sponsored by Women's Services and helps both male and female students who are either beginning or reentering college. New Directions offers campus orientation sessions, workshops and support groups.

The Bibliographic Instruction program has established a liaison with each of these programs and works directly with program staff to provide library orientations and instruction.

These orientations may have from twenty to sixty students. We try to have a ratio of one librarian for each group of fifteen students. This may mean recruiting librarians from other departments. The focus of these tours is to give the students a general introduction to the library, introduce and emphasize the availability of public services staff, and identify and stress the importance of learning about library computer systems.

Tutorial services, mathematics, reading, and computer labs are all housed on the fourth floor of the library. Included in the tour is an introduction to these services, and whenever possible the coordinators of these labs meet briefly with the students to introduce their programs.

Many of these students are enrolled in developmental English classes. In conjunction with these classes, additional instruction in using the library is provided. Instruction librarians discuss library research assignments with the instructors of these classes. Students are introduced to Illinet Online, the online catalog, and general research skills.

As I stated earlier, 35% of the students entering Northeastern during 1990-91, were adults aged twenty-six or older. The Library Survival Seminars were established to meet the needs of these students.

I first became aware of the needs of these adult students while a graduate student intern in Reference at the University of Illinois - Chicago Main Library, during the mid 1980's. At that time, UIC had three public access computer systems; Illinet Online, OCLC and LUIS/NOTIS.

The returning adult students would come up to the reference desk with panic in their eyes asking what happened to the library they once knew. Where was the card catalog? Many of these students were returning for graduate study. Programs to introduce these students to the library were not available at UIC, which often meant one on one instruction.

After completing my internship at UIC, I accepted a position at Northeastern as a Bibliographic Instruction Librarian.

One of the programs I developed is the Library Survival Seminars for adult students.

Instructive session 9 (Gawrych) cont.: part 3 - Presentation

These seminars have evolved during the past four years. Changes have been implemented based on student feedback. The seminars cover the following:

Seminar One - Tour and General Introduction to the Library

Seminar Two - Library Computer Systems: Illinet Online, ERIC, PsychLit, InfoTrac.

Seminar Three - Research process: overview of library research, developing a bibliography, locating materials.

Seminar Four - Ask the Librarian: addressing specific questions students have.

Seminars are scheduled approximately three weeks after the beginning of the term and are offered both during the day and evening.

The general focus of each seminar has been established. However, I ask each student if they are working on a research project or are interested in locating information on a particular topic. I will then focus on these topics when teaching the seminar.

The concept of the "Electronic Library" is stressed in all these seminars. I explain to students that libraries are no longer bound by four walls. Technology connects libraries to each other and allows access to a vast world of resources. I stress the importance of overcoming anxiety about computers and learning to use these resources.

I also try to teach students how to identify computer systems (i.e. Silver Platter) so that they may go into any library, identify systems they have used at Northeastern, and not feel so overwhelmed by the technology.

I have presented a general overview of special student programs and library services at Northeastern. Suggestions on how to establish a similar program in an academic library are listed below:

1. Identify special programs and student groups on campus that might benefit from specialized library instruction.

2. Contact faculty and staff who are involved in these programs. Discuss the availability of library instruction and the implications of library technology.

3. Establish number of seminars to be offered and what is to be taught in each. I have found that one seminar is not sufficient.

4. Promote the seminars. Flyers, letters to faculty, and assistance from the special programs staff are all ways to promote.

5. Evaluate - ask students to evaluate the seminars and to indicate what they would like to learn. A sample evaluation form is provided.

6. Revise - review student evaluations and feedback and revise seminars as needed.

Based on ongoing feedback from students who have participated in these seminars, Advanced Library Survival Seminars: The Electronic Library and Beyond, may be offered during the next academic year. Many students have expressed an interest in learning about online systems like Prodigy, CompuServe, BRS Afterdark and how to access the online catalog from their home or office. Many of these students own microcomputers and modems or are planning to purchase them.

I would also like to incorporate a greater emphasis on critical evaluation of all resources in future seminars.

These classes take time to plan and teach, since I wear many hats at Northeastern, time is often something I feel I don't have enough of.

However, I have found it very rewarding to teach these students. They are bright, motivated and have many diverse interests. They also come back to share their success in using the library.

Instructive session 9 (Gawrych) cont.: part 3 - Presentation (continued)

— ELAINE GAWRYCH —

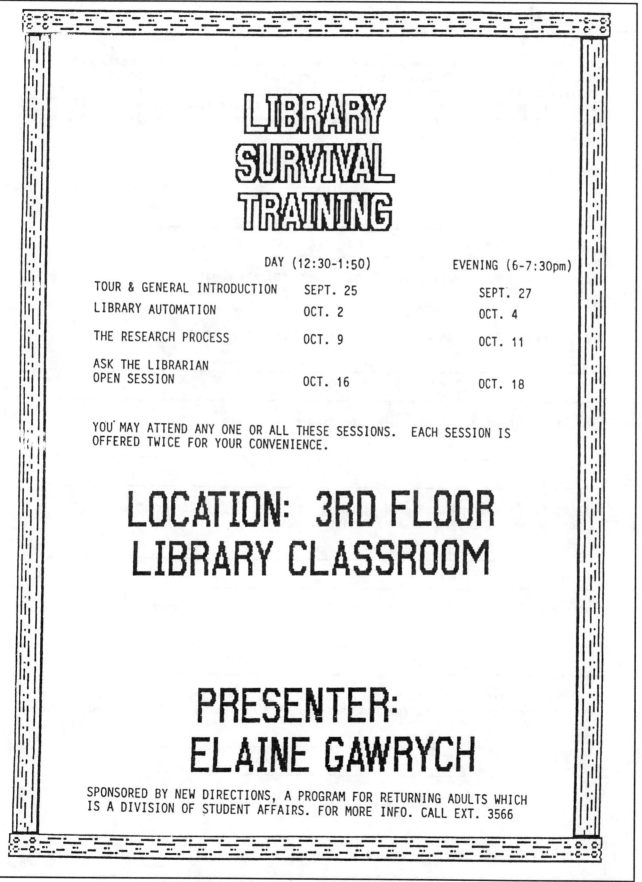

LIBRARY SURVIVAL TRAINING

	DAY (12:30-1:50)	EVENING (6-7:30pm)
TOUR & GENERAL INTRODUCTION	SEPT. 25	SEPT. 27
LIBRARY AUTOMATION	OCT. 2	OCT. 4
THE RESEARCH PROCESS	OCT. 9	OCT. 11
ASK THE LIBRARIAN OPEN SESSION	OCT. 16	OCT. 18

YOU MAY ATTEND ANY ONE OR ALL THESE SESSIONS. EACH SESSION IS OFFERED TWICE FOR YOUR CONVENIENCE.

LOCATION: 3RD FLOOR LIBRARY CLASSROOM

PRESENTER: ELAINE GAWRYCH

SPONSORED BY NEW DIRECTIONS, A PROGRAM FOR RETURNING ADULTS WHICH IS A DIVISION OF STUDENT AFFAIRS. FOR MORE INFO. CALL EXT. 3566

Instructive session 9 (Gawrych) cont.: part 4 - Flyer

NEW DIRECTIONS: A Program For Returning Adults
EVALUATION OF   PROGRAMS

Evaluations of programs offered by NEW DIRECTIONS are important as a basis for
planning the content and format of future programs. Your cooperation in
completing this brief form is greatly appreciated. If you wish to respond more
fully, please use the back of this sheet. Return this evaluation to a NEW DIRECTIONS
staff member before you leave the program or return it to the NEW DIRECTIONS Office
(D-213). Thank you very much.

- -

EVALUATION

Name of Program: _____

Date: ___ __ . _____

What is your overall rating of this program? (Circle one)

    Excellent   Good   Fair   Poor

What content/information did you find most potentially helpful?

_____

_____

What, if anything, might have been modified or omitted?

_____

_____

Was the format appropriate? (Circle one)   Yes   No
If not, could you suggest an alternative format?

_____

_____

What types of programs should NEW DIRECTIONS offer in the future?

_____

_____

If you would like to be placed on the NEW DIRECTIONS mailing list, please provide
your name, address, and year/period that you started (Fall, Winter, Spring, Summer).

NAME _____

ADDRESS _____

CITY, STATE, ZIP _____

PLEASE CIRCLE   FALL   WINTER   SPRING   SUMMER   19____

Instructive session 9 (Gawrych) cont.: part 5 - Evaluation Form

— ELAINE GAWRYCH —

New Directions

RETURNING ADULT STUDENTS WE NEED YOU !

The New Directions Program was originally designed to assist men and women returning to college. You may ask, "Who is the returning adult student?" The returning adult student can be male or female. They may be married, widowed, legally separated, divorced, or never married. They may or may not have children, a household and a job to juggle, along with their additional responsibilities of school. They are at least twenty-five years of age. Do any of these criteria sound familiar? Does any of this possibly describe you?

You may also ask, "Why is there a returning adult program?" Studies have shown that there are more adults returning to academia than ever. Adult students comprised 28 percent of the nationwide student body in 1970. This same age group increased to 37 percent by 1980, and according to the most recent 1989 statistics, adult students account for 42 percent of the student body enrolled in courses for credit. Here at Northeastern, returning adults make up approximately one half of the student body.

Since there has been such an increase in the number of returning adult students, we feel it is necessary to re-assess our goals, so that our goals will more directly reflect your needs. In essence, the New Directions staff is looking for a new direction! We feel that you have a wealth of knowledge to contribute, as well as problems and concerns that need to be addressed. We want the program to be for you and about you. For this to be accomplished, we need your help. You, the returning adult student, have the expert knowledge and power. With this student expert knowledge in mind, we are opening the newsletter as a forum for returning adult students.

The Newsletter staff now consists of 75% returning adult students and a New Directions staff member as a consultant. We are inviting you to send us articles, suggestions, tips, and feedback. Please answer the questions we ask you through the newsletter. We feel that you, the returning adult student (RAS), should have the power to impact the goals and directions of a program designed especially for you. Use your voice and the New Direction Staff will be able to better serve you by listening to, reading and publishing what you have to say. We are looking forward to working with you.

Patricia Johnson

Instructive session 9 (Gawrych) cont.: part 6 - New Directions Newsletter

NEW DIRECTIONS GIVES BIRTH

At the beginning of this term New Directions gave birth to its own advisory committee. The committee consists of nine seats. Six are held by faculty and/or staff from departments familiar with the issues and needs of returning adult students. There are two seats for returning adult students; however, these seats have not been filled yet. If you are interested or know someone who is interested please ask them to contact the New Directions Office.

The committee will meet approximately three times per term, dates and times to be announced. The committee will mainly be involved with programming suggestions for the New Directions Office. The committee will be evaluating existing services as well as making recommendations for new ones. All returning adult students are invited to the committee meetings.

IT'S NEVER TOO LATE

Do you ever mean to get around to something for the longest time? Then when you do, you wish that you'd done it a long time ago? Well, that's what happened when I found out about New Directions and all the services they offer.

The New Directions office serves returning adult students (RAS). They are here to help you get in school, and help keep you in school. They provide personal and academic counseling. If they cannot solve a problem you have in their office, they will know just the right person to assist you.

They provide study skills workshops to help you learn or re-learn necessary skills that help you in school. Some of these workshops are about: writing term papers; studying and taking tests; reading and notetaking, resume writing, and library research.

Other helpful workshop topics include: assertiveness training, math anxiety, and time management. They also have workshops to help

---

Instructive session 9 (Gawrych) cont.: part 6 - New Directions Newsletter (continued)

— ELAINE GAWRYCH —

you develop your self-esteem; handle stress; apply for scholarships; and develop leadership qualities.

There's even a Returning Women's Support Group that meets on a weekly basis.

If you haven't declared a major, don't worry. Ask them about a seminar where you'll earn one credit-hour, examine your life experiences, identify your career interests, and tie them into educational opportunities.

They have scholarship information on grants and loans offered around the country and through the university.

Keep up with what's going on, and check out your New Directions bulletin boards. One is located outside room B114. The other is just west of the Center Desk opposite of the bookstore. Or just call the New Directions Office and ask for Jacquie or Cassandra, extension 3567. Let them know what you need, and they will do their best to get it.

Mary Vasquez

Dear Returning Adult Students,

The New Directions staff is please to welcome both returning and newly enrolled adults to the Spring term. We hope you had a relaxing and enjoyable Spring break.

This is a special edition of the Newsletter. This newsletter was designed and published by return-ing adult students. They are dedicated to making this newsletter a voice for all returning adult stu-dents. For that to become a reality, they will need lots of help from you.

We sincerely hope that the information provided in this newsletter will be beneficial to you.
Good Luck,

New Directions Staff

TOWN MEETINGS ?

No, we haven't been transported back to Mayberry or Green Acres. The New Directions Advisory Com-mittee decided that it would be nice to have a group of returning adult students sitting around talking about what it is that they need and want. So the committee scheduled two such meetings in March.

The attendance for these meetings was far below what we expected, but those RAS who did attend were very informative. We were able to get a good idea of what some RAS think. However, we would still like to hear from more of you.

So with that in mind, we are asking that you take some time out of your busy day and answer a few questions for us. This way when we sit down to make recommendations for the fall, we can also present your views. Please answer the following questions and either drop the reply by the New Directions Office or in the mail. We would certainly appreciate hearing from you.

1. Have you participated in any recent campus activities? If yes, what were these activities?

2. What do you see as the biggest problem for returning adult students participating in on-cam-pus events?

3. What kinds of services/activities do you feel should be provided for RAS?

One of the issues talked about at the Town Meet-ing was childcare. If you need child care or are interested in this issue, call:
Cassandra at (312) 583-4050 ext. 3699 and let us hear your voice.

We look forward to hearing from you.

The New Directions Advisory Committee

Instructive session 9 (Gawrych) cont.: part 6 - New Directions Newsletter (continued)

NEW DIRECTIONS

ADULT RE-ENTRY PROGRAM
A DIVISION OF STUDENT AFFAIRS

NORTHEASTERN ILLINOIS UNIVERSITY
5500 N. ST. LOUIS AVENUE
CHICAGO, ILLINOIS 60625

NORTHEASTERN ILLINOIS UNIVERSITY
5500 N. ST. LOUIS AVENUE
CHICAGO, ILLINOIS 60625
(312) 583-4050 EXT. 3566

Want More Information?

Watch for flyers posted on bulletin boards throughout the university announcing the dates and times of our activities. Sign up for the NEW DIRECTIONS newsletter, (published each term), for receipt of information on university programs and upcoming events. Remember, we are here to serve you. If you have questions or just wish to talk, visit or call our office.

LOCATION: Room D-213. Take the elevator to the second floor (M level) above Admissions and Records (Administrative Building).

PHONE: 583-4050, extension 3566.

HOURS: 8:30 - 6:00 p.m. Monday through Wednesday (or later by appointment) and 8:30 - 4:30 p.m. Thursday and Friday.

Northeastern Illinois University subscribes to the principles of equal opportunity and affirmative action and does not discriminate against any individual on the basis of age, color, handicap, national orgin, race, religion, sex or veteran status.

Instructive session 9 (Gawrych) cont.: part 7 - New Directions Brochure

— ELAINE GAWRYCH —

We also confront fears and reservations about returning to college. We allow ample time for your questions. In addition you can request a campus tour from a member of our staff.

A PROGRAM FOR YOU....

NEW DIRECTIONS is designed specially for returning adult students. Our program assists men and women returning to college and eases the transition to the university environment.

The NEW DIRECTIONS Program will help you continue the life-long process of growth and learning. Once you are settled at Northeastern Illinois University you will enjoy and benefit from the educational experience. We can help you get started, ease any difficulties that may occur in the transition, and chart your new path.

HOW THE NEW DIRECTIONS PROGRAM CAN ASSIST YOU

Getting Started

We offer individual counseling to adults planning to return to college. We will assess your individual situation: your work history, your previous academic experience, your career goals, and your family responsibilities. We then refer you to appropriate resources, including Northeastern's adult degree programs.

Once you enroll we offer evening orientation workshops to acquaint you with university academic requirements, policies and procedures. Participants meet representatives of the adult degree programs.

Developing Your Academic Abilities

Experience shows that adults are generally excellent students. You can be, too! NEW DIRECTIONS offers a series of study skills workshops each term to help you determine your strengths, identify your weaknesses, and learn new study methods. Some of the topics we've covered include: "Writing A Term Paper", "How To Study For And Take Tests", "Reading And Notetaking Skills", and "Using A Computer to write Your Next Paper".

Deciding On Academic Or Career Goals

Exploring your interests and goals is an intergral part of your education. Workshops on decision making and career planning can help steer you in a more satisfying direction. Two of our staff members are Academic Advisors and can assist you in planning your academic program.

Dealing With The Everyday Pressures of Being A Student, A Worker, A Parent

New Directions currently offers a Returning Women's Support Group and a Parenting Support Group. These informal groups meet weekly and provide a place where members can share concerns, explore possible solutions, and develop friendships. Additionally, we offer workshops on time management, assertiveness training, balancing multiple roles, and other topics to help you get organized and better your many responsibilities.

Are You An Evening Student In Need Of Services

A member of the New Directions staff is available for advising, counseling, and referrals Monday through Wednesday until 6:00 p.m. (later by appointment). Our workshops and courses are offered in the evening as well as during the day.

Instructive session 9 (Gawrych) cont.: part 7 - New Directions Brochure (continued)

NORTHEASTERN ILLINOIS UNIVERSITY
RONALD WILLIAMS LIBRARY

LIBRARY SURVIVAL TRAINING
THE RESEARCH PROCESS
A SELECTIVE GUIDE TO RESOURCES

LIBRARY RESEARCH GUIDES

Beasley, David R. How to Use a Research Library. New York:
Oxford University Press, 1988.
Z675 R45 B42 1988

Felknor, Bruce L. How to Look Things Up and Find Things Out.
New York: Morrow, 1988.
REF.Z710 F44 1988

Hauer, Mary G. Books, Libraries, and Research. Dubuque,
Iowa: Kendall/Hunt Publishing Co., 1987.
Z710 B7 1987

Mann, Thomas. A Guide to Library Research Methods. New York:
Oxford University Press, 1987.
Z710 M23 1987

Smith, Robert M. The Independent Learners Sourcebook. Chicago:
American Library Association, 1987.
REF.Z1035.1 S577 1987

ON–LINE COMPUTER DATABASES

Bowen, Charles and David Peyton. CompuServe Information Manager:
The Complete Sourcebook. New York: Bantam Books, 1990.
QA76.57 C65 C65 1990

How to Get the Most Out of CompuServe. New York: Bantam
Books, 1989.
QA76.57 C65 B6931 1989.

Dvorak, John C and Nick Anis. Dvorak's Guide to PC
Telecommunications. Berkeley, California: Osborne-
McGraw Hill, 1990.
QA76.25 D9 1990
Guide to installing a modem and accessing electronic mail, bulletin board systems, and
on-line databases such as CompuServe, BRS AFTER DARK, Prodigy and other on-line
systems. Also includes information on shareware and freeware programs. This book has
accompanying diskettes; Modem Tutor and Telix SE telecommunications program. The
diskettes are available at the Curriculum Materials Center, 3rd floor. The software is non-
circulating, but may be used in the Computer Lab on the 4th floor of the Library.

Glossbrenner, Alfred. The Complete Handbook of Personal Computer
Communications. New York: St. Martin's Press, 1990.
QA76.5 G535 1989

How to Look It Up On-line. New York: St. Martin's
Press, 1987.
QA76.55 G57 1987

5500 N. ST. LOUIS AVENUE
CHICAGO,ILLINOIS 60625–4699

Instructive session 9 (Gawrych) cont.: part 8 - Bibliography

RESEARCH AND REPORT WRITING GUIDES

Berry, Ralph. How to Write a Research Paper. New York:
Pergamon Press, 1986.
LB2369 B38 1986

Cash, Phyllis. How to Develop and Write a Research Paper.
New York: Arco, 1988.
LB2369 C36 1988

Hubbuch, Susan M. Writing Research Papers Across the
Curriculum. New York: Holt, Rinehart and Winston, 1989.
LB2369 H83

Hult, Christine A. Researching and Writing: An Inter-
disciplinary Approach. Belmont, California: Wadsworth
Publishing Co., 1986.
LB2369 H84 1986

Roth, Audrey. The Research Paper: Process, Form, and
Content. Belmont, California: Wadsworth Publishing Co.,
1988.
LB2369 R66 1988

West, Pamela. The Commonsense Guide to Writing the Research
Paper. New York: Macmillan Publishing Co., 1986.
LB2369 W43 1986

PUBLICATION STYLE MANUALS

Chicago Guide to Preparing Electronic Mauscripts. Chicago:
University of Chicago Press, 1987.
REF.Z286 E43 U54 1987

Gibaldi, Joseph. MLA Handbook for Writers of Research
Papers. 3rd ed. New York: Modern Language Association,
1988.
REF.LB2369 G53 1988

Publication Manual of the American Psychological
Association. 3rd ed. Washington: American Psychological
Association, 1983.
REF.BF76.7 P83 1983

Sorenson, Sharon. Webster's New World Student Writing
Handbook. New York: Simon and Schuster, 1988.
REF.PE1408 S6577 1988

Turabian, Kate L. A Manual for Writers. 5th ed. Chicago:
University of Chicago Press, 1987.
REF.LB2369 T8 1987

Compiled by: Elaine Gawrych
February - 1991
a:resear

Instructive session 9 (Gawrych) cont.: part 8 - Bibliography (continued)

**POSTER
SESSIONS**

THE ELECTRONIC LIBRARY: A FACULTY SEMINAR

Marsha Forys
The University of Iowa Libraries
Iowa City, Iowa 52242
319 335-5301   cadrysts@uiamvs

The University of Iowa Libraries began presenting faculty seminars in fall 1988 in order to introduce to its faculty and graduate students a variety of information sources on a wide range of topics. One of the most popular seminars has been *The Electronic Library*. This topic was chosen because advances in technology have produced a large number of bibliographic and non-bibliographic databases and CD-ROM products that many researchers are unfamiliar with. It allows librarians to demonstrate some of these new sources and to answer questions about them.

The Electronic Library lasts 2 1/4 hours (including a 15 minute break) and consists of an introduction, six presentations, and a summary. A number of database searches are done and projected onto a screen. The librarians participating in this seminar also create bibliographies and other handouts which are given to those who attend. The audience is given the opportunity to ask questions after each speaker has finished as well as at the end of the seminar. Evaluation forms filled out by those who have attended have been favorable, and indicate that the seminar has increased their awareness of the possibilities of electronic sources.

Poster session 1 (Forys): part 1 - Faculty Seminar

Faculty Seminar Planning

Every May, librarians interested in being involved in faculty seminars get together with the User Education Coordinator to discuss which topics would make good seminars. Two topics are chosen for the fall semester and two for the following spring. Librarians interested in each topic become a team or a committee that will be responsible for the development of the topic into a seminar.

Each committee and the User Education Coordinator have their own responsibilities.

The committee is responsible for:
* Selecting a chairperson
* Deciding how the topic will be developed
* Selecting the title of the seminar
* Recommending a date and time
* Deciding who will be responsible for what
* Creating bibliographies and other handouts
* Recommending which departments and individuals should receive publicity
* Deciding which visual material would help them present the seminar most effectively
* Providing high quality bibliography and handout masters to the User Education Coordinator
* Attending the rehearsal
* Making the presentation

The User Education Coordinator is responsible for:
* Setting a timetable
* Creation and dissemination of publicity
* Registration
* Duplicating the bibliographies and other handouts
* Assembling the packets containing the bibliographies, handouts, and evaluation forms
* Reserving and setting up the room
* Providing equipment
* Attending the rehearsal
* Compiling the results of the evaluations

2

Poster session 1 (Forys) cont.: part 1 - Faculty Seminar (continued)

The chairperson begins with a brief introduction, and ends with a brief summary and a reminder to fill in the evaluation forms. The six presentations are:

GEORGE BOOLE AND THE ELECTRONIC LIBRARY

This presentation begins with a brief biography of George Boole, the 19th -century British philosopher and mathematician, and then introduces the idea of using the Boolean operators, **and, or, not**, to retrieve information stored in electronic databases.

Visuals: Transparencies demonstrating the Boolean **and, or, not** concepts are shown.

> Prepared & presented by:
> Jim Julich
> Reference Department
> The University of Iowa Libraries

FEE-BASED ONLINE SEARCHING

Fee-based online bibliographic database searching is described, including: the advantages and disadvantages of doing a search; how the various costs are determined; the search interview; expanding and limiting a search; print options; and updating a previous search on a regular basis.

Visuals: Two bibliographic database searches are projected onto a screen.

> Prepared & presented by:
> Rebecca Johnson
> Reference Department
> The University of Iowa Libraries

NON-BIBLIOGRAPHIC DATABASE SEARCHING

Non-bibliographic databases are sometimes referred to as "source" databases because they contain actual sources rather than pointing you to another source. The different types of non-bibliographic databases that are described are: full text; directory; graphic; and numeric.

Visuals: Three non-bibliographic database searches are projected onto a screen.

> Prepared & presented by:
> David Martin
> Business Library
> The University of Iowa Libraries

CD-ROMS IN THE LIBRARY

This presentation covers several topics: a definition of the term; a description of the equipment and software involved; the major strengths and limitations of CD-ROM indexes and full text services; and user aids(manuals, handouts, etc.). There is also a brief discussion of the search possibilities of the format. An attempt is made to keep a balance

3

Poster session 1 (Forys) cont.: part 2 - Contents of Seminar between what CDs can do and cannot do, especially in terms of coverage.

Visuals: Transparencies are used to highlight the points being made.

Prepared & presented by:
Sandra Ballasch
Hardin Library for the Health Sciences
The University of Iowa Libraries

OASIS UPDATE

The University of Iowa Libraries' online catalog is called OASIS. This presentation includes a brief history of the NOTIS installation at Iowa; an explanation of keyword searching on OASIS; and information on the new multiple database feature, WILS, which contains five Wilson indexes.

Visuals: A demonstration of keyword searching is projected onto a screen. When discussing WILS, transparencies are used since WILS can only be searched from a dedicated terminal and we use dial up access for the seminar.

Prepared & presented by:
Suzanne Olson
Automation Office
The University of Iowa Libraries

THE RESEARCH LIBRARIES GROUP

This is a discussion of library consortia-- their purpose and the ever-growing need to share resources. It includes a description of RLG, an in-depth discussion of the various databases in RLIN, and the plans for RLIN to expand world-wide. There is also a description of the services available to individual researchers.

Prepared & presented by:
Helen Ryan
Reference Department
The University of Iowa Libraries

Poster session 1 (Forys) cont.: part 2 - Contents of Seminar (continued)

NUMBERS

We offered *The Electronic Library* four times in the fall of 1989 and twice in the fall of 1990.

Number of sessions	6
Number who registered	186
Number who attended	136
Number of evaluations turned in	83

EVALUATIONS

What did we learn from the 83 evaluations? From questions 1-3, we learned the following:

1. Who attended?

U of I faculty	44
U of I graduate students	25
Other U of I staff	12
Other researchers	2

2. How did they rate this program?

Very useful	50.6%
Useful	47.0%
Not very useful	1.2%
Left answer blank	1.2%

3. How much of the material did they already know <u>before</u> the session?

Some of it	92.77%
None of it	4.82%
All of it	2.41%

5

Poster session 1 (Forys) cont.: part 3 - Evaluation

Questions 4-7 solicit a narrative response. Just some of the answers are below.

4. What one thing stands out in your mind about this seminar?

Boolean concept entirely new to me.

How much info is available through the electronic library. Wow!

It offers a good sampling of what can be done, whetting the appetite. Good demos, good overview.

5. To what extent did the seminar cover what you expected?

Very well.

50%

100%

6. How could this seminar have been more useful to you?

Subject specific.

Hands on work with searches etc.

I wish I'd heard it months ago.

7. Please make any additional comments below.

You made users feel comfortable in seeking more information later.

A well organized and informative seminar. Thank you.

Follow up sessions with more time & specific focus (e.g. by major discipline or by type of database).

6

Poster session 1 (Forys) cont.: part 3 - Evaluation (continued)

The Dana Faculty-Librarian Partnership Workshops at Wheaton College, Norton, Mass.

In the spring of 1989 Wheaton College was awarded a $71,000 matching grant from the Charles A. Dana Foundation to strengthen the teaching role of the library and to promote "Information Literacy" among Wheaton students. The Faculty-Librarian Partnership Program has three objectives:

1) To incorporate library instruction skills into the curriculum, through faculty/librarian collaboration;
2) In that process, to also teach students to develop critical thinking skills; and
3) To incorporate use of the new technology into the curriculum.

A series of faculty-librarian workshops was a key element in stimulating faculty to include a library component in the transformation of their courses . The workshops were designed to provide forums to discuss the concept of faculty-librarian partnerships, the important issues of the role of the library at liberal arts colleges, and the need to develop critical thinking skills in students, especially in an age when seemingly limitless amounts of information are available to students through information databases. The new technology was also presented with the opportunity for hands-on experience with new CD-ROM databases.

Margaret Gardner and Marcia Grimes, reference librarians, displayed agendas for two workshops held at Wheaton College: (May 1990) "Shaping Student Research Assignments: Technology and the Need for Critical Thinking" and (January 1991:) "Improving the Quality of Student Work: Dana Course Transformation Projects". They also provided hand-outs from workshop packets given to all participants and answered questions about the project.

Poster session 2 (Grimes and Gardner): part 1 - Abstract

JANUARY WORKSHOP! JANUARY WORKSHOP!

DATE: December 17, 1990

TO: All Faculty Members

FROM: Sherrie Bergman

RE: January Dana Faculty/Librarian Workshop:
             Registration Information

Enclosed are the agenda and registration form for the next Dana Faculty/Librarian Partnership Workshop to be held the morning of Thursday, January 24, 1991.

The workshop is entitled "Improving the Quality of Student Work: Dana Library Course Transformation Projects." We will continue discussions begun during our Dana workshop last May, of how faculty members and librarians together can transform courses to teach students about library research. Faculty who received funding to transform courses taught this past semester, will report on their projects with their librarian partners, and assess the projects' effect on the quality of students' work.

I especially look forward to the workshop because we will introduce ELIZA, the new Wheaton library catalog on CD-ROM, which will replace the microfiche catalogs early this spring.

The morning will end with a free hour in the reference room for hands-on time with an ELIZA prototype, reference CD-ROM databases, new reference books, or for teaming up with librarians to plan course transformation projects.

The workshop discussions should be of special interest to faculty members who are preparing to teach a revised course in the spring, but we believe all faculty members will benefit from this opportunity to discuss the role of the library in the teaching process.

Faculty attending the workshop will be eligible to and are encouraged to work with a librarian to design a course transformation proposal for funding in summer 1991. The Library Committee has established Friday, February 15th as the first submission deadline for the next round of proposals. Proposals should be sent to Ed Tong, Chair.

For more details about the course transformation opportunities, or background information on the Dana project, please call me at extension 518.

A tear-off registration form appears on the bottom of the agenda. I hope many of you plan to attend.

Happy Holiday wishes from the Library Staff.

SB:dmz
attachments

Poster session 2 (Grimes and Gardner) cont.: part 2 - Handout #1

IMPROVING THE QUALITY OF STUDENT WORK:
DANA LIBRARY COURSE TRANSFORMATION PROJECTS

Thursday, January 24, 1991

Wallace Library
Cole Room

AGENDA

8:30 a.m.   Coffee

9:00   Welcome and Overview: Hannah Goldberg and Sherrie Bergman

Review of Dana Course Transformation Projects - Fall 1990

Library components for Lower Level Courses:

Classics 223A -5th Century Athens
Ann Marshall, Sherrie Bergman

English 256A - American Fiction Since World War II
Richard Pearce, Sherry O'Brien

Religion 316A - Islam: Faith and Practice
Charles Forman, Marcia Grimes

9:45   Library Components for Upper Level Seminars:

History 302 - Junior Colloquium: The Uses of History
Paul Helmreich, Zephorene Stickney

Sociology 402 - Senior Seminar
Ira Gerstein, Margaret Gardner

Political Science 401 - Comparative Politics - Senior Seminar
Lesego Malepe, Marcia Grimes

10:15   Break

10:30   Discussion

11:15   Introduction to ELIZA, the Wheaton catalog on CD-ROM
Sherrie Bergman and Mary Whelan

Free time in the Reference Room:
Try ELIZA, use CD-ROM databases, examine new reference books

12:30 p.m.   Lunch through the line at Chase Round - tickets provided

- -

Registration Form

Name _____   Department _____

____ I plan to attend the Dana Faculty/Librarian Workshop on Thursday, January 24.

Please return to Sherrie Bergman by Friday, January 11, 1991.

Poster session 2 (Grimes and Gardner) cont.: part 2 - Handout #1 (continued)

Office of the Provost
and Academic Vice President
Wheaton College
Norton, Massachusetts 02766
(508) 285-7722
FAX (508) 285-2908

Date: March 19, 1990

To: All Faculty Members

From: Hannah Goldberg

Re: Course Transformation Support for
             Dana Faculty/Librarian Partnership Program
             Full-day workshop: Thursday, May 24, 1990
             Follow-up half-day workshops: Friday, May 25, 1990

I am pleased to be able to offer financial support for course
transformation projects through the Faculty/Librarian Partnership
Program grant awarded to the Wallace Library by the Charles A.
Dana Foundation. The goal of the grant is to strengthen the
teaching role of the library and promote information literacy by
encouraging faculty/librarian collaboration to integrate library
components into individual courses.

This goal will be achieved through a new series of faculty
workshops and course transformation projects, to be offered over
two years, beginning this May. All interested faculty will
receive per diem support at the usual rate of $80 for full-day
and $40 for half-day workshop attendance, plus $80 per day for
10-20 faculty for up to two and one half days of course
transformation work over the summer 1990. Funding is available
to support 10 additional faculty members doing course
transformations in summer 1991.

The project will provide faculty and librarians with an
opportunity to work together as partners to design experiences
for our students that transform their understanding of what a
library is, and how to use it, with a particular emphasis on
mastery of the newest technologies. Over two years we expect
this project will create a new prominence for the library within
the curriculum and that the approach will be shown to be a useful
model for teaching critical thinking skills through library
instruction.

The Faculty Workshops

Workshops will consist of two parts: one all-day workshop on
Thursday, May 24, and two half-day workshops on Friday, May 25.

The May 24 workshop will be divided into two parts. The morning
session on the teaching role of the library in the curriculum
will be led by Evan Farber, College Librarian, Earlham College,

Poster session 2 (Grimes and Gardner) cont.: part 3 - Handout #2

— MARCIA GRIMES AND MARGARET GARDNER —

and a leader in successfully integrating library instruction into the curriculum. He will moderate presentations by Wheaton faculty/librarian teams who will describe collaborations to date. In the afternoon, hands-on demonstrations of CD-ROM and online database technologies will be provided by Wheaton's reference librarians. Lunch will be provided.

You may also attend a half-day discipline-based workshop the next day in order to work closely with librarians in hands-on demonstrations of resources and technologies specific to your field and to explore ways to incorporate a library component into a specific course.

The Course Transformation Projects

The goal of the course transformation projects is to teach students to utilize critical thinking skills as they develop library research strategies and master the use of both traditional library resources and the newer online and CD-ROM database technologies.

You are invited to submit a proposal, in collaboration with a librarian, to integrate a library component into one of your courses. Since the long-range goal is to involve faculty from all academic departments, preference will be given to making the awards over as broad a range of departments as possible. In addition, you are encouraged to revise courses required for the major. Faculty members submitting proposals under this grant must attend the May 24th workshop, but attendance at that workshop does not require submission of a proposal.

Proposals should be submitted to Steve Dworetz, Chair, Library Committee, before one of the following deadlines:

    Round 1:   by Monday, May 7 (for faculty who already have a
               project in mind). Award notification date: May 17

    Round 2:   by Wednesday, May 30 (for faculty who wish to plan
               the course transformation project after attending
               the May workshops). Award notification date:
               June 4

    Round 3:   Spring 1991.

The proposal, which must be submitted by a faculty/librarian team, should describe the course which would be used for the project, when that course will be offered, and a description of how a library component would be incorporated into the course.

Following the first two semesters of teaching a revised course, each faculty member who receives a stipend will be asked to submit a report to the Library Committee evaluating the success of the transformation effort.

Poster session 2 (Grimes and Gardner) cont.: part 3 - Handout #2 (continued)

Librarians can be contacted for further explanation of the
Partnership Program, as well as to work on specific course
transformation projects. Subject specialty areas are indicated
for the reference librarians:

Sherrie Bergman, College Librarian (ext. 518)
Margaret Gardner, Reference Librarian (ext. 502)--Psychology,
     Sociology, Anthropology
Marcia Grimes, Reference Librarian for Interlibrary Loan
     (ext. 500)--History, Religion, Philosophy, Political
     Science, Economics, German, Mathematics
Faith Dickhaut Kindness, Fine Arts Librarian (ext. 529)--
     Music, Art
Sherry O'Brien, Reference Librarian for Computer-Based Services
     (ext. 502)--Natural Sciences, Literature and Languages,
     Education, Women's Studies
Jean Pearce, Readers' Services Librarian (ext. 512)
Mary Whelan, Associate Librarian & Director of Technical Services
     (ext. 511)

In a future mailing you will receive a registration form with a
more detailed agenda for the full-day workshop on Thursday, May
24th and a schedule for the discipline-based demonstrations of
new technologies the next day. For now, please mark the dates on
your calendars and, for those submitting Round 1 proposals, meet
with a librarian to begin to design your course transformation
projects.

Poster session 2 (Grimes and Gardner) cont.: part 3 - Handout #2 (continued)

Madeleine Clark Wallace Library
Wheaton College
Norton, MA

The Dana Faculty/Librarian Partnership Workshop
Thursday, May 24/Friday, May 25, 1990

Day 1 - Thursday, May 24:

FINAL AGENDA

8:30 a.m.	Coffee	Holman Room
		Mary Lyon

9:00   Introduction -- Hannah Goldberg
                              -- Sherrie Bergman

9:15 - 10:15 Faculty/Librarian Collaboration:
               Teaching Research Skills Across the Curriculum
               Evan Farber, College Librarian, Earlham College

10:15 - 10:30 Break

10:30 - 12:00 Noon Faculty/Librarian Partnerships at Wheaton:
                     Works in Progress

                    Evan Farber, Moderator
                     -Chemistry Senior Seminar (Chemistry 400)
                      Myrna Pearson and Sherry O'Brien

                     -Psychology as a Social Science (Psychology 101)
                      Derek Price and Margaret Gardner

                     -Approaches to Literature (English 202)
                      Kathleen Vogt and Sherry O'Brien

                     -Labor Economics and Industrial Relations (Economics 240)
                      Hilda Kahne and Marcia Grimes

                     -Spirituals, Blues and All That Jazz:
                      Afro-American Originals (Music 272)
                      Ann Sears and Faith Dickhaut Kindness

12:15 - 1:30 p.m. Box Lunch

1:30 - 3:00   Shaping Students' Research Assignments: Library-Reference Room
              Technology and the Need for Critical Thinking
       1:30 - 2:00   Introduction - Sherrie Bergman
                     The CD-ROM Search - Sherry O'Brien and Jeffrey Mann
       2:00 - 2:30   Small Group Discussions
       2:30 - 3:00   Summaries of Group Reports and Wrap-up

3:00 - 4:00 p.m. Hands-on Computer Searching:
                   CD-ROM Technology

                  Wine and cheese   Cole Room

FUNDED THROUGH THE GENEROSITY OF THE CHARLES A. DANA FOUNDATION, INC.

Poster session 2 (Grimes and Gardner) cont.: part 4 - Agenda

The Dana Faculty/Librarian Partnership Workshop

Day 2 - Friday, May 25, 1990:

You have been assigned to either the morning or the afternoon session.
Please check the assignment sheet.

FINAL AGENDA

MORNING SESSION: Social Sciences, Religion, Philosophy and History

8:30 a.m.   Coffee (available throughout the morning)   Library
                                                                          Cole Room

9:00   Introduction: Sherrie Bergman   Cole Room

                             Concepts in Searching: Cole Room
                               Research Technology at Wheaton
                               Sherry O'Brien

9:30 - 11:00   Discipline-based Searching of   Reference Room
                               CD-ROM and Online Databases

                             (small group hands-on sessions)

11:00 - 12:00 Noon   Faculty/Librarian Meetings on
                               Course Development and Library Assignments

AFTERNOON SESSION: Fine Arts, Natural Sciences, Mathematics,
                     Literature - English and Foreign Languages

1:00 p.m.   Introduction: Sherrie Bergman   Cole Room

                             Concepts in Searching: Cole Room
                               Research Technology at Wheaton - Sherry O'Brien

1:30 - 3:00   Discipline-based Searching of   Reference Room
                               CD-ROM and Online Databases

                             (small group hands-on sessions)

3:00 - 4:00 p.m.   Faculty/Librarian Meetings on
                               Course Development and Library Assignments

                             (cold drinks will be available in the afternoon)

Poster session 2 (Grimes and Gardner) cont.: part 4 - Agenda (continued)

Dana Faculty/Librarian Partnership Workshop

Suggested Group Discussion Topics
Thursday, May 24th, 1990

1.   What methods can we use to encourage students to develop a focused topic for their library assignments?

2.   How can we as librarians and faculty help students to critically evaluate the citations found in a literature search?

Tips?   Pointers?   Strategies?

Poster session 2 (Grimes and Gardner) cont.: part 5 - Suggested Group Discussion Topics

MADELEINE CLARK WALLACE LIBRARY
WHEATON COLLEGE
Norton, MA

<u>The Dana Faculty/Librarian Partnership Workshop</u>

EVALUATION FORM
Friday, 25 May 1990

1. From an overall perspective did the workshop meet your expectations? YES ____ NO ____

2. Have you had previous experience with CD-ROM searching? YES ____ NO ____
          Often ____   Occasionally ____   Seldom ____

3. Have you had previous experience with On-line searching? YES ____ NO ____
          Often ____   Occasionally ____   Seldom ____

4. How effective was the librarian's instruction/demonstration in explaining computer search strategies?

5. How effective were the sample searches provided for the individual CD-ROM databases?

6. Was enough time provided for hands-on searching?

7. How frequently will you use CD-ROM searching for your own teaching and research?
          Often ____   Occasionally ____   Seldom ____

8. How frequently will you use On-line searching for your own teaching and research?
          Often ____   Occasionally ____   Seldom ____

9. How frequently will you recommend CD/ROM searching for your students?
          Often ____   Occasionally ____   Seldom ____

10. How frequently will you recommend On-line searching for your students?
          Often ____   Occasionally ____   Seldom ____

11. Did you learn about a database or CD-ROM disk that will be of help to you or your students?
    Please give title of database/disk:

11. Has the workshop inspired you to transform a course through faculty/librarian partnership?

12. General comments:

PLEASE PLACE THIS EVALUATION IN BOX ON REFERENCE DESK

Poster session 2 (Grimes and Gardner) cont.: part 6 - Evaluation Form

ABSTRACT

COMMUNICATING WITH FACULTY IN THE NEW ELECTRONIC ENVIRONMENT
Nancy Young and Bill Coons

The Stouffer Hotels Library, serving the 800 faculty, students, and staff of Cornell University's School of Hotel Adminstration, is connected with the School's Digital Equipment Corporation's VAX and its ALL-IN-1 electronic mail and word processing system. In February 1991, the Library began using this e-mail system to distribute an electronic library newsletter.

Several reasons for selecting the electronic rather than the print medium were to:

—Take advantage of available technology
—Disseminate timely information and provide a mechanism for immediate feedback
—Reach everyone and not just those who ordinarily use the library
—Make the library and its services and staff more visible (and to change attitudes toward the library)
—Save paper.

Before the first issue was sent, we formulated our goals, searched the literature for reviews of similar projects, and identified the possible contents and categories of the newsletter.

Possible contents or components of each electronic newsletter are drawn from the following list (an asterisk indicates a top priority component). Each issue is limited to 2-3 screens; therefore, a single issue usually includes only four or five of these possible categories of information:

—Recent inquiries from industry (questions from our fee-based service)*
—New acquisitions (selective/representative samples)*
—Announcements of new services or policy changes*
—Library publications (such as bibliographies and handouts)
—Assistance offered to faculty/staff
—Collection development (potential purchases and cancellations, call for suggestions, news/help on special projects)
—Highlights (one service/person described in detail)
—Professional activities and contributions of library staff
—Solicitation of feedback about library hours, services, etc.
—Announcement of new issues of electronic journal (Journal of the Internationl Academy of Hospitality Research)

A biweekly production schedule calls for alternating responsibility for newsletter issues between the two reference librarians, who jot down ideas in a notebook, compose the drafts in Microsoft Word for editing, and then input the final version into the ALL-In-1 system.

Response from the faculty and staff has been favorable and interesting. As a result of a suggestion from a reader, the title of the newsletter was changed. The original title, SHA Library Link, reminded the reader of an unglamourous food product. Therefore, the new title is SHA Library Entree, which lends itself more easily to an appropriate acronym: Electronic Newsletter to Researchers, Educators and Employees. The newsletter has also engendered requests for copies of journal articles, for more information about new publications and technical innovations, and for submission of information about library activities for inclusion in the Hotel School alumni newsletter.

Poster session 3 (Young): part 1 - Abstract

We have learned that there are both advantages and disadvantages to producing a library newsletter electronically. The major advantages are:

—Speed (information is current)
—Reliable delivery (no one can avoid receiving an e-mail message and most recipients probably read at least a portion of it.)
—Novelty factor (because it is a new format, people tend to pay attention).

The disadvantages of an electronic newsletter are:

—Lack of graphics (technology for word processing on the ALL-IN-1 system is limited)
—Unavailability of back issues (unless readers print them themselves)
—Inability to edit for errors once the e-mail message is sent
—Exclusion of students from access to the e-mail system.

In an effort to overcome some of these disadvantages, our goals for the future of the SHA Library Entree include working out a method for distributing the newsletter to students, becoming more familiar with the system's word processing capabilities and improving print quality and variety, and making the newsletter a separate menu choice on the system, so that it is not grouped with the general e-mail messages--an "Entree" unto itself.

Poster session 3 (Young) cont.: part 1 - Abstract (cont.)

GOALS

*To Educate and Inform

*To Change Attitudes Toward the Library (To Make Library, People and Services Visible)

*To Reach Out to Those Whose Shadow Doesn't Darken Our Threshhold

*To Participate in the SHA Family Community Network

*To Take Advantage of the Existing Technology

*To Save Paper

*To Disseminate Timely Information by Eliminating the Middlemen (Printers and Mailroom)

*To Provide a Mechanism for Immediate Feedback

Poster session 3 (Young) cont.: part 2 - Outline #1

PLANNING

*Formulate and State Goals

*Literature Search

*Equipment Capability Survey

*Outline Possible Categories and Set Priorities

*Suggest Idea on E-Mail System; Solicit Feedback Re. Content, Frequency, Usefulness, Etc.

*Study Use of E-Mail for Weekly Newsletter from Associate Dean for Acadmeic Affairs

Poster session 3 (Young) cont.: part 3 - Outline #2

CONTENT/COMPONENTS

*Recent Inquiries from Industry (HOSTLINE Questions)

*New Acquisitions (Selective/Representative)

*Announcements of New Services or Policy Changes

*Library Publications (Bibliographies, Class Handouts, etc.)

*Assistance Offered to Faculty/Staff (Who We've Helped With Research, Instruction, Factfinding)

*Collection Development: Potential Purchases and Cancellations, Call for Suggestions, News/Help on Special Projects

*Highlights: Choose One Service/Person and Describe in Detail

*Professional Activities and Contributions of Library Staff: Conferences, Workshops, Publications, Etc.

*Solicit Feedback Re. Library Hours, Services to Faculty, Etc.

*Announce New Issues of Electronic Journal (Journal of the International Academy of Hospitality Research)

Poster session 3 (Young) cont.: part 4 - Outline #3

LAYOUT, COMPOSITION AND PRODUCTION

*Alternate Responsibility for Newsletter Issues

*Make Production Schedule

*Notebook for Ideas

*First Draft Input Into Microsoft Word

*Hard Copy Routed to Staff for Editing and Review

*Final Copy Input Into All-IN-1 System

*Distribute Via Electronic Mail

Poster session 3 (Young) cont.: part 5 - Outline #4

SAMPLE NEWSLETTERS AND RESPONSES

*Title Change From SHA LIBRARY LINK To SHA LIBRARY ENTREE

*Requests for Copies of Articles

*Requests for More Information about New Publications

*Requests for More Information About Technical Innovations

*General Comments of Support and Thanks

*Request for Submission of Library Activity Information for Issues of the Hotel School Alumni Newsletter

Poster session 3 (Young) cont.: part 6 - Outline #5

WHAT WE'VE LEARNED: ADVANTAGES AND DISADVANTAGES

Advantages of an Electronic Newsletter

*Speed: Information is Current

*Everyone Gets It and Probably Reads at Least Part of It

*Novelty Value; Attention Getter

Disadvantages of an Electronic Newsletter

*No Graphics: Technology for Word Processing is Limited

*Back Issues Unavailable Unless Readers Print Them

*Inability to Edit for Errors; Once It's Mailed, It's Gone

*Students Not on E-Mail System

Poster session 3 (Young) cont.: part 7 - Outline #6

FUTURE: WHERE DO WE GO FROM HERE?

*Work Out Method for Distributing Newsletter to Students

*Become More Familiar with Word Processing Capabilities; Improve Print Quality and Variety

*Separate Newsletter from General E-Mail Messages

*Make Newsletter a Separate Menu Choice

Poster session 3 (Young) cont.: part 8 - Outline #7

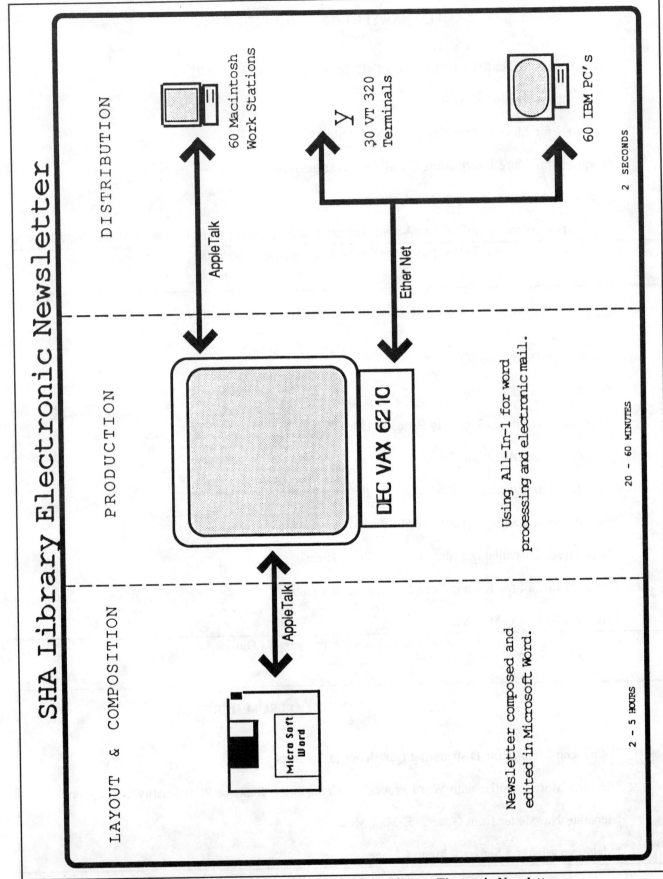

Poster session 3 (Young) cont.: part 9 - SHA Library Electronic Newsletter

— NANCY YOUNG —

PANEL
SUMMARY

LOEX CONFERENCE—PANEL SUMMARY

To conclude the program of the 19th annual LOEX Conference, six participants were asked to provide brief reactions to the content of this year's presentations, in light of the conditions of their bibliographic instruction programs and the personal interaction with teaching faculty on their own campuses.

First to speak was Rachel Gardner of Monmouth College, a small liberal arts institution in Randolph, New Jersey. As the BI Librarian, she keeps up with the literature and has attended other library instruction-related meetings. At this year's LOEX Conference, Rachel has noticed four shifts in focus:

- a renewed emphasis on outcomes assessment for bibliographic instruction within the context of higher education, an emphasis driven by a number of recent studies delineating "what's wrong with higher education." These BI outcomes include what students really learn about the value of information as well as the practical skills, knowledges, and attitudes they acquire.

- increasing requirements for institutional support of academic BI and information literacy service programs. To be successful, these programs should be included among administrative priorities. In addition to working more closely with administrators, librarians also need to consider regional accrediting association interests.

- importance of librarians' mastering, teaching, and integrating new computer and communications technologies into the more traditional BI programs. These new technologies not only provide research tools, but are also drawing cards that motivate faculty to get involved in the information literacy effort. Rachel finds that students respect images and that using technologies provides an element of "seduction" that the print medium does not match.

- the need to link library programs and services to the changing currents of curricula in higher education. Rachel notices a politicization and revision of the curricula brought about by the infusion of multicultural content and the multidisciplinary nature of many areas of study. Librarians should adjust their activities and services to support evolving academic programs and the educational mission of their institution.

Rachel outlined the Middle States Accreditation Association's (Monmouth College's regional accrediting body) effort to establish new criteria that stress the quality of a library's BI program and deemphasize the more traditional quantitative criteria such as the number of volumes in the collection. The evaluating team's methods might include interviewing students about their research experiences as well as assessing the quality of their actual papers and bibliographies.

Literature documenting the Middle States Association's commitment to information literacy was distributed to a number of interested administrators at Monmouth College. Along with the literature went a proposal to establish a faculty committee charged with exploring the feasibility of implementing a concrete information literacy initiative: teaching faculty of each major-granting department would establish information literacy objectives appropriate to that discipline. These objectives would then be implemented by incorporating specially designed assignments in the major's course sequence. Working under the aegis of the Middle State's mandate, given adequate time, and beginning with one key department, Rachel and the other librarians hope to develop a model program for their institution.

Concluding, Rachel also offered a final admonition: the almost mind-boggling increase in information access made possible by new technologies is only one factor in the acquisition of knowledge and should not be confused with knowledge itself. The medium is by no means the message.

Abigail Loomis of the University of Wisconsin-Madison continued the panel presentation by sharing the following concerns:

It seems clear after listening to the presentations of this LOEX Conference that the faculty-librarian partnership is alive and well and still the cornerstone of our BI programs. But it also seems clear that if the seeds of this partnership that we are sowing are to bloom fully and broadly, we—the front-line librarians—and not the library administrators need to build coalitions with campus administrators. Library directors actually may not fully understand the details which this work involves.

There are a number of reasons why I think this administrative support is essential, one of which relates directly to the theme of this Conference, and that has to do with the nature of the faculty-librarian partnership. This relationship, while it provides the foundation for much of what we do in user education, is often—programmatically speaking—a tenuous affair.

Typically, and for a variety of reasons, a faculty member recognizes and responds to the need to teach her students how to find and use information, and works with the user education librarian to integrate such instruction into her syllabus. This is an individual and not a departmental contact or initiative. When that faculty member leaves, or when her course assignments are changed, there is no programmatic guarantee that information literacy will continue to be a component of the syllabus of her successor. The teaching faculty/librarian relationship is primarily personality-dependent.

The same uncertainties can threaten the library side of this partnership. Faculty often get used to working with one user education librarian. If this librarian leaves or is reassigned, faculty are sometimes reluctant to pick up with her successor, particularly if the departing librarian was a star in the classroom. Instead, the reaction is often, "I'll just do it myself." Obviously, the successor needs to be extra sensitive and responsive to this resistance to change. In either case, the faculty/librarian partnership is often personality-dependent rather than programmatically dependent.

If our programs are to have the continuity, the consistency, the broad integration into the curriculum that they need to flourish, they need institutional support of campus administrators and not just individual faculty support. Again, we front-line librarians and not just our library directors need to be involved in building that coalition.

Several presentations here at the LOEX Conference have referred to recent educational reports calling for reform within higher education. All of these reports emphasize the need to improve the quality of teaching in higher education. And, significantly, they all indicate that in order to do this, faculty must put more energy and creativity into their teaching. Many may have to learn to incorporate new pedagogical methods into their teaching. Most importantly, these reports all admit that administrative support is absolutely essential if such reforms are to take place. In order for faculty to be willing to devote great time and energy to teaching reform, administration must create a reward system and an underlying value system as well, which will make it desirable for them to do so, and, implicitly, undesirable for them not to.

It seems to follow, therefore, that because information literacy programs demand significant and very similar changes in the way many faculty teach (no more lecture and reserve reading-dependent instruction, no more passive classes of spoonfed information regurgitated periodically on machine-graded, multiple choice exams), it, too, requires major support from the top down in order to implement. Even faculty members who are sympathetic to the cause of library instruction and information literacy can only afford, both literally and figuratively, to invest so much time to integrating it into their classroom if the reward system on their campus concentrates on research rather than on teaching. Faculty who are indifferent or even hostile to incorporating any change such as information literacy into their syllabi have no incentive in such a system, while those faculty who espouse the change, because of research demands can only invest limited time to integrating innovative teaching methods.

Continuing the discussion in a practical and descriptive vein was Marsha Miller from Indiana State University at Terre Haute. She described herself as a front-line BI librarian who has presented 246 library sessions during 1989 and 1990. NOTIS was introduced at Indiana State in 1985, rendering their environment definitely electronic. They have happily enjoyed steady faculty support for advances in electronic information access, with concomitant strong support for incorporating BI into freshman-level composition classes.

Library workshops to assist users in writing term papers were discontinued several years ago. Individualized instruction is promoted via new student orientation, contact with graduate and international students and faculty. More than 70% of the freshman composition courses receive formal library instruction, usually in two lectures (online catalog; indexes). Other undergraduates may receive a one-hour lecture in their physical education, library science, speech classes, etc. A library science course entitled Libraries and their Use (not taught by library staff but through the Department of Library Science) is rumored to be on the way out.

Whether or not an equivalent offering could be sustained by the library has not been addressed.

In her situation, reaching out is all-important. Librarians need to market themselves and their BI services so that teaching faculty will recognize their expertise and also the benefits that students in their courses derive from incorporating BI in teaching sessions. She finds that she has been targeting campus administrators to a higher degree than previously, as well as continuing contact with teaching faculty. A recent contact was with and academic department's accreditation team (Recreation & Leisure Studies). This is an additional opportunity to highlight a library's resources and promote the formal instruction needed to adequately put them to use.

University of Detroit Reference Librarian Shirley Black continued the panel presentations:

Shirley introduced herself as a first-time LOEX Conference participant. Her brief remarks are based on her initial assumption that Conference attenders already know how to teach. BI librarians teach interactively, and Shirley feels that with this teaching skill, we have a lot to say to those in higher education.

BI sessions, being not strictly in total lecture format, can challenge students in a variety of ways through the use of CAI, consultation and interaction, and electronic technology. BI librarians can serve by example as good teachers, especially with our general emphasis and concentration on student learning outcomes. Librarians ought to be engaged in honest, open and sincere dialogue about the value and priorities of teaching, talking not just among ourselves but with teaching colleagues and campus administrators. Contact with the latter is absolutely crucial, but we cannot wait for the trickle-down effect to occur, or for word-of-mouth about the value of incorporating instruction in information use in the curricula to reach these administrators by happenstance.

At the University of Detroit, a needs assessment based on the ACRL BIS Model Statement of Objectives was used in contacting and working with the teaching faculty, not the department head. Further, contact was made with the university's Core Curriculum Committee. Objectives, plans and needs assessment findings were presented to the Committee for a model program that would teach library users how to find, gather and evaluate information. The program was developed for use in English composition and research methods classes. Shirley related that the effort was a successful one because the librarians approached the Core Committee with an advantageous proposal to complement and improve instruction. Copies of the project are available through the LOEX Clearinghouse.

Sharon Mader, Associate Director at DePaul University Libraries, continued the reactive panel presentations by describing the situation today:

She noted that, increasingly across the country, practicing BI librarians are becoming administrators and library directors and taking more positions of "power" in academic libraries.

Sharon echoed other panel members when she further described the growing emphasis on the importance of teaching in higher education and the resulting tension that has surfaced between the ongoing demands for improving teaching and for conducting and publishing research. Sharon quoted a recent survey from the *Chronicle of Higher Education*: when American college teachers were asked to list their top professional goals, 58.5% included *Research*; 98.2% included *Good Teaching*.

She also exhorted the audience to become a very strong voice in higher education and in our profession by collaborating with and taking positions in regional, state and national organizations; by working on committees within ACRL; by forming networks on campus and within the profession; by reporting on our experiences and research in professional journals such as *Research Strategies*; and by forming alliances within higher education—so that interest in and awareness of the benefits of bibliographic instruction can be heightened.

Librarians can play a unique role in spearheading reforms. By the nature of our own work, we are accustomed to working across disciplines.

Sharon stressed that much discussion has occurred relating to the gaps and misunderstandings about what students should know and learn. She advised that we need to step back and form new and stronger lines of communication with faculty. It is essential to sit down and talk—to see which faculty perceptions surface about problems students are having with the research process, and to include perceptions of student mentors and of the librarians as well. Librarians and teaching faculty play complementary roles in the teaching process. We also need to talk about *definitions* of concepts: what it means to integrate critical thinking and research skills within a syllabus.

At DePaul, faculty and librarians met together in a workshop designed to facilitate communication. Together they worked through assignments based on Carol Kuhlthau's interpretation of the stages of the research process. As well as working with supportive teaching faculty on our own campuses, Sharon conclud-

ed, we need to ask ourselves how we can make an impact on a larger local, state and even national level.

Keynote speaker and Earlham College Library Director Evan Farber wrapped up the panel presentations by summarizing the program:

He notes a recurring emphasis on the necessity of beginning with the individual librarian/teaching faculty relationship which then spreads to the department and to an ongoing BI program. One has to start here, and the more individuals contacted and sold on the program, the better.

Evan feels that an excellent example of this tenet is the program described by the Ohio State University speakers at this Conference. Implementation of their broad instructional efforts has been impressive, and illustrates the importance of garnering administrative support. Evan thinks that the OSU program points this out as well as has any other academic BI endeavor he knows of.

The OSU Director of Libraries and the library administrators have confidence in the User Education Office Director, Virginia Tiefel, and the University administrators have been *equally* generous is supporting the program, both financially and philosophically.

One of the thrusts of the OSU program that Evan particularly admires is the way in which the program and the librarians help students overcome the initial hurdle of library anxiety. This is a vital BI concept—that the library user feels comfortable using the facility and services. BI programs should raise this consciousness and then build on that, so that users feel good about using the library.

Evan also expressed his admiration that the OSU User Education program has been so successful at a very large institution. This effort, compared to mounting a BI initiative at a smaller academic library, requires widespread and comprehensive support, initiative, and dedication. Such projects take time; Earlham College has spent 25 years and OSU has taken 20 years to develop their library instruction programs.

He cautioned the participants not to become impatient with implementing their own programs. Instead, concentrate on building relationships with teaching faculty and administrators, and continue to develop them.

In conclusion, Evan commented that he was impressed with a rather remarkable esprit de corps among the BI librarians attending the LOEX meeting. He exhorted us to persevere in achieving our BI objectives, for our expectations will be rewarded.

BIBLIOGRAPHY

LIBRARY ORIENTATION AND INSTRUCTION—1990

Hannelore B. Rader

The following is an annotated list of materials dealing with information literacy including instruction in the use of information resources, research, and computer skills related to retrieving, using, and evaluating information. This review, the seventeenth to be published in *Reference Services Review*, includes items in English published in 1990. A few are not annotated because the compiler could not obtain copies of them for this review.

The list includes publications on user instruction in all types of libraries and for all levels of users, from small children to senior citizens and from beginning levels to the most advanced. The items are arranged by type of library and are in alphabetical order by author (or by title if there is no author) within those categories.

Overall, as shown in figure 1, the number of publications related to user education decreased by 16 percent between 1990 and 1991.

These figures are approximate and based on the published information that was available to the reviewer. However, since the availability of this information does not vary greatly from year to year, these figures should be reliable.

Publications dealing with user instruction in academic libraries continue to be the most numerous, and the number of publications in this category decreased by three percent. The number of publications about public libraries decreased by 75 percent; about school libraries decreased by 6 percent; and about

Rader is director, University Library, Cleveland State University, Cleveland, Ohio.

Type of Library	# of 1989 Publications	# of 1990 Publications	% Change
Academic	105	102	-03%
Public	08	02	-75%
School	18	17	-06%
Special	14	06	-57%
All Types	13	05	-62%
TOTAL	158	132	-16%

Figure 1: Number of Publications Related to User Education, 1989 and 1990

special libraries decreased by 57 percent. Publications about all levels decreased by about 62 percent.

User education publications in libraries continue to deal with teaching users how to access and organize information, including online searching, online system use, and bibliographic computer applications. An increasing percentage deal with evaluative research of user education. It is noteworthy that more user instructional articles are appearing in non-library journals.

This year's publications continue to refer to the importance of teaching library users to be information literate in a technological society. The focus on information literacy has continued to grow; librarians are becoming very interested in teaching users how to evaluate information and how to obtain critical thinking skills.

ACADEMIC LIBRARIES

Adledigba, Yakub. "User Education in Research Institutes' Libraries in Nigeria." *Quarterly Bulletin of the International Association of Agricultural Librarians and Documentalists* 35 (1990): 73-76.

Baker, Susan. "Providing Library Services to Overseas Students." *Library Association Record* 92 (July 1990): 509-10.

Summarizes a survey of international students at the Liverpool School of Tropical Medicine to assess their needs regarding bibliographic and library skills. Results from the survey were used to approximate user instruction for the students.

Banks, Julie, and S. Higgesson. "Conceptual and Mechanical Aspects of Subject Headings: A Brochure." *Show-Me-Libraries* 41 (Winter 1990): 25-29.

Describes a brochure prepared at Southeast Missouri State University to aid students in doing more successful subject searches in the online catalog.

Bell, Steven J. "Using the 'Live Demo'." *Online* 14 (May 1990): 38-42.

Discusses live demonstrations of online searching during instructional sessions. Provides advantages and helpful planning advice, from equipment availability to classroom techniques to troubleshooting hints.

Bessler, Joanne, et al. "Do Library Patrons Know What's Good for Them?" *The Journal of Academic Librarianship* 16 (May 1990): 76-85.

Author advocates that academic libraries should not try to teach patrons what they think is good for them, but what patrons want from the library. Six librarians respond to Bessler's argument in short opinion articles that follow.

Bodi, Sonia. "Teaching Effectiveness and Bibliographic Instruction: The Relevance of Learning Styles." *College and Research Libraries* 5 (March 1990): 113-19.

Examines learning styles of university students as well as Kolb's theory of experimental learning. Provides information on the use of Kolb's theory in the freshman library instruction program at North Park College.

Bodi, Sonia. "Through a Glass Darkly: Critical Thinking and Bibliographic Instruction." *Catholic Library World* 61 (May-June 1990): 252-56.

Argues that bibliographic instruction can be used to teach students critical thinking skills. Describes a practical application of this at North Park College.

Boenau, A. Bruce. "Introducing Students to Reference Sources in Comparative Politics." *Political Science Teacher* 3 (Summer 1990): 12-14.

Outlines a project designed to inform students about library reference sources essential to an introductory course in comparative politics. Suggests how the project can incorporate current topics. Stresses the importance of student familiarity with periodical guides, newspaper indexes, standard biographical sources, and yearbooks.

— HANNELORE B. RADER —

Boosinger, Marcia. "Associations between Faculty Publishing Output and Opinions Regarding Student Library Skills." *College and Research Libraries* 51 (September 1990): 471-81.

This study investigated the relationship between faculty publishing output, faculty instructional practices, and faculty perceptions of student needs and abilities related to the library. A positive relationship was found between publishing output and classes taught that require library use.

Bostian, Rebecca, and A. Robbins. "Effective Instruction for Searching CD-ROM Indexes." *Laserdisk Professional* 3 (January 1990): 14-17.

Examines the relationship between successful searching of databases on CD-ROM by undergraduate students and the various types of instruction provided by the library staff.

Bourne, Donna. "Computer-Assisted Instruction, Learning Theory, and Hypermedia: An Associative Language." *Research Strategies* 8 (Fall 1990): 160-71.

Reviews computer-assisted instruction and its application to user instruction in the future.

Breivik, Patricia S. "Information Literacy: Revolution in Education." In *Coping with Information Illiteracy: Bibliographic Instruction for the Information Age*, ed. by G.E. Mensching and T.B. Mensching, 1-6. Ann Arbor, MI: Pierian Press, 1989.

Discusses resource-based learning as a fundamental approach to restructure education in order to prepare students of today for lifelong learning and active citizenship in our information society. Gives numerous challenges to librarians, the most important being that librarians must convince faculty and campus administrators that information literacy can make the learning process more active.

Brothman, May, and M. Loe. *The LIRT Library Instruction Handbook.* Englewood, CO: Libraries Unlimited, Inc. 1990.

This handbook, written by a member of the ALA Library Instruction Roundtable, provides practical advice and recommendations to plan, evaluate, and improve library instruction programs in academic, school, public, and special libraries. Includes a selective bibliography and an index.

Bruce, Christine, and G.H. Brameld. "Improving the Quality of Fourth-Year Civil Engineering Research Projects through Bibliographic Instruction." *Research Strategies* 8 (Summer 1990): 129-36.

Describes a library instruction program at Queensland University of Technology in Australia to improve library research projects done by civil engineering students.

Bruce, Christine. "Information Skills Coursework for Postgraduate Students: Investigation and Response at the Queensland University of Technology." *Australian Academic and Research Libraries* 4 (1990): 224-32.

Describes an intensive course on information retrieval skills for college students at Queensland University of Technology in Australia. Course planning was based on a survey of postgraduate students and their supervisors.

Bush, Renee, and M. Wells. "Bibliographic Instruction for Honor Students: The University at Buffalo Experience." *Research Strategies* 8 (Summer 1990): 137-43.

Provides a description of a library instruction program for fifth-semester honor students at SUNY-Buffalo, including future plans for expanding this instruction.

Canelas, Cathryn, and L. Westbook. "B.I. in the Local High School." *College and Research Libraries News* 51 (March 1990): 217-20.

Describes in detail the planning and implementation of a bibliographic instruction program between the University of Michigan Undergraduate Library and the local high school to prepare students for college.

Cardman, Elizabeth. "The Gender Gap in Computer Use: Implications for Bibliographic Instruction." *Research Strategies* 8 (Summer 1990): 116-28.

Discusses the gender gap in computer utilization. Addresses disadvantages of female campus library users in regard to computerized library resources and what to do about this.

Charles, Susan, and K.E. Clark. "Enhancing CD-ROM Searches with Online Updates: An Examination of End-User Needs, Strategies, and Problems." *College and Research Libraries* 51 (July 1990): 321-28.

Reports a research project conducted at Texas A&M University Library involving searching patterns and search behavior of CD-ROM databases. End-user searching methodology and search strategies were found to be underdeveloped indicating a need for more and better user instruction.

Collins, Donald, et al. *Libraries and Research. A Practical Approach.* 2d ed. Dubuque, IA: Kendall/Hunt, 1990.

Dennis, Nancy, and N.D. Harrington. "Librarian and Faculty Member Differences in Using Information

Technologies." *Reference Services Review* 18, no. 3 (Fall 1990): 47-52.

Examines current status of library programs for teaching information technologies and how they fulfill librarians' views of what users need rather than faculty's or users' ideas of what they need. Provides techniques on how to remedy this situation.

Dennis, Nancy. "New Technologies for Libraries and Classrooms: An Information Fair." *Research Strategies* 8 (Winter 1990): 37-39.

Librarians at Salem State College put on a special fair about new technologies for libraries to familiarize faculty and students about existing computer technologies in the library and in the classroom.

Dimitroff, Alexandra, et al. "Alliance for Information: Michigan Librarians and Library Faculty Join Forces for the Future." *Research Strategies* 8 (Spring 1990): 52-58.

Describes a program at the University of Michigan where librarians and library school faculty are cooperating to enhance the information literacy of all students and to overcome institutional barriers to the information created by and of concern to non-mainstream populations.

Eadie, Tom. "Immodest Proposals." *Library Journal* 115 (15 October 1990): 42-45.

Presents arguments against the value of user instruction by calling it marginal and redundant. Offers reference service as an alternative to user instruction. Points out many problems with user instruction and its futility.

Eisenberg, Phyllis. "Going Out on a Limb and Falling Off." In *Coping with Information Illiteracy: Bibliographic Instruction for the Information Age*, ed. by G.E. Mensching and T.B. Mensching, 91-93. Ann Arbor, MI: Pierian Press, 1989.

Describes a one-credit library course at Piedmont Virginia Community College to teach students library literacy.

Elsbernd, Mary E., et al. "The Best of OPAC Instruction: A Selected Guide for the Beginner." *Research Strategies* 8 (Winter 1990): 28-36.

Reviews library instruction literature from 1980-1989. Selected materials include value of OPAC instruction, teaching methods, staffing needs, faculty education, and serving remote users.

Engeldinger, Eugene A., and P. Stuart. "The Library in Social Work Research: A Review of Social Work Research Textbooks." *RQ* 29 (Spring 1990): 369-79.

Because instruction in library search strategies is often neglected in social work education, about 75 major social work and social science textbooks were reviewed and divided into three groups by the amount of coverage of library research skills. Strengths and weaknesses along with suggestions for a model orientation to library use are provided.

Fister, Barbara, and K.R. Huber. "Recreating the Renaissance: Dramatic Presentations in an Art History Class." *Research Strategies* 8 (Fall 1990): 200-203.

Describes a library instruction project at Gustavus Adolphus College for art history students to help them do real research using primary sources and to present findings.

Fjallbrant, Nancy. "Why User Education and How Can Information Technology Help?" *IFLA Journal* 16 (1990): 405-13.

Examines the effects of information technology as applied to user education, specifically in the Nordic academic libraries. Discusses how online databases, optical storage devices, document delivery, systems, electronic publishing, and electronic mail affect user education globally.

Fox, Lynne. "Partnership for the Future: Information Literacy in Nursing Education." *Colorado Libraries* (September 1989): 26-27.

This column on bibliographic instruction, edited by Jon Grate, describes how the ACRL Model Statement of Objectives for Academic Bibliographic Instruction has been applied to the University of Northern Colorado's nursing program.

Fox, Lynne, et al. "Pathways to Information Literacy." *Journal of Nursing Education* 28 (November 1989): 422-25.

Provides detailed information on how librarians at the University of Northern Colorado worked with the nursing faculty to integrate information literacy into the nursing curriculum.

Fox, Lynne. "Teaching the Wise Use of Information - Evaluation Skills for Nursing Students." *Western Journal of Nursing Research* 11 (December 1989): 773-76.

Describes a strategy for teaching nursing research to nursing students utilizing evaluation of information skills.

Frank, Polly. "Information Literacy through Interactive Instruction: Using the Online Catalog to Teach Basic Concepts of Information Organization and Access." In *Coping with Information Illiteracy: Bibliographic*

Instruction for the Information Age, ed. by G.E. Mensching and T.B. Mensching, 96-99. Ann Arbor, MI: Pierian Press, 1989.

Explains how to use the online catalog to teach students basic concepts of organizing information at Mankato State University.

Frick, Elizabeth. "Qualitative Evaluation of User Education Programs: The Best Choice?" *Research Strategies* 8 (Winter 1990): 3-13.

Discusses qualitative assessment of user education as a valid alternative to statistical evaluation. Suggests methods and processes such as interviewing, observing, and collecting descriptive data, with inductive analysis of the data gathered, to make qualitative evaluation relatively rigorous.

Garcha, Rajinder, and J.N. Gatten. "Preliminary Observation of Non-traditional University Students' Library Skills." *Library Review* 39 (1990): 13-20.

Discusses the needs of non-traditional students (re-entering adults) for library skills. Compares library skills and library attitudes of traditional and non-traditional freshman students based on a study conducted at Kent State University in 1989.

George, Mary W. "Instructional Services." In *Academic Libraries: Research Perspectives*, ed. by Mary Jo Lynch, 106-142. Chicago: American Library Association, 1990.

Reviews the literature on library instruction services for the last 30 years.

Glasberg, Davita, et al. "The Library Scavenger Hunt: Teaching Library Skills in Introductory Sociology Courses." *Teaching Sociology* 18 (April 1990): 231-34.

Argues that library skills instruction should be an integral part of the undergraduate sociology curriculum. Provides practical strategies for teaching library skills.

Gold, Michael. "The Mathsci CD-ROM at Purdue University: Video Instruction." In *National Online Meeting Proceedings*, 131-36. Medford, NJ: Learned Information, 1990.

Describes the preparation of a seven-minute video to familiarize library users with the use of Mathsci CD-ROM.

Hoover, D.G., and V. Clayton. "Graduate Bibliographic Instruction in ERIC on CD-ROM." *Behavioral and Social Sciences Librarian* 8 (1989): 1-12.

Describes a bibliographic instruction program for master's candidates in education that trains students to be independent information seekers using traditional print-based materials as well as ERIC on CD-ROM.

The rationale for the course is discussed, and the materials and methods used in the course are described in detail.

Hunter, Rhonda, and C. Levine. *Library Research Workbook*. ERIC Reproduction Service, 1990. ED320 584.

Includes ten chapters on library research such as doing the research paper, locating information in various reference, and indexing sources and planning a research strategy. It was developed for students at North Carolina State University.

Iroka, Luke. "Library Orientation and Instruction for Students in Nigerian Medical Schools." *Research Strategies* 8 (Spring 1990): 82-84.

Describes user instruction and library orientation in Nigeria medical schools where these efforts are just beginning.

Jackson, Rebecca. "Transforming the ACRL Model Statement of Objectives into a Working Tool." In *Coping with Information Illiteracy: Bibliographic Instruction for the Information Age*, ed. by G.E. Mensching and T.B. Mensching, 61-80. Ann Arbor, MI: Pierian Press, 1989.

Describes how the librarians at the University of Maryland adopted the ACRL Model Statement of Objectives for Bibliographic Instruction in order to help evaluate the effectiveness of their bibliographic instruction program.

Jacobovits, Leon, and Diane Nahl-Jacobovitz. "Measuring Information Searching Competence." *College and Research Libraries* 51 (September 1990): 448-62.

Uses a taxonomy of instructional objectives for information searching behavior that includes affective, cognifices, and sensorimotor items to test three types of university students. Provides implications for bibliographic instruction and appropriate teaching activities.

Kirkendall, Carolyn. "Competencies for Short-Term or Lifelong Learning?" In *Coping with Information Illiteracy: Bibliographic Instruction for the Information Age*, ed. by G.E. Mensching and T.B. Mensching, 81-95. Ann Arbor, MI: Pierian Press, 1989.

Features a discussion by Richard Feinberg on how short-term library skill competencies are the only possible goals in library instruction. Carolyn Dusenburg argues that it is possible to teach lifelong learning skills through user instruction by imparting generalizable skills for information utilization.

Koehler, Boyd, and K. Swanson. "Basic Writers and the Library: A Plan for Providing Meaningful Bibliographic Instruction." *Journal of Basic Writing* 9 (Spring 1990): 56-74.

Describes a way to help basic writers, including English-as-a-Second-Language (ESL) students, learn and enjoy the fundamentals of bibliographic instruction. Outlines the pretest for readiness, the in-library practicum, and the posttest to measure progress.

Lawson, V. Lonnie. "A Cost Comparison between General Library Tours and Computer-Assisted Instruction Programs." *Research Strategies* 8 (Spring 1990): 66-73.

Provides information on the cost of methods of library orientation at Central Missouri State University. Provides specific data on cost.

Lawson, V. Lonnie, and C.E. Slattery. "Involvement in Bibliographic Instruction among Technical Services Librarians in Missouri Academic Libraries." *Library Resources and Technical Services* 34 (April 1990): 245-48.

Reports a survey in Missouri of selected academic libraries to determine the degree to which technical services librarians were involved in bibliographic instruction and how public and technical services librarians felt about it.

Lents, Ben, and C. Pracht. "The New General Education and Bibliographic Instruction at Southeast Missouri State University." *Show-Me-Libraries* 41 (Winter 1990): 20-22.

Describes the university's general education program as part of an independent college requiring a core curriculum of 48 credited hours. The program includes a major bibliographic instruction component.

Lewis, Patricia, and D. Postlethwaite. "Another Time Another Place: Personal/Public History." *Research Strategies* 8 (Spring 1990): 90-93.

Presents term paper assignments that meet class goals and teach library use but take a non-traditional approach.

Liestman, Daniel, and C. Wee. "Library Orientation for International Students in Their Native Language." *Research Strategies* 8 (Fall 1990): 191-96.

At Rutgers University, librarians provide international students with library orientation in English, Chinese, and Korean. Evaluations have shown this instruction to be effective.

Lowry, Anita. "Beyond BI: Information Literacy in the Electronic Age." *Research Strategies* 8 (Winter 1990): 22-27.

Discusses the need for more complex user instruction because of the new information technologies. Describes a graduate course at Columbia University for humanities students that incorporates computer-based resources, information retrieval, scholarly communication, and analysis of primary sources.

Lutzker, Marilyn. "Bibliographic Instruction and Accreditation in Higher Education." *College and Research Libraries News* 51 (January 1990): 14-18.

Discusses the Middle States Commission on Higher Education's new requirement for accredited institutions to have a bibliographic instruction program and implications for academic librarians. Provides information on bibliographic instruction as part of accreditation, self-studies, syllabi, and library objectives.

MacAdam, Barbara. "Information Literacy: Models for the Curriculum." *College and Research Libraries News* 51 (November 1990): 948-51.

The challenge of information literacy is prompting librarians to rethink their instructional programs to foster independent analytical thinking. Librarians must become trained to teach understanding of the nature and principles of library-based research.

Mandernack, Scott. "An Assessment of Education and Training Needs for Bibliographic Instruction Librarians." *Journal of Education for Library and Information Science* 30 (Winter 1990): 193-205.

A study of Wisconsin librarians finds that they have not had sufficient training for bibliographic instruction. Suggests methods based on librarians' needs for continuing education. The questionnaire used is appended.

Maynard, J. Edmund. "A Case Study of Faculty Attitudes Toward Library Instruction: The Citadel Experience." *Reference Service Review* 18, no. 2 (Summer 1990): 67-76.

Reviews a survey of the faculty at Citadel, the Military College of South Carolina, to assess the English faculty as well as other faculty regarding their perception of library instruction. Results indicated a major division between integrated library instruction (English faculty) and a credit course (other faculty).

Mensching, Teresa. "Dialogue and Debate." *Research Strategies* 8 (Winter 1990): 44-47.

This column discusses the relationship between bibliographic instruction and information literacy as presented by Joan Kaplowitz from UCLA, Diana Shonrock from Iowa State University, Donald Kenney from Virginia Tech University, and Anne Roberts from SUNY-Albany.

Mensching, Teresa. *Library Instruction Clearinghouse: A Directory, 1989. Updated/Revised*. ERIC Reproduction Service, 1990. ED 320 600.

Lists directory information for academic library instruction resources, such as state clearinghouses, newsletters, salaries, and program information.

Miller, Steven, and M. Warmkessel. "Bibliographic Instruction, History of the Book and Post-Structuralism: An Unlikely Combination Helps to Expand the Critical Thinking Skills of Undergraduates." *Research Strategies* 8 (Spring 1990): 59-65.

Describes a joint effort between a librarian and a faculty member at Millerville University to teach students critical thinking skills.

Moran, Barbara B. "Increasing Active Learning in Undergraduate Education." *College and Research Library News* 51 (June 1990): 511-14.

Advocates close cooperation between the library and classroom teaching similar to the library college idea but in the new technological environment.

Nahl-Jacobovits, Diane, and Leon A. Jacobovits. "Learning Principles and the Library Environment." *Research Strategies* 8 (1990): 74-81.

Discusses the broadest possible application of learning principles to bibliographic instruction. The authors see motivation, responding, and reinforcement as necessary conditions for effective learning. Both reinforcement and self-regulatory behavior are key factors in creating positive attitudes and outcomes for patrons.

Obenhaus, Bruce. "Maps: Knowing Enough to Help Users Help Themselves." *Research Strategies* 8 (Summer 1990): 144-49.

Discusses the need for map use instruction in academic libraries and how librarians can accomplish this.

Olsen, Jan K., and B. Coons. "Cornell University's Information Literacy Program." In *Coping with Information Illiteracy: Bibliographic Instruction for the Information Age*, ed. by G.E. Mensching and T.B. Mensching, 7-13. Ann Arbor, MI: Pierian Press, 1989.

Describes the library's information illiteracy program at Cornell's Mann Library dealing with the development of agricultural economics. The program includes goals and objectives for four years of instruction, evaluation, and anticipated outcomes.

Patterson, Charles, and D.W. Howell. "Library User Education: Assessing the Attitudes of Those Who Teach." *RQ* 29 (Summer 1990): 513-24.

Summarizes a 1987 survey of bibliographic instruction librarians to assess their procedures and attitudes. It was found that librarians are not prepared in their professional education for teaching nor do they have administrative support for it. B.I. librarians were found to be very resourceful in self-improvement, self-evaluation, and other problems.

Penchansky, Mimi, and L. Schneider. *Instructional Perspectives: A Dialogue between High School and College Librarians. Promoting Student Independence in the Library. An Annotated Selective Bibliography on the Theme of the 1990 LACUNY Institute*. ERIC Reproduction Service, 1990. ED 322 917.

This is a five-part annotated bibliography to promote cooperative library instruction between high school and college librarians to promote information literacy.

Poe, Retta. "A Strategy for Improving Literature Reviews in Psychology Courses." *Teaching of Psychology* 17 (February 1990): 54-55.

Describes an intervention program to teach undergraduates to write literature review papers in psychology.

Puttapithakporn, Somporn. "Interface Design and User Problems and Errors: A Case Study of Novice Searchers." *RQ* 30 (Winter 1990): 195-204.

This article deals with problems inexperienced searchers encounter in using CD-ROM products. Provides recommendations based on a small study that used observation, questionnaires, and interviews. Proposed system design improvements and training program changes.

Rader, Hannelore. "Bibliographic Instruction or Information Literacy?" *College and Research Libraries News* 51 (January 1990): 18-20.

Points out the importance of information literacy in preparing citizens for the twenty-first century. Shows that information literacy builds on bibliographic instruction but also broadens it.

Rader, Hannelore. "Bringing Information Literacy into the Academic Curriculum." *College and Research Libraries News* 51 (October 1990): 879-80.

Describes the establishment of a comprehensive information literacy program at Cleveland State University.

Ream, Dan. "Using Tabloid Literature to Teach Critical Reading Skills." In *Coping with Information Illiteracy: Bibliographic Instruction for the Information Age*, ed. by G.E. Mensching and T.B. Mensching, 112-13. Ann Arbor, MI: Pierian Press, 1989.
     Describes how tabloid literature can be utilized to teach students critical thinking skills to evaluate information.

Reichel, Mary. "Library Literacy." *RQ* 29 (Spring 1990): 348-53.
     This column was prepared by Nancy Totten on "Teaching Students to Evaluate Information: A Justification." It reviews the literature on critical thinking in relation to library instruction and provides a practical description of a teaching session on information evaluation at Indiana University Southeast.

Reichel, Mary. "Library Literacy." *RQ* 29 (Summer 1990): 505-9.
     This column deals with "teaching research as a social act: collaborative learning and the library" and was written by Barbara Fisher. The author describes how she teaches students the research process in her B.I. sessions through the use of collaborative learning. This instruction helps students to become aware of knowledge as a network of relationships that is interdependent and changing.

Reichel, Mary. "Library Literacy." *RQ* 30 (Fall 1990): 46-49.
     This column is written by Lori Arp and deals with "information literacy or bibliographic justification: semantics or philosophy?" The author clarifies the context in which either term is used and gives relevant political and educational implications. Shows the challenge of information literacy to libraries.

Reichel, Mary. "Library Literacy." *RQ* 30 (Winter 1990): 189-92.
     This column is written by Gemm Devinney who describes an effective communication model about bibliographic instruction at the State University of New York at Buffalo's seven major library units.

Reinhart, Billie, and G. Thompson. "Sailing the Seas of Information at Cleveland State." *College and Research Libraries News* 51 (February 1990): 112-15.
     Describes an innovative library orientation program for new freshmen at Cleveland State University using the nautical theme.

Ridgeway, Trish. "Information Literacy: An Introductory Reading List." *College and Research Libraries News* 51 (July-August 1990): 645-48.
     Provides a definition of information literacy, explains the need for coalitions to bring about national information literacy, and highlights major publications on this topic.

Ridgeway, Trish. "Integrating Active Learning Techniques into the One-Hour Bibliographic Instruction Lecture." In *Coping with Information Illiteracy: Bibliographic Instruction for the Information Age*, ed. by G.E. Mensching and T.B. Mensching, 33-42. Ann Arbor, MI: Pierian Press, 1989.
     Describes how active learning can be integrated into a library instruction service. Using cognitive and affective objectives can help improve teaching effectiveness as demonstrated by practical examples.

Rohfeld, Rae, et al. *How Are Libraries and Archives Different? Introduction to Archival Research*. ERIC Reproduction Service, 1990. ED 324 005.
     Explains the difference between library and archival research. Details the type of materials available in the archives and their use for primary research.

Royse, Molly, and R.M. Sands. "Bibliographic Instruction and Afro-American Music: An Experience in Faculty-Librarian Cooperation." *Research Strategies* 8 (Winter 1990): 40-43.
     Describes a unique research experience for undergraduates at Berea College; team-taught by faculty and librarian.

Santa Vicca, Edmund. "A Case Study of Bibliographic Instruction in France: Bibliotheque des Letres, Universite de Nice, Sophia-Antipolis." *Research Strategies* 8 (Fall 1990): 181-90.
     Examines user instruction at a French university in the area of French language and literature. Compares it to user instruction in U.S. academic libraries.

Sheridan, Jean. "The Reflective Librarian: Some Observations on Bibliographic Instruction in the Academic Library." *Journal of Academic Librarianship* 16 (March 1990): 22-26.
     Argues for the use of collaborative learning in B.I. Methods are discussed and specific applications are given. Special needs of students are considered.

Sherratt, Christine, and M.L. Schlabach. "The Applications of Concept Mapping in Reference and Information Service." *RQ* 30 (Fall 1990): 60-69.
     Describes the importance of concept teaching and learning in reference, instruction, and research.

Provides concept maps to help librarians learn conceptual approaches to various areas of librarianship.

Shirato, Linda. "Dialogue and Debate." *Research Strategies* 8 (Spring 1990): 94-97.

This column focuses on use of video in user instruction and features comments from Marsha Forys from the University of Iowa, Jean Smith from the University of California, San Diego, Virginia Tiefel from Ohio State University, Joan Clarke from St. Louis Community College, Mary Beth Bell from the Community College of the Finger Lakes, and Jim Vasstine from the University of South Florida-Tampa.

Shirato, Linda. "Dialogue and Debate." *Research Strategies* 8 (Spring 1990): 150-52.

This column addresses specific difficulties in bibliographic instruction and ways to address them. Responses were provided by Helene Williams from Michigan State University, Lynell Buckley from Louisiana Tech University, and Barbara Fister from Gustavus Adolphus College.

Shoolbred, Michael. "Writing a Project: A Library User Education Package for Engineering Students." *Education for Information* 8 (March 1990): 33-40.

Summarizes a current writing project in the United Kingdom to prepare a user instruction learning package in a polytechnic library for engineering students. The material consists of six booklets designed for open learning and structured writing techniques. The material is available to librarians on floppy disk for helping them customize their library needs.

Somerville, Arleen. "Perspectives and Criteria for Chemical Information Instruction." *Journal of Chemical Information and Computer Services* 30 (1990): 177-81.

The American Chemical Society's Committee on Professional Training has guidelines for library resources and chemical information instruction. However, chemistry departments have problems implementing the instruction guidelines. Provides ideas for overcoming these problems.

Stachacz, John, and T. Brennan. "Bibliographic Instruction in an Undergraduate Biology Course." *Research Strategies* 8 (Winter 1990): 14-21.

Describes course-integrated bibliographic instruction designed to introduce undergraduate biology students to methods of searching the literature at Dickinson College.

Staines, Gail. "Articulation Agreements for Bibliographic Instruction." *Community and Junior College Libraries* 7 (1990): 17-22.

Describes an articulation agreement in the area of bibliographic instruction between Clinton Community College and SUNY-Plattsburgh. A one-credit course was provided for community college students to teach them library skills to prepare them for transfer to the four-year university.

Still, Julie. "A Boring Approach to Library Research: Boring's Mother-in-law as an Introduction to Psychology Sources." *Research Strategies* 8 (Spring 1990): 85-89.

Describes an innovative search strategy to teach psychology students library research methods at the University of Richmond.

Tomaindo, Nicholas G. "Reconsidering Bibliographic Instruction for Adult Reentry Students: Emphasizing the Practical." *Reference Services Review* 18, no. 1 (Spring 1990): 49-54.

Presents surveys of educational needs of reentry students in regards to bibliographic instruction. Discusses reentry students' learning styles and life experiences and how to incorporate them into library instruction.

Tucker, Dennis. *Finding Sociology (in the Library). A Student Manual of Information Retrieval and Utilization Skills.* Bristol, IN: Wyndham Hall Press, 1990.

Provides instruction in the basic skills needed to do research in sociology including using libraries and finding information related to sociology.

Tuckett, Harold. "Computer Literacy, Information Literacy, and the Role of Instruction Librarians." In *Coping with Information Illiteracy: Bibliographic Instruction for the Information Age*, ed. by G.E. Mensching and T.B. Mensching, 21-31. Ann Arbor, MI: Pierian Press, 1989.

Explains the relationship between computer and information literacy and implications for teaching students to become literate in both areas. Points out complexities for instruction librarians and advocates broadening of institutional goals.

Turner, Ann. "Computer Assisted Instruction in Academic Libraries." *Journal of Academic Librarianship* 15 (January 1990): 352-54.

Provides 12 situational characteristics for computer-assisted instruction application in organizations.

Walters, John. "Federal Documents for Undergraduate Students in Public Administration." *Research Strategies* 8 (Fall 1990): 197-99.

Describes how U.S. documents can be used by undergraduate students to teach them how to do original research using primary sources.

Welsch, Erwin K., and Abigail Loomis. "Research Assistant: A HyperCard Approach to Library Instruction." *OCLC Micro* 6 (April 1990): 20-25.

Provides an in-depth examination and review of "Research Assistant," a HyperCard stack designed to provide computer-assisted instruction for the research process. Looks at the program both pedagogically and technically and raises questions about the role of technology in library instruction.

Whitaker, Cathy Seitz. "Pile-Up at the Reference Desk: Teaching Users to Use CD-ROMs." *The Laserdisk Professional* 3 (March 1990): 30-34.

Reports the results of a survey of 38 librarians, who had experience in training CD-ROM end-users to determine the most effective way to train patrons in the use of CD-ROMs. Covers a wide range of CD-ROM-related instructional issues.

Wilson, Linda. "A Graduate Course in Information Literacy." In *Coping with Information Illiteracy: Bibliographic Instruction for the Information Age*, ed. by G.E. Mensching and T.B. Mensching, 114-22. Ann Arbor, MI: Pierian Press, 1989.

Describes a graduate course on information literacy to education students. Provides several innovative approaches to teaching students valuable information skills.

Wittkopf, Barbara. "BI Librarians and Information Literacy." Editorial. *Research Strategies* 8 (Spring 1990): 50-51.

Comments on ALA's report on information literacy and its impact on bibliographic instruction librarians.

Wittkopf, Barbara. "Proficiencies for BI Librarians: Who Defines Them?" *Research Strategies* 8 (Spring 1990): 102-3.

Discusses proficiencies for institution librarians and who should define them.

Wittkopf, Barbara. "White House Conferences and B.I." Editorial. *Research Strategies* 8 (Fall 1990): 158-59.

Reviews outcomes of the first White House Conference on Library and Information Services and discusses the second one regarding instruction librarians.

Wood, Judith, and M.E. Tucker. "Online Education Project: Library and Information Science Intermediaries for Environmental Science and Engineering Students." In *National Online Meeting Proceedings*, 461-65. Medford, NJ: Learned Information, 1990.

Describes a cooperative project between the University of North Carolina's School of Information and Library Science, the Department of Environmental Sciences and Engineering (ESE), and the Health Sciences Library to provide bibliographic instruction to ESE graduate students and give them experience in online searching.

Wright, Carol, and Mary Ellen Larson. "Basic Information Access Skills: Curriculum Design Using a Matrix Approach." *Research Strategies* 8 (Summer 1990): 104-15.

Describes a matrix to identify conceptual gaps in traditional instruction programs to help individuals become information literate.

Yee, Sandra. "Information Literacy Skills: How Students Learn Them and Why." In *Coping with Information Illiteracy: Bibliographic Instruction for the Information Age*, ed. by G.E. Mensching and T.B. Mensching, 43-59. Ann Arbor, MI: Pierian Press, 1989.

Provides a definition of information literacy and how to teach information literacy skills by utilizing appropriate learning theories. Provides an example of teaching information skills to minority students at Eastern Michigan University.

PUBLIC LIBRARIES

Good, Julanne. "Term Papers: Where to Turn." *School Library Journal* 36 (August 1990): 102.

Describes how the St. Louis Public Library copes with students who need library instruction to do term papers. A series of orientation workshops taught by a retired school librarian has helped to alleviate the problem.

Haigh, Bernard. "Behind the Stacks: Derby Central Library's User Education Course." *Library Association Record* 92 (January 1990): 41-43.

Describes an eight-week user education course at Derby Central Library, a British public library.

SCHOOL LIBRARIES

Berry, Margaret, and P. Morris. *Stepping into Research. A Complete Research Skills Activities Program for Grades 5-12*. Center for Applied Research in Education, 1990.

Designed to prepare students in various grade levels for research assignments. Can be used as course of study or by individual units. Provides objectives, activities, and tests.

Daniel, Twyla. "Extending Literacy with School Libraries." *Language Arts* 67 (November 1990): 746-49.

Discusses how one school library functions as a natural setting for extending the literacy of students, even though the library has no librarian.

Di Betta, Chrystal. "The Poetry of Science." *The School Librarian's Workshop* 10 (March 1990): 12-13.

Describes a library skills teaching unit combining science and humanities for grades five to eight.

Gerhard, Brenda. "De-mystifying the Media Center." *School Library Journal* 36 (June 1990): 67.

States that it is the librarian's role to initiate and implement library orientation.

Intner, Sheila. "The Public and Bibliographic Instruction: Missed Opportunities in Creating a Positive Information Environment." *Reference Librarian* 31 (1990): 15-30.

Discusses the public need for bibliographic instruction in libraries, what they are learning, who is not being served, and what the implications of that failure are. It is suggested that bibliographic instruction should create a public knowledgeable about the information environment, including its principles, structure, systems, and libraries as integral parts.

"Into the Curriculum." *School Library Media Activities Monthly* 7 (December 1990): 16-26.

Provides seven fully developed library media activities to be used in conjunction with specific curriculum units in French, mathematics, reading/language arts, science, and social studies. Grade levels, objectives, curriculum objectives, resources, instructional roles, activities and procedures for completion, evaluation, and follow-up are described for each activity.

Keppel, Mildred. "Presidents in Perspective." *The School Librarian's Workshop* 10 (February 1990): 6-7.

Outlines a library skills teaching unit on the presidents for sixth-grade social studies students. Uses worksheets and activities to teach research and critical thinking skills.

Kuhlthau, Carol. "Information Skills for an Information Society: A Review of Research." *Information Reports and Bibliographics* 19 (1990): 14-26.

Summarizes a study to assess which information technologies are useful in schools and reviews interna-

tional information literacy programs to prepare students for the information age.

Lamb, Annette. "Dictionary Skills Go High Tech: Using Webster's Dictionary on CD-ROM." *School Library Media Activities Monthly* 7 (January 1991): 40-42.

Describes the Macintosh CD-ROM edition of *Webster's Ninth New Collegiate Dictionary* and discusses advantages and disadvantages of using the electronic dictionary in library media skills instruction. Use in large group instruction is discussed and advantages are highlighted, including the large print feature, sound feature, and ability to search cross-references.

Lamb, Annette. "Hyper about HyperCard? An Introduction to HyperCard in the School Library Media Center." *School Library Media Activities Monthly* 6 (June 1990): 32-34.

Briefly describes the elements of HyperCard and discusses its potential as an easy authoring tool for library media specialists to use in creating professional quality, computer-based instructional materials. Suggestions for the development of presentations, tutorials, information exploration exercises, and desktop instruction using HyperCard are offered.

McCutcheon, Randall. "Library Scavenger Hunts: A Way Out of the Bewilderness." *Wilson Library Bulletin* 64 (January 1990): 38-40.

An English teacher at Albuquerque Academy teaches his students information literacy and critical thinking skills through scavenger hunts.

Neuman, Delia, and R. Jackson. *MAJIK/1: Hyperland Introduction to the Use of Periodicals, Final Report.* ERIC Reproduction Service, 1990. ED 323 964.

Describes a HyperCard program at the University of Maryland to provide individual instruction to use periodicals. Includes pre- and posttests.

Pennsylvania Online: A Curriculum Guide for School Library Media Centers. ERIC Reproduction Service, 1990. ED 324 009.

This is a curriculum guide for teaching library media skills in all schools in Pennsylvania. It includes goals and objectives to prepare students for information and lifelong learning skills and incorporates online access information skills.

"Proof of Teaching." *The School Librarians' Workshop* 10 (January 1990): 1-3.

Demonstrates how library media skills instruction should have the cumulative effect of creating lifelong learners. Describes an application with seventh graders in U.S. history and politics.

Ross, Shirley L. "Information Skills in the Information Laboratory." *School Library Media Activities Monthly* 6 (March 1990): 31-33.

Describes a process approach to library media skills instruction that would focus on the development of students' critical thinking skills and give them the ability to examine and utilize information. The importance of instructing students in database searching and ways that database searching will enhance information skills development are also addressed.

Santeford, Deborah, et al. "Into the Curriculum." *School Library Media Activities Monthly* 7 (October 1990): 18-27.

Provides seven fully developed library media activities to be used in conjunction with specific curriculum units in mathematics, music, science, and social studies. Grade levels, objectives, curriculum objectives, resources, instructional roles, activities, and procedures for completion, evaluation, and follow-up are described for each activity.

Waddle, Linda. "School Media Matters." *Wilson Library Bulletin* 64 (April 1990): 84-86.

Discusses teaching strategies for the online catalog in school media centers.

SPECIAL LIBRARIES

Callinan, Ellen. "Research Protocols in Reference Service: Informal Instruction in Law Firm Libraries." *Law Library Journal* 82 (Winter 1990): 39-59.

Discusses how the former mentoring system for attorneys to teach them bibliographic and research skills is disintegrating. Formal in-house training is taking its place; however, formal legal research training serves more effectively at the point-of-need during reference service.

Dorsch, Josephine, et al. "A Multidisciplinary Approach to Information and Critical Appraisal Instruction." *Bulletin of the Medical Library Association* 78 (January 1990): 38-44.

Provides information on a ten-week critical appraisal course for third-year medical students taught by the library and the department of medicine at the University of Illinois. The course teaches selection, evaluations, and application of information to patient care.

Getaz, Joan. "Library Orientation for College Secretarial Staff." *College and Research Libraries News* 51 (May 1990): 427-28.

Describes a library orientation project for secretaries on campus to familiarize them with library resources.

Hardy, Trotter. "Project Clear's Computers in Legal Education; Assistance with Research: Paper Choice, a Hypertext System for Giving Advice about Legal Research." *Law Library Journal* 82 (Spring 1990): 209-37.

Levene, Lee. "Health Educators and Library Resources." *Health Education* 21 (September/October 1990): 25-29.

Wood, Elizabeth, et al. "Drug Information Skills for Pharmacy Students' Curriculum Integration." *Bulletin of the Medical Library Association* 78 (January 1990): 8-14.

Describes an interactive user education program for pharmacy students at the University of Southern California between the School of Pharmacy and the Norris Medical Library. The program involves all four years and incorporates advanced technology.

ALL LEVELS

Blake, Virgil, and R. Tjoumas. *Information Literacies for the Twenty-First Century*. Boston: G.K. Hall, 1990.

Includes a variety of papers written by scholars from diverse disciplines, addressing oral, visual, and print communication and the effects of computer technology on the information environment, culture, and society. Literacy is the major theme of the papers.

Breivik, Patricia. "National Forum on Information Literacy." In *ALA Yearbook of Library and Information Services*, 209. Chicago: ALA 1990.

Describes the formation and progress of the National Forum on Information Literacy as a coalition to promote information literacy.

Kimball, John, et al. "Providing Reference Assistance for Machine-Readable Materials: The Library of Congress Completes a One-Year Pilot." *Reference Librarian* 31 (1990): 31-38.

The Machine Readable Collections Reading Room of the Library of Congress is described with an emphasis on the reference assistance required and how it compares with assistance required in other areas of the Library of Congress. The interaction between users and librarians is shown to be like that of bibliographic instruction.

Kuhlthau, Carol. "The Information Search Process: From Theory to Practice." *Journal of Education for Library Information Science* 31 (Summer 1990): 72-75.

Kuhlthau, Carol, et al. "Validating a Model of the Search Process: A Comparison of Academic, Public and School Library Users." *Library and Information Science Research* 12 (January-March 1990): 5-31.

Reports a study funded by the U.S. Department of Education to determine whether the search for information process in the school library setting is generalizable to other types of libraries. Academic, school, and public libraries were studied to determine information seekers' search processes. Changes in thoughts and feelings were noted.

Nicholls, Paul Travis. "CD-ROM in the Library: Implications, Issues and Sources. *Laserdisk Professional* 3 (March 1990): 100-103.

Briefly discusses six issues related to the use of CD-ROM in libraries and provides sources of information on each issue. The issues discussed are pricing and costs; user preferences for CD-ROM; networking as a means of meeting high demand for CD-ROM; media options; strategic planning to meet demands; and bibliographic instruction.

Rader, Hannelore. "Library Orientation and Instruction 1989." *Reference Services Review* 18, no. 4 (Winter 1990): 35-48.

Gives annual review of library instruction literature for all types of libraries and all levels of users.

PARTICIPANTS

ROSTER OF PARTICIPANTS

Barbara Kay Adams
J. D. Williams Library
University of Mississippi
University, MS 38677

Jamileh Amirzafari
Library
Bloomfield College
Bloomfield, NJ 07003

Judith M. Arnold
Library
St. Xavier College
Chicago, IL 60655

Larry Baerveldt
Duggan Library
Hanover College
Hanover, IN 47234

Betsy Baker
Library
Northwestern University
Evanston, IL 60208

William Baker
Library
Miami University
Oxford, OH 45056

Mary Barton
Livingston Lord Library
Moorhead State University
Moorhead, MN 56563

Georgia Baugh
Pius XII Library
St. Louis University
St. Louis, MO 63108

Jeane Beccone
DeWitt Wallace Library
Macalester College
St. Paul, MN 55105

Patricia Berge
University Library
Marquette University
Milwaukee, WI 53233

Goodie Bhullar
158 Ellis Library
University of Missouri
Columbia, MO 65201

Marilee Birchfield
Library
Northwestern University
Evanston, IL 60201

Shirley Black
106 Kresge Library
Wayne State University
Detroit, MI 48202

Cheryl Blackwell
Library
Albion College
Albion, MI 49224

Carlene Bogle
University Library
California State Polytechnic
University
Pomona, CA 91768-3090

Mary Bopp
Main Library
Indiana University
Bloomington, IN 47401

Jane Bradford
Library
Stetson University
DeLand, FL 32720

Ann Breitenwischer
Library
Ferris State University
Big Rapids, MI 49307

Allison Bryant
Woodhouse LRC
Aquinas College
Grand Rapids, MI 49506

Lori Buchanan
Austin Peay State
Woodward Library
Clarksville, TN 37044

Lynell Buckley
Library
Louisiana Tech University
Ruston, LA 71270

Chester Bunnell
Pius XII Library
St. Louis University
St. Louis, MO 63108

Jane Burchfield
Bertrand Library
Bucknell University
Lewisburg, PA 17837

Paul Burnam
Ohio Wesleyan University
Library
Delaware, OH 43015

Gale Burrow
Honnold/Mudd Library
Claremont Colleges
Claremont, CA 91711

Renee Bush
Science/Engineering Library
SUNY-Buffalo
Buffalo, NY 14260

Judy M. Butler
Library
David Lipscomb University
Nashville, TN 37204

Jeff Coon
Library
Indiana University at Kokomo
Kokomo, IN 46904

Betty Dance
Merrill Library
Utah State University
Logan, UT 84322

Nancy Davidson
Dacus Library
Winthrop College
Rock Hill, SC 29733

Susan DeGregory
Library
University of North Alabama
Florence, AL 35632

Kathleen Donovan
Gutman Library
Harvard University
Cambridge, MA 02138

Eileen Douglas
Library
John Abbott College
McGill University
Ste. Anne De Bellevue
Quebec, Canada H9X 3L9

Sue Dubois
Library
Gull Lake High School
9550 East M-89
Richland, MI 49083

Linda Durfee
Wessell Library
Tufts University
Medford, MA 02155

Nancy Enright
English Department
Seton Hall University
South Orange, NJ 07079

Evan Farber
Lilly Library
Earlham College
Richmond, IN 47374

Valerie Feinman
Library
Adelphi University
Garden City, NJ 11530

Suzanne Fitzsimmons
Pius XII Memorial Library
St. Louis University
St. Louis, MO 63108

Faith Fleming
Olin Library
Cornell University
Ithaca, NY 14853

Marsha Forys
University Library
University of Iowa
Iowa City, IA 52242

Polly Frank
Mankato State University Library
Mankato, MN 56002

Donna Gagnier
Galvin Library
Illinois Institute of Technology
Chicago, IL 60616

Margaret Gardner
Wallace Library
Wheaton College
Norton, MA 02766

Rachel Gardner
Guggenheim Library
Monmouth College
West Long Branch, NJ 07764

Elaine Gawrych
Northeastern Illinois University
Library
Chicago, IL 60625

Betty J. Glass
Getchell Library
University of Nevada-Reno
Reno, NV 89557

Linda Goff
Library
California State University
Sacramento, CA 95819

Elaine Gordon
Library
DePaul University
Chicago, IL 60614

Steve Gowler
Teszler Library
Wofford College
Spartanburg, SC 29303

Marcia Grimes
Library
Wheaton College
Norton, MA 02766

Margaret Groesbeck
Library
Amherst College
Amherst, MA 01002

Julia Gustafson
Andrews Library
College of Wooster
Wooster, OH 44691

Ruth Gustafson
Biomedical Library
University of California
at San Diego
La Jolla, CA 92093

Carol Hansen
Stewart Library
Weber State University
Ogden, UT 84408

Marilyn Hautala
Library
University of Nebraska
Omaha, NE 68105

Margaret Hendley
Library
University of Waterloo
Waterloo, Ontario
Canada N2L 3G1

Patricia Herrling
Steenbock Library
University of Wisconsin
at Madison
Madison, WI 53706

Randall Hoelzen
Library
University of Wisconsin
at LaCrosse
LaCrosse, WI 54601

Patricia Hogan-Vidal
Moellering Library
Valparaiso University
Valparaiso, IN 46383

Diane Hunter
Lauinger Library
Georgetown University
Washington DC 20013

Alexa Jaffurs
Science Library
Wesleyan University
Middletown, CT 06459

Karen Jaggers
Cline Library
Northern Arizona University
Flagstaff, AZ 86011

Ann Jerabek
Library
Sam Houston State University
Huntsville, TX 77340

Judy A. Johnson
Library
Cedarville College
Cedarville, OH 45314

Miriam E. Joseph
Pius XII Memorial Library
St. Louis University
St. Louis, MO 63108

Jane Keefer
University Library
Eastern Michigan University
Ypsilanti, MI 48197

Linda Keltner
Walker Library
Drury Library
Springfield, MO 65802

Jean Kent
Learning Resources Center
North Seattle
Community College
Seattle, WA 98103

Carolyn Kirkendall
Library
Eastern Michigan University
Ypsilanti, MI 48197

Lynn Klekowski
Branch Library
DePaul University
Westchester, Il 60154

Pamela Lakin
Herrick Library
Alfred University
Alfred, NY 14802

Judy Lee
Rivera Library
University of California-Riverside
Riverside, CA 92517

Soo Lee
Library
Messiah College
Grantham, PA 17027

Ben Lents
Southeast Missouri State
University Library
Cape Girardeau, MO

Alison Levene
Memorial Library
Mankato State University
Mankato, MN 56002

Anne G. Lipow
University Libraries
University of California-Berkeley
Berkeley, CA 94105

Julie Long
Cushwa-Leighton Library
St. Mary's College
Notre Dame, IN 46556

Abigail Loomis
Memorial Library
University of Wisconsin-Madison
Madison, WI 53706

Myra Lowe
Wise Library
West Virginia University
Morgantown, WV 26506

Sharon Mader
Library
DePaul University
Chicago, IL 60657

Beth Mark
Library
Messiah College
Grantham, PA 17027

Alba Martinez
Library
Aguadilla Regional College
University of Puerto Rico
Aguadilla, PR 00605

Faye Maxwell
Education Library
University of Alberta
Edmonton, Alberta
Canada T6G 2G5

Frank McBride
Herrick Library
Alfred University
Alfred, NY 14802

Susan McMillan
Schmidt Library
York College of Pennsylvania
York, PA 17403

Gloria Meisel
LRC
Westchester Community College
Valhalla, NY 10595

Vanaja Menon
Donnelley Library
Lake Forest College
Lake Forest, IL 60045

Glenn Mensching
Library
Eastern Michigan University
Ypsilanti, MI 48197

Marsha Miller
Library
Indiana State University
Terre Haute, IN 47804

Susan Miller
Milner Library
Illinois State University
Normal, IL 61761

Sally Jo Milne
Good Library
Goshen College
Goshen, IN 46526

Thomas Minnick
University College
Ohio State University
Columbus, OH 43210

Jacqueline Mirabile
Falvey Memorial Library
Villanova University
Villanova, PA 190985

Anna Jane Moyer
Library
Gettysburg College
Gettysburg, PA 17325-1493

Nancy Turner Myers
Ellis Library
University of Missouri
Columbia, MO 65201

Lynette Nickum
Milner Library
Illinois State University
Normal, IL 61761

Thomas Nixon
Sterling Library
Yale University
New Haven, CT 06520

Fran Nowakowski
Killam Library
Dalhousie University
Halifax, Nova Scotia
Canada B3H 4H8

William Orme
Library
IUPUI
Indianapolis, IN 46202

James Pegolotti
Haas Library
Western Connecticut
State University
Danbury, CT 06810

Michael Perkins
Library
San Diego State University
San Diego, CA 92182

Mary Piette
Merrill Library
Utah State University
Logan, UT 84322

Gayle Poirier
Library
Louisiana State University
Baton Rouge, LA 70803

Mary Pagliero Popp
University Libraries
Indiana University
Bloomington, IN 47405

Betsy Porter
Coe Library
University of Wyoming
Laramie, WY 82071

Carl Pracht
Kent Library
Southeast Missouri State University
Cape Girardeau, MO 63701

Penny L. Pugh
Wise Library
West Virginia University
Morgantown, WV 26506

Linda Randolph
Pellissippi State Technical
Community College Library
Knoxville, TN 37933

Marea E. Rankin
Lupton Library
University of Tennessee
at Chattanooga
Chattanooga, TN 37403

Carol Reed
Carlson Library
University of Toledo
Toledo, OH 43606

Katharine T. Reichert
Griswold Library
Green Mountain College
Poultney, VT 05764

Billie Joy Reinhart
University Library
Cleveland State University
Cleveland, OH 44115

Janet Reit
Bailey Howe Library
University of Vermont
Burlington, VT 05405

Loretta J. Rielly
Kerr Library
Oregon State University
Corvallis, OR 97331

Catherine M. Rod
Burling Library
Grinnell College
Grinnell, IA 50112

Eleanor Rodini
Memorial Library
University of Wisconsin
Madison, WI 53706

Fred Roecker
Library
Ohio State University
Columbus, OH 43210

Sandra Rosenstock
Firestone Library
Princeton University
Princeton, NJ 08544

Pam Ross
Library
Iowa Wesleyan College
Mt. Pleasant, IA 52641

Patricia Rothermich
Library
Otterbein College
Westerville, OH 43081

Fern Russell
Humanities & Social Science
Library
University of Alberta
Edmonton, Alberta
Canada T6G 2J8

Michele Cash Russo
Library
Indiana University
South Bend, IN 46634

Kathy Schulz
Thomas Library
Wittenberg University
Springfield, OH 45501

Kathleen Scott
Learning Resources Center
Washtenaw Community College
Ann Arbor, MI 48106

Kim Sether
Library
Teikyo Westmar University
LeMars, IA 51031

Ruth C. Shoge
Library
Washington College
Chestertown, MD 21620

Vaswati R. Sinha
Skillman Library
Lafayette College
Easton, PA 18042

Craig Smith
Walker Library
Drury College
Springfield, MO 65802

Diane Smith
Robarts Library
University of Toronto
Toronto, Ontario, Canada
M5S 1A5

Karen V. Smith
Library
Southwestern College
Chula Vista, CA 91910

Nathan M. Smith Jr.
Merrill Library
Utah State University
Logan, UT 84322-3000

Keith Stanger
Eastern Michigan University
Library
Ypsilanti, MI 48197

Glenn Ellen Starr
Belk Library
Appalachian State University
Boone, NC 28608

Tom Stave
Library
University of Oregon
Eugene, OR 97403

Susan Swords Steffen
Schaffner Library
Northwestern University
Chicago, IL 60611

Arena L. Stevens
IUN Library
Indiana University NW
Gary, IN 46408

Athena Stone
Library
University of Tennessee
at Chattanooga
Chattanooga, TN 37403

Paula Storm
Mardigian Library
University of Michigan
Dearborn, Mi 48128-1491

Sister Anita Talar
McLaughlin Library
Seton Hall University
South Orange, NJ 07079

Charles Terbille
Carlson Library
University of Toledo
Toledo, OH 43606

Dot S. Thompson
Bertrand Library
Bucknell University
Lewisburg, PA 17837

Ron Titus
Morrow Library
Marshall University
Huntington, WV 25755

James E. Ward
University Library
David Lipscomb University
Nashville, TN 37204

Kappa Waugh
Library
Vassar College
Poughkeepsie, NY 12601

Priscilla Wentworth
Cooper Library
Clemson University
Clemson, SC 29634-3001

Donna Wertheimer
Library
Elmira College
Elmira, NY 14901

Norm Weston
Library
Northwestern University
Evanston, IL 60208

Marilyn Whitmore
Hillman Library
University of Pittsburgh
Pittsburgh, PA 15260

Susan Whyte
Northrup Library
Linfield College
McMinnville, OR 97128

Robert Woodley
Library
Philadelphia College of Pharmacy
Philadelphia, PA 19104

Kristine Wycisk
Zimmerman Library
University of New Mexico
Albuquerque, NM 87123

Ying Xu
Mansfield Library
University of Montana
Missoula, MT 59812

Sandra Yee
Library
Eastern Michigan University
Ypsilanti, MI 48197

Nancy Young
Stouffer Hotels Library
Cornell University
Ithaca, NY 14853

WITHDRAWAL